Pindar

The Complete works of Peter Leslie

Pindar

THE COMPLETE WORKS

OF

PETER LESLIE

THE LOCHGELLY POET

Compiled by

James Campbell

GRACE NOTE PUBLICATIONS

PORTRAIT OF THE AUTHOR
Pindar: The Complete Works of Peter Leslie
This edition is published by
Grace Note Publications in collaboration with
Grace Notes Scotland and James Campbell, 2016

Grace Note Publications C.I.C.
Grange of Locherlour,
Ochtertyre, PH7 4JS,
Scotland

ISBN 978-1-907676-83-3

books@gracenotereading.co.uk
www.gracenotepublications.co.uk

preface©James Campbell, 2016
copyright©Grace Note Publications, 2016

The content of this book was published between 1877 and 1905,
and it was collected by James Campbell from different sources

The publisher thanks Margaret Bennett, Ros and Russell Salton
for editing and proofreading the manuscript

A catalogue record for this book is available
from the British Library

In memory of Peter Leslie,
The Lochgelly Poet
(1835–1905)

CONTENTS

Part I

AUTOBIOGRAPHY OF A PRIVATE SOLDIER

Part II

Random Rhymes

Part III

Unpublished Poems by John Pindar

PREFACE

John Pindar
(Peter Leslie)
The Lochgelly Poet

I first came across the writings of John Pindar, the Lochgelly Poet, in 1987, while reading through papers and other material that had been entrusted to me by Mrs Jenny Mitchell, as they once belonged to her father, Alex Westwater, the Editor and owner of "The Cowdenbeath and Lochgelly Times & Advertiser".

At the time I had just begun to search "The Cowdenbeath and Lochgelly Times & Advertiser" from 1895 to 1897, looking for snippets of news regarding the actual story and events concerning the local and surrounding areas, when I noticed that there seemed to be a fairly regular supply of poems being submitted by Pindar.

Among the material I had been given by Mrs Mitchell was a copy of a collection of poems by Pindar entitled "Random Rhymes", published in 1893. As none of the poems that I came across in the local newspaper appeared in the "Random Rhymes" it occurred to me that it would be worth compiling these original Pindar poems from the newspapers into a small booklet, which I duplicated and gave to the local library.

I was later fortunate enough to be able to obtain a rare copy of Pindar's life-story, "The Autobiography of a Private Soldier", published in 1877. As copies of Pindar's autobiography and his collections of poems are now difficult to find, I decided to put together this book to make sure the writings of this remarkable person do not get lost in the mist of time. I hope that others might find the world of one of the Sons of Lochgelly as interesting as I did, and that the work of John Pindar will live in people's memory for a wee while longer.

In considering an introduction that would do justice to the poet, I realised, after a great deal of thought, that no better introduction could be provided than one from the pen of Mr Alex Westwater, "Mr Lochgelly" himself.

With this thought in mind, and the knowledge that Alex Westwater has given quite a few talks to various organisations in Lochgelly, I made a point of checking if he had ever given a talk on Pindar. With the greatest respect and gratitude to Mr Alex Westwater, I am now delighted to present, as the introduction to my book, the talk he once gave to a church group in Lochgelly.

I would like to take this opportunity to thank most sincerely Professor Margaret Bennett of Grace Notes Scotland and Dr. Gonzalo Mazzei of Grace Note Publications for their continuous help and advice. Without their belief in me as an individual this book would never have seen the light of day. I would also like to thank Jim Stark of the *Central Fife Times* for the access he so generously gave me to the old copies of *The Cowdenbeath and Lochgelly Times & Advertiser*. Finally, my heartfelt appreciation goes to one of Fife's most stalwart local historians, Arthur Nevay, whose encouragement and friendship has sustained me over many years of research into our history, culture and heritage.

James Campbell
Crosshill, 2016

INTRODUCTION

A generation ago Lochgelly had many real worthies, and when I use the term, I mean it literally.

We also had characters. Today, common to all Scottish towns and villages, we are not so rich in such personalities as we once were. The race of worthies and characters seem to have died out, unless it may be said that some of us, without knowing it, are carrying on the tradition!

The subject of our talk, John Pindar, was a combination of both the worthy and the character. He illuminated the life of our community and was altogether an outstanding personality. He died nearly thirty-three years ago, (1905) so that to many here he would be unknown; but I see here quite a number who would know him well.

Those who do remember him will recall a tall, stalwart figure with a slight limp. That limp was the result of a pit accident shortly after he had returned from the army and was working in a pit along Lumphinnan's Road. He was brought to his lodging in a coal cart filled with straw, as was the custom at that time. His doctor was the late Dr. Nasmyth who resided at Cowdenbeath, and who was later Medical Officer for the County of Fife, and still later, a prominent Edinburgh citizen and Councillor. There were no ambulances in these days; the first one in the district being established in Lochgelly about 35 years ago.

Pindar was laid on a folding iron bed, a handy piece of furniture which was in nearly every home in these days. It was some time ere the doctor arrived to set the limb. When the break was almost healed, Pindar, being a restless man, fell out of the couch, and so made the break worse, which left him with a slight deformity, hence the limp.

Pindar was born in auld Launcherhead; an old Raw that was demolished many years ago. They were then the eldest houses in Lochgelly. His mother was a farm servant at Dothan Farm, and she later married David Baxter, from one of the oldest families in Lochgelly, who was grandfather of the well-known Lochgelly Baxter family who have been closely identified with instrumental music in the town. The late David Baxter, whom I can recall from boyhood playing his beloved coronet round about Cartmore Braes, was a half-brother. Two other brothers were also soldiers.

His real name, or at least the name under which he joined the army was Peter Leslie. The pen name of Pindar was doubtless suggested by his reading acquaintance with John Wolcott, who wrote satires and lampoons around the end of the eighteenth century under the pseudonym of Pindar, or it may have suggested itself from the French poet Pindar. In Lochgelly he was never known by any other name than Pindar.

He never married though he had many a romance.

He early showed a taste for rhyme and literature though he had not much of an early education. In his book "The Autobiography of a Private Soldier" he states that he was born in the beautiful village of Glenvale, which of course is Lochgelly. The term Glenvale he would take from the little Glen that runs between the Bishop and the West Lomond Hills, a romantic spot where a roving laddie with such a temperament as Pindar would be likely to visit. The year of his birth was 1836, one year before Queen Victoria came to the throne.

> "My parents," he writes, "were of humble origin, belonging to that hard working class who earn their livelihood in the subterraneous caverns of the earth. School Boards were of the future and there was no outside pressure to cause parents

to send their children to school; hence what little knowledge was installed into my youthful mind was only gathered round the parental fireside, leaving me in blissful ignorance of those intellectual and educational attainments without which no man is able to raise himself to a respectable position in life."

When ten years of age, he was sent to work in the pit, as his forefathers had done before him, and at that early age he found himself driving a pony in a coal mine for sixpence a day.

Being of a studious nature he could manage to read Solomon's Proverbs even before his pony driving days, and he eagerly embraced the advantages of an evening school in the village and at the age of 16 he began to write. His old schoolmaster doubtless sensed some ability in the lad. He would be one of the lads o' pairts, in whom old Scottish dominies took a special interest, and he took great pains with Pindar. It was a proud moment when he was able to write his first letter in a half text hand, whereafter received the congratulations of the schoolmaster. He refers to him as "old Johnnie" without giving his name and I expect it would be John Ewing who kept a school in the Well Road or Church Street.

Johnnie Ewing schule
Where mony a scholar guid cam oot
And aiblins mony a ful!

With growing years and growing knowledge Pindar got restless working in the pits. There was yet no library in the village but he managed to borrow or buy books and before he was twenty, had read through, he says, nearly all the works of the British poets. He craved to see something beyond his environment. Apparently he had a particular liking for martial poems. Professions requiring education were denied to him and so he decided to adopt the profession of a soldier. Recruiting parties had not been successful in the village though, he says, the Queen was badly needing men. It was considered in Lochgelly then, as he puts it, that a determined youngster who bubbled after reputation at the cannon's mouth was little better than a ne'er do well. Pindar had no sympathy with that point of view. What, he writes, can be the cause of so much antipathy towards a red coat in religious and covenanting Scotland?

So in the end he definitely decided to be a soldier and proceeded on that to Edinburgh.

Pindar, like most poets I suppose, was always given to flowery or poetic language. Listen to this poetic prose:

> *"On a smiling morn in 1885, I bade farewell to*
> *Fifeshire's pleasant*
> *Fields and forests clad in green. The sun was shedding*
> *its refulgent*
> *Beams over the laughing earth; the lark high up in the*
> *blue sky was*
> *Pouring forth its merry lay in the calm stillness of the*
> *summer morn.*
> *All nature rejoiced with a cheerful voice when I left my*
> *native village."*

Arriving in Edinburgh he sauntered along the High Street and was accosted by a recruiting sergeant, Paddy Foley, as follows – "Well young man I'm the boy that's willing to give yeh a job. Come in to Rutherfords and let us have a social crack over a sparkling glass of frotheen. Be jabbers it's a nice young fellow that ye are with the mark of a Marshall's baton on yer brow. Its just fellows like you we want to fight the Sepoys in India. Oh, they've kilt all our women and children at Cawnpore and then drowned them in the well. Bad luck to the black hearted spaleens, but its thundering vengeance we'll have before long." And so on, finishing up with four lines (doubtless Pindar's own composition)

> *"Come drink a glass, my young spaleen*
> *I see that thou art willing*

To serve our loving gracious Queen
Come, here my lad's the shilling."

Pindar took the shilling and joined the Fusiliers. After 15 months training at home he joined a draft to proceed to India. On the troopship he sang songs of his own composition. Here are two verses of his

FAREWELL TO SCOTLAND

"Twas was when the flowers o' summer were bonnie
An' birdies sang sweetly frae ilka green tree
When I taen fareweel o' dear Caledonia
An' gaed oot tae India, a sodger to be.
I had wrocht in the pits sin' I was a wee callan
An' keen, keen I was the big world tae see;
I've seen noo my folly and tears fast are fa'in
For those I hae left in my ain countrie.

Beloved Caledonia, dear land o' my childhood
Thou glorious land o' the brave and the free
Aften I've wandered thy glens and sweet wildwood
An' sported wi' lassies upon the green lea.
But those days are gane never more to return
While I, a puir wanderer, bound now to roam
Far frae companions, which maks me to mourn
An' sigh for the joys o' my auld Scottish home."

After singing that song Pindar reports the sailors would have drowned him in grog, but at that time he says his temperance principles prevented him from tasting any stimulant. Pindar later fell steeply from that high estate.

In India he transferred to the Highland Light Infantry, a regiment that he served in until his 21 years were up.

The story of his service in India is of general interest. The mutiny was just over and he tells of visiting placed rendered famous by the occurrence, and with how reverent and tearful an eye he gazed on the bloody well of Cawnpore.

In his new regiment he was under a captain who belonged to Dunfermline and who knew many people in Lochgelly. He shunned the common life of a soldier, he says, finding more pleasure in the barrack room poring over the inspired lays of Milton, Cowper and Thomson, which he preferred to the attractions of all the gin palaces in the world.

He had his baptism of fire on the northwest frontier, known as the battle of the Umbeylah Pass. He told me of how he felt on that occasion. He was so nervous and excited that his rifle quivered like a wand until the man lying next to him hit him a resounding smack on the jaw and that steadied him up.

On 14th December 1864 the battalion started its march for home and on 4th February 1865 embarked at Calcutta. On the way round he was one of the favoured few allowed to disembark at Capetown. Pindar by then had apparently ceased to be a teetotaller for he says there was nothing worth seeing in Capetown, and after drinking a couple of glasses of "Cape Smoke", a sort of whisky, he returned to the vessel.

After four months at sea they reached Plymouth and re-embarked for Granton and Edinburgh Castle. Imagine, he writes, the delightful feelings with which we again beheld the coast of our dear native land. While rounding the Berwick Law, many an anxious glance I cast over to the tranquil plains of Fife, that sweet wee Kingdom that contained all I held dear in the world. Five days afterwards he had the unfeigned pleasure of meeting his aged mother.

"I at once", he writes, "knew the music of that dear tongue which was wont to instil into my soul the principles of love and self-respect." He celebrated the occasion in verse –

> *Lang years hae gane by*
>   *Sin' I left my dear hame*
>   *An' the freens o' my early days;*
>   *But noo I'm at hame nae mair will I roam*

Awa frae my sweet native braes.
Though aince on the blood-stained field I did lie
Surrounded by comrades slain,
Its noo, thank God, I am able to cry –
Is this bonnie Scotland again!"

Pindar had still to serve many years ere his full service was up. He was stationed for a time at Aldershot and on the outbreak of the Fenian disturbances was sent to Ireland. There he became addicted to the poteen and the bewitching Irish colleens.

He says that the Irish County girls made more impression on his heart than any he had met elsewhere.

He reached the rank of corporal but lost his stripes after a foolish adventure. He had been sent to Cork with a prisoner whom he delivered safely at the jail. He then got on the spree and spent the day and night in Cork. In the morning he set out to walk the 20 miles back to camp but went in the opposite direction, and found himself 40 miles from his destination with 6d in his pocket. This he spent on porter and bread. It was, he says, the crushing point of his career when in front of the regiment he was reduced to the ranks and sent to the same prison at which he had delivered his prisoner, to undergo a sentence of 56 days with hard labour.

On his discharge in 1879 he returned to Lochgelly, his beloved "Glenvale". He brought with him a number of testimonials from officers of his regiment, the 71st H.L.I. He was very proud of them. They are in the possession of his nephew, Harry Baxter, and are splendid testimony of his record as a soldier. With one of his commanding officers, Col. Hope of Pinkie, he maintained a lifelong correspondence, and occasionally visited Pinkie House from which he never came away empty handed. Indeed, it was well known that it was from Pinkie House that he got the well cut tweeds which he wore.

And so he settled down to live on his pension of 1/- a day. He restarted work in the pits along with his half-brother, David

Baxter, but after the accident of the broken leg already referred to, he never returned there.

He got odd jobs. For a time he worked at the little Gas works in the Main Street assisting Andrew Leitch, and was caretaker at the music hall before it was purchased by the late Provost Reid. In addition to his "Autobiography of a Private Soldier" he published in 1893 a selection of his verses under the title of Random Rhymes. The little book was edited by the late Dr. Houston, Auchterderran. Pindar went round the town and countryside selling it.

He was guy, fond of a dram and numbered among his cronies others of a like temperament. A great admirer of Burns, he was in the Lochgelly Club that formed in the early nineties and which met in Andra Dunsires public house in the Main Street, site of the Bay Horse hotel. I recall attending a Burns celebration there in 1894, forty-three years ago, in the capacity of a reporter. All the village was there. In the course of the evening Pindar was called on to propose the toast of the Press and of course I was to reply. A shy, bashful lad I was then, and still am, and I can almost feel yet the state of nerves I got at the thought of having to make what would be my maiden speech. I hastily wrote out a reply on the back pages of my notebook. Pindar, like all versifiers, was fond of using flowery language and he could indeed be very eloquent. I rose to reply and turned to my book. But lo and behold what I had so hastily written I could not read. The sweat broke over me as I collapsed in the chair. Pindar, however, was sympathetic. He got up again and recalled that on one similar occasion

Sandy Russell, the famous editor of the Scotsman responded to a similar toast by a simple "thank you" and next day a full column of his speech appeared in the Scotsman. He suggested that I should follow his example; but of course I was too modest to do that!

His output of verse was prolific. When Pindar got short of cash he addressed a poem to someone and was generally rewarded, at least he looked for a money reward. What he got generally went to swell a licence holders drawings.

Though never a church-goer he was on very friendly terms with the ministers of the district. Mr Dewar of this church, Duncan Brown of the Free, David Jamie of Ballingry, and A.M Houston of Auchterderran.

To Mr Dewar he addressed this epigram –

> *Mr Dewar, Mr Dewar, your sermon is pure*
> *Yes, eloquent, learned, sublime*
> *But mankind is jolly, wicked, unholy*
> *They treat with contempt what's divine.*

Like most old soldiers he was strongly conservative in politics. I recall the general election when Wemyss of Wemyss and Yellowlees of Stirling had a staunch supporter in Pindar at the meetings. Pindar always commanded an audience at the cross for he could use eloquent language.

Some here will recall a Miss Hay who came from Dunfermline and carried on for months a really successful evangelistic campaign. She held open air meetings at the cross, and then adjourning to the masonic hall. Pindar joined her band and appeared at the open air meetings, speaking and singing hallelujah rhymes. In the course of one address he gave at one of these gatherings he said "If you don't repent you will disappear into hell like midgies on Contle burn."

Some years after he returned from the army he set out with two friends, drouthy cronies, to walk round Loch Leven. All the money they had was spent in refreshment at the Shank o' Navity, so that when they reached Scotlandwell they were unable to quench their thirst, so they proceeded to raise the wind. Pindar took up stance in the village and in eloquent language declaimed against intemperance and related his own experiences of the evil effect of strong drink. They got a fair lot of coppers as a result of a round with the hat. They went on to Kinnesswood and went through the same performance there with a similar result, and from there made for Cuthil Muir, which was then an Inn kept by a Lochgelly man named Smith. The collection was laid down, and well, you know the rest. Pindar and his friends were driven home that night from Milnathort, where,

> *"They fell in wi' Mr White*
> *An' had a friendly dram*
> *He gave his gig to them that night*
> *As they had far tae gang."*

Sometimes Pindar was on the verge of a breakdown by overindulgence. He stayed in his later years in a garret in Main Street opposite the Free Kirk and his sister-in-law, Mrs Baxter, who was very kind to him, sent over his meals.

One of her daughters arrived one day with his dinner. Pindar had just returned from the pub and was in a great rage because a certain publican had refused him any more drink on credit. On the mantlepiece opposite was a timepiece. Working up his indignation to a frenzy, he lifted the unoffending clock and with the remark, "well, if there's nae tick for me there's nae tick for you." He dashed it to the floor smashing it to uselessness.

I have already said that Pindar was either up in the heights or down in the depths. He led a chequered life, and if he fell short in virtue he had, like Burns the "pangs of keen remorse!" In a longish poem, which he calls, "A Misspent Life", there is much that would have done credit to Burns himself.

Alex Westwater
Lochgelly, 1938

PART ONE

AUTOBIOGRAPHY
OF A
PRIVATE SOLDIER

BY

JOHN PINDAR
(PETER LESLIE)

==============

CUPAR: FIFE
PRINTED IN THE *"FIFE NEWS"* OFFICE

———

MDCCCLXXVII

Chapter I

Birth – School Days – in the Mine – Enlistment

The beautiful Village of Glenvale, in the "Kingdom of Fife," was the place destined to hear my first wailing cry, for there, about the year 1836, I made my *debut* upon the stage of life. My parents were humble origin, belonging to the hard-working class who earn their livelihood in the subterranean caverns of the earth. School Boards at that time only looming in the distant future, there was no outside pressure to cause parents to send their children to school; hence what little knowledge was instilled into my youthful mind was only gathered around the parental fireside, leaving me in blissful ignorance of those intellectual and educational attainments without which no man is able to raise himself to a respectable position in life. Happy years of infancy, however, I enjoyed until about my tenth, when it was destined that, like my forefathers, I should first learn to toil in the bowels of the earth, for at that early age I found myself driving a pony in a coal mine for sixpence a day. Proud, of course, I was to be able to add even this sum to the family exchequer; but as I grew in years and strength I was promoted to the position of a real miner. Being of a studious nature I could manage to read Solomon's Proverbs even before my pony driving days, and now I eagerly embraced the advantages of an evening school in the village. At the age of sixteen I began to learn to write. My old schoolmaster used to take great pains with me, and I felt prouder than I had ever done before when I wrote my first letter to him in a half-text hand. How cordially he congratulated me upon my wonderful progress. Dear old Johnnie! Many years have passed since then; still I remember the kindly smile that was wont to illumine thy sonsie face. Where thou art now I cannot tell; but should this meet thy waning eye it will tell thee that the wanderer loves thee still.

Although I toiled on for years without murmuring I was never content with my position as a miner. I felt a craving to see something beyond the circles of my little home, for I had now spent twenty years of my life without ever passing the confines of the "Kingdom;" yet daring all that time I had never once entertained the notion of becoming a son of Mars. I was considered by my friends to possess a pusillanimous kind of soul, as I never took any interest in the sports of the village, and the gay-hearted companions of my youth were wont to bestow upon me the endearing appellation of "calf." None ever dreamt of the likelihood of me ever leaving the quiet and calm seclusion of my village home to mingle in the strife and turmoil of a martial life. Yet such are the unknown ways of Providence – "Man proposes, but God disposes." As my mind became enlightened by the few books I managed to buy or borrow (there being no public library in the village) to read, I began to feel more and more dissatisfied with my monotonous life, and had now managed to wander through nearly all the works of the British poets, finding they all therein spoke proudly of the British soldier, and sang his praise in soul-stirring strains. How often does our national bard sing of a "sodger laddie," ranging from his "I am a Son of Mars" down to his mournful and plaintive song about the weary and warlike soldier returning to the scenes of his youth and passing the trystin' tree "where Nancy first he courted." Tannahill, also, in his "Wallace's Lament," tells as how the soldier's deeds

> "Shall' make immortal the place where he fell.
> And his name be enrolled with the sons of the brave."

And Campbell's "Soldier's Dream," the grandest of all our martial poems! Who cannot, in imagination, see the war-broken soldier sleeping on his pallet of straw, dreaming of home and early youth? He wanders o'er the heathery hills; he hears his father's goats bleating amongst the well-remembered scenes of early youth; he strains his weeping wife to his bosom; his children are kissed a thousand times o'er, but, alas! He awakes from his sanguinary bed to find himself surrounded by comrades slain. Indeed all the poets I had read, from Byron to Macneal, had some encouraging word to say in favour of a soldier's life.

Whether or not these authors had aught to do in bending my inclination towards the army I cannot exactly say, but I began to look around me for some occupation more congenial to my mind than that of a miner. Profession requiring education were closed against me, and I began to perceive I had no prospect of being able to maintain myself in a respectable position above ground unless I enlisted for a soldier. I knew Her Majesty was at the time greatly in want of men for the army, for these were no "piping times of peace." France and Austria were drenching the fair fields of Italy with the blood of their bravest sons, while our own gallant little army was contending against the blood-thirsty savages of India's terrible mutiny. Recruiting parties had on several occasions paid a visit to our village but without any success, for although a few young fellows belonging to it did enlist, the young men generally had repaired either to Kirkcaldy or Dunfermline before taking that important step, as any determined youngster who longed after bubbled reputation at the cannon's mouth was considered in his native quarter little better than a *black-guard*, though he should have been honoured with the proud designation of a *brave* guard.

What can be the cause of so much antipathy towards a red-coat in religious and covenanting Scotland, a deeper learned man than myself will require to tell; for where the Bible is the primary book of a country, and where infant lips are taught to prattle the heroism of old Abraham in gathering together his trained servants and pursuing the army of the leagued kings to rescue Lot; of Moses and Joshua's routing the Amalekites and Canaanites; of the Sweet Singer of Israel's oft-repeated encounter with the Philistines, and especially his onslaught and destruction of Goliath; of Gideon, Samson, Barak, and Jephthah, down to the destruction by the hordes of ancient Rome of the city and its beautiful Temple that were wept over so lovingly – it seems to me more of Christian charity ought to be bestowed upon those who take their life in their hand to keep an insulting foe within bounds.

Soldiering is thus seen to be of very great antiquity, and even now, in this boasted age of civilisation and intellectual refinement, there is little appearance of the Millennium morn dawning on our war-stricken world. Rather, indeed, many things in the world, both religious and political, indicate that the profession of arms will be a popular occupation up to the time of the great battle of Armageddon.

Having at last made up my mind and determined to be a soldier, one bright smiling morning in June 1858 I bade farewell to Fifeshire's pleasant fields and forests clad in green. The sun was shedding his refulgent beams o'er the laughing earth; the lark, high up in the blue sky, was pouring forth his merry lay in the calm stillness of that summer morn; all nature rejoiced with a cheerful voice as I left my native village *en route* to the Scottish capital to "take the shilling" and serve my Queen and country. Arriving there and walking leisurely up the High Street, I was accosted by a recruiting sergeant – Paddy Foley by name, who was well up to his business – in the following manner: – "Well, young man, looking for employment to-day? I'm the boy that's willin' to give ye's a job. Come into Rutherford's and let us have a social crack over a sparkling glass of potheem. Be jabbers, it's the nice young fellow you are, born with the mark ov a Marshal's baton on your brow. It's jist sich young fellows like ye's that we want to foight the Sepoys in India. Oh! They've kilt all our poor women and children at Cawnpore, and then drowned them in the well. Bad luck to the black-hearted spalpeens, but it's the thundering vengeance we'll have before long. My ould Crimean General, Sir Colin Campbell, has gone out to India, and he's jist what we call in Ireland 'the real broth of a boy.' I would have been there with my regiment now only the ould doctor tould me that the wound I got in the Crimea would prevent me from ever serving in action again. I soldiered in India long before the Mutiny, and it's a nice country indeed – no dirty fatigues ov orderly- man to do there; just keep yourself clean, and you can shoot bears and tigers all day in the jungle; but there's plenty of cowardly Sepoys to shoot at present, and as I think you intend to be a gentleman by becoming a soldier yon can't do better than join my brave ould Hieland Regiment. Though born near the Galtee Mountains in ould Ireland, twenty-three years in a Hieland Regiment have nearly made me forget my ould mother's tongue."

Sergeant Foley was every inch a soldier. He had four medals for service in face of his country's foes, and during his long career in the army, had served in all parts of the world – East and West Indies, China, Canada, Corfu, Mediterranean, and the Crimea.

> Come drink a glass, my young spalpeen,
> I see that thou art willing
> To serve our loving, gracious Queen—
> Come, here my lad's the shilling.

Paddy's eloquence fairly floored me, for I there and then became a soldier; but not in his regiment, as I selected one of the Fusiliers which was at the time bravely defending their country's honour and glory before the gates of Lucknow.

CHAPTER II

Embarks for India – Paddy M'Cann Discourses on Songs and Sings an Irish One – A Scotch Song – Lands at Calcutta

Having now voluntarily become a soldier of Her Majesty, I had a few days I could call my own before the usual preliminaries of "passing the doctor" and "swearing in" took place, of which you may be sure I took every advantage to explore the beauties of "Auld Reekie." There is no Scotchman now-a-days, I believe, but has seen it for himself, and must have felt much the same as I did on his first visit, so that my ideas of it are unnecessary here, and I have no doubt are better wanting, as the gorgeous descriptions of the Indian cities that were being "dinned" into my head daily at this time caused our own capital to look but second class at best. But now my longings to be out in the world are about to be realised, for after being fairly attested I am sent on to Colchester in England to join the depot of my regiment. Here I was doomed to linger for fifteen months getting instructed in the "goose step," handling and using the rifle, &c., with nothing to break the monotonous life save an occasional stroll about the town to show off my red coat and bushy, thinking oft that Foley's dreams of India were never to be realised.

But "it's a long lane that has no turning" and we are at last to get a taste of life, for an order has been received for a draft to be sent on to Gravesend for embarkation to join the regiment. Accordingly I was one, and, along with some other 500 soldiers, women, and children, bound for all the different corps then in India, I embarked on board the sailing transport "Algiers," on the 12th September 1859, the whole of us being under the command of Colonel (now General) Sir P. Grey, E.C.B. Few unless those who have seen it can conceive the scene of commotion and confusion to be witnessed on the crowded deck of a troop ship preparatory to sailing. Here are a huddled knot of women and children looking wistfully out at the shore of their native land, perhaps never more to be beheld by them. There you see a few half tipsy soldiers shaking hands in parting with some old comrades who have not been permitted to accompany them; while in every corner baggage is lying, and sailors bustling hither and thither to make things straight, every now and then coming tilt against some tear-begrimed mother looking anxiously for her straying children. There was one very touching episode which I may here mention. A handsome English girl got permission to go on board ship to take farewell of her young husband. Their parting was indeed heartrending. They had a little boy two years old, who despite his tender age seemed to realise the situation. When his father, kissed him the innocent tears flowed down his chubby cheeks. Five months afterwards I saw the father of that little boy laid by the banks of the yellow Ganges. Their parting on board ship was the last on earth. When the grave yields up its charge the re-union of these fond hearts will, methinks, be a scene over which angels will preside.

After everything has been put to rights, hatches battened down, and the good ship and tight merrily ploughing her way through the briny sea, life on board, without that grim enemy, sea-sickness, is rather of a joyous nature to those who lore a stirring and active life. We weighed anchor and sailed next day, and having a favourable breeze soon left the white cliffs of Albion far behind us. Now was the time for every one on board to find out ways and means to beguile the long, weary voyage, and none was more energetic in this than Paddy McCann. He was leading man in everything, and whenever languor seemed to oppress us, Paddy was sure to have some drama to rehearse for an amateur theatre, or might be seen flying about choosing his men to take part in an embryo concert. One evening, after we had been long at sea and were drawing near the line, a group of us, quite languid with the sultry heat, were crouched in a comer with weary spirits longing once more for a sight of land – which we had entirely lost sight of since leaving the Channel. The good ship was moving lazily before the light breeze, when one exclaimed, "I think Paddy McCann should favour us with a good old Irish song."

Paddy, always willing, replied, "Well, boys, I'm not much of a singer, but I'm a bit of a poet, although I never composed a rhyme in my life. An ould poet, Wordsworth by name, once said that there were thousands of poets who had the

> 'Vision and the faculty divine,
> Yet wanting the accomplishment of verse.'

But, boys, I'm one of those poets who see beauty and love in every land where I've been, and I've soldiered in every country which acknowledges Queen Victoria as its ruler. I'm now an old soldier, the oldest of the 500 now aboard this ship. I fought on the banks of the Sutlej twelve years ago, an', let me tell you, India is a glorious country. Don't drink too much; be careful of your health, and be temperate in everything and you'll all do well."

"But, Paddy, you once sung me a beautiful song in Preston Barracks about some nice girl in Templemore," cried Jim Lockton of the 20th.

"Let me off once more an' I'll give you a song – a good ould Irish song – written by a genial- hearted Irishman who has made the whole world laugh wid his wit an' humour. Well, my young boys, if long familiarity wid the glory an' grandeur of external nature ought to make a man a poet I should be classed along wid Byron and Shelley. Like these distinguished poets I've seen some ov the most sublime scenes in the world. I've been the hero of moving an' romantic adventure; I've been familiar with death on the sanguinary field of battle; I've sailed more than once o'er the wild wide sea, an' slept in the midnight stillness of foreign forests; I've trodden the pine-covered hills of the Punjaub, an' lived for years under the hoary head of the heaven-kissing

Himalayas; I've swam in the yellow Ganges, an' reposed amongst royal groves on the banks of the rapid-rolling Indus; I've been a wanderer in distant lands; I've seen the sun rise and set on the sunny coast of Africa; I've beheld the stars come forth in the fragrant Isles of the Southern Seas; I've lived in the populous cities and mingled 'midst the assembled multitude of mankind; I've been intoxicated with the rosy charms of female beauty; I've drunk inspiration from some of the moat romantic scenes in the world; yea, I've even pressed to my bosom the lovely flowers from the Cashmere hills, an' yet Paddy McCann is no poet. I've never, its true, conversed with living men of genius, but I've read the poets an' historians ov Ancient Greece an' Rome, while the poets ov my own country have been to me like the majestic beauties ov Nature, a pleasure an' enjoyment."

"Go on, Paddy," cried a hundred voices at one time.

"A few words more, boys, an' I've done. Now, without disrespect to the young English boys who're now listening to me, I must say that England has no national songs – that is songs like Ireland an' Scotland. Eliza Cook wrote some nice songs, but her two best are Irish an' Scotch – Norah McShane' and the 'Star o' Glengarry.' Ould Ireland has her Tom Moore, and bonnie Scotland her Robbie Bums, but English song writers are still in the future. Tom Moore, the national poet ov my country, has immortalised in his beautiful songs the virtuous beauty that adorns the daughters of my own bright Emerald Isle. Och! my bright boys, these songs ov ould Ireland shall find an echo in the heart of my countrymen while there's leaves in the forest and foam on the river. Look again at the sweet songs o' bonnie Scotland – songs that are sung wherever a Scotchman's foot has trod. I've listened to the sweet music of a Scotch melody in the stillness of an Indian jungle, an'. Irishman though I be, I've felt something like a Scottish spirit stirring within my soul as I've listened to that grand martial song ov auld Scotland –

'Scots wha hae wi' Wallace bled.'

"Well done, Paddy; it's at home in Parliament yon su'd be instead o' fechtin' the battles o' yer country," cried young Sandy Murray, a recruit going to join the Gordon Highlanders.

"Well, boys, I'll speechify no more, but sing you the song I promised sometime since."

FORGET NOT YOUR KATHLEEN

Forget not your Kathleen
When on the wide sea,
Remember, dear Dennis,
She lives but for thee.
I know that 'tis duty
Alone bids thee go,
And leave me behind ye
In sorrow and woe.

Though far you may wander
From home and from me,
My blessings and prayers
Shall be ever with thee.
In good or in evil.
In each changing scene.
Remember me, dearest,
Forget not Kathleen.

Forget not your Kathleen
Where'er you may roam.
Nor kind hearts that love ye –
The old friends at home
Remember, dear love,
In the hour of distress,
When dangers surround thee,
Or sorrow oppress.

Though fortune frown on thee
Your Kathleen will smile,
 And a home you will find
In your own native isle,
In storm or in sunshine,
In each changeful scene,
Remember me, Dennis-
Forget not Kathleen.

Old Paddy's song was well received by us young fellows, and he claimed the right to call for the next song and pitched upon a young Scotchman named Baxter of the 88th for it.

"Weel, my lads," says Baxter," I'll try an' sing ye a bit sang, but min' ye ye're no to expect a great speech frae me sich like as ye've had the pleasure o' listenin' tae frae the lips o' oor frien' Mr M'Cann. I feel I ocht tae return him my very sincere thanks for the kindly manner he spak o' my dear country, an' oor national bard, Bobbie Burns. I ne'er heard oor minister, the Bev. Mc M'Fitt, speak at ony o' oor soirees wi' half the eloquence that charactereeses the speeches o' oor frien', M'Cann. Su'd I fin' my future companions- in-arms in the Rangers as kindly disposed towards a puir Scotch laddie as Paddy M'Cann is, I'll ha'e nae cause tae regret my enlisting in the best o' Irish Regiments."

FAREWEEL TO SCOTLAND.

'Twas whan the flowers o' the summer were bonnie,
An' birdies sang sweetly frae ilka green tree,
Whan I tane fareweel o' my dear Caledonia,
An' gaed oot tae India a sodger tae be.
I had wrocht i' the pits sin' I was a wee callan',
An' keen, keen I was the big warld tae see;
I've seen noo my folly, an' tears fast are fa'ing
For those I ha'e left in my ain countrie.

I little kent then what was't to be a sodger —
I had heard his life was a' glorious an' fine;
But aften he's lain on the cauld grun' a lodger
Whan marching at nicht in a far foreign clime.
I aften ha'e tho'cht since I put on a red coat,
A bonny blue bannet wi' plume hangin' o'er,
A waistbelt an' bayonet, although they look bonnie.
Are but a puir change fur the claes I ance wore.

Childhood's day o'er my memory rushes —
Oh, sweet pleasant day nae mair tae return —
When I roamed 'mang groves o' bonnie brown bushes,
An' pu'ed the gowans on the banks o' the burn.
Oh I then I was happy, blythesome, an' cheery,
In life's early mornin' nae sorrows kent I;
But noo my life is aye stern and dreary,
Tho' beauteous an' sweet is the bright Orient sky.

Beloved Caledonia, dear land o my childhood,
Thou glorious land o the brave an' the free,
Aften I wandered thy glens an' sweet wildwood,
An' sported wi' lasses upon the green lea.
But those days are gane never more to return.
While I, a pair wanderer, bound now to roam
Far frae companions, which mak's me tae mourn,
An' sigh for the joys o' my auld Scottish home.

The young Scotchman sang his song in a very modest and creditable manner. The sailors would have drowned him with grog, but Baxter's temperance principles prevented him from tasting either grog or any other stimulant. Teetotallers are very common in the army now-a-days;' but, like their brethren in civil life they are rather hard towards those who do not think as they do. If a man considers a glass of porter or ale beneficial to his health by all means let him take it. But the law should be very severe with those who make beasts of themselves or exhibit themselves in a state of intoxication. This has been done in the British army, and what is the result? Why, the British Army is a pattern of sobriety. We don't keep drunkards in it; they are discharged the first opportunity. Man being reasonable gets drunk, said Lord Byron, but he only shows his unreasonableness when he drinks fire-water until he forgets his manhood and respectability. In many such cases he sinks

> "Into the vile dust from whence he sprung,
> Unwept, unhonoured, and unsung."

Such scenes as these led on by Paddy's genial, round Celtic countenance, were the means of keeping away ennui during the long voyage round the Cape, for we had no Suez Canal then. Now and again we would see turtle and porpoise sporting in the water, and have visits from the flying fish and "Mother Carey's chickens." Twice also had we sport assisting the sailors to haul on board a large shark they had caught. One of these creatures measured no less than 15 feet, and did wallop the deck well with its mighty tail before he was fairly despatched, after which all of us partook of parts of its flesh, and gave the remnant to its hungry brethren of the sea.

We had only one death all the way, and never will I forget the impressiveness of the funeral at sea. The corpse, sewed up in its canvas coffin, with the shot attached, is stretched upon the sloping plank, and when the chaplain comes to the words, "We therefore commit his body to the deep," one heavy plunge and we see our comrade no more, until "The sea shall give up its dead." For a while this causes a calmness and solemnity to reign over us, but shortly cheerfulness resumes its sway, and the dead is soon forgotten amongst us, though there will be lamentation and wailing in that little cabin in the south of Quid Ireland when the melancholy news reaches there.

Although we were all enjoying good health and were very comfortable in our floating house we again began to long to see land, never having seen any since we took the last glimpse of England. However, on the morning of the 20th January 1860,

India's coral plains were seen on our right. Such a ringing cheer it called forth. By evening we were anchored at the mouth of the Ganges. Next morning we were towed gently up the river, the banks of the Houghly being beautifully dotted with splendid mansions and very pretty gardens on both sides; but many a sickening scene is observed on its bosom owing to the numerous dead bodies in every stage of decomposition floating down the sacred stream – a thing it took me a long time to erase from my memory. At six the same evening we cast anchor opposite Fort William and had the "City of Palaces" (Calcutta) spread, out before our admiring eyes.

CHAPTER III

Joins Another Regiment in India – March 1100 Miles – The Majestic Wonders of Nature – Soldiering in India and Opportunities for Intellectual Culture

Next morning (21st January 1860) we were all disembarked and marched to the military station of Dum Dum, about 7 miles from Calcutta, to be forwarded from thence to the stations of our different regiments. And now came a tinge of sadness after the hilarity we had revelled in for the last four months, for we were to be scattered far and wide – parted, many of us, never to meet again on this side of the grave. It was little else but a recapitulation of what most of us had had to undergo when leaving home. Comrades from the same village home who had wandered and frolicked together o'er the tranquil hills of their native land had to bid a long adieu, while promises of remembrance in the future and earnest prayers for each other's success were the main topics of the hour. I found that the regiment I had come out to join was on the eve of embarkation for home, and those of us who were destined to serve in the Fusiliers were to remain here until it came down from Allahabad to Calcutta on the way to England. We had, therefore, three months' duty to perform in Dum Dum before we joined the head-quarters of the regiment in Fort William Barracks, Calcutta. Arrived there I was posted to Captain Walpole's company, and though I found out I had only two countrymen of my own in the whole regiment, I liked the Fusiliers exceedingly well, and learned that I could not well have selected a more distinguished regiment, as they had fought in nearly all the bloody battles of Europe, and for their bravery and the great services they had rendered in the Mutiny, received the distinguished approbation of the Commandeer-in-Chief (Lord Clyde), and the Governor-General (Lord Canning). As is usually the case on a regiment leaving India any of us wishing to prolong our service in that country were allowed to volunteer to any of the other regiments under the strength. As I had been but a few months out and did not altogether relish the idea of returning to England so soon without seeing something of a country I had heard so much about, and whose terrible deeds of a year or two back were still fresh in every one's memory, I made one of a party of volunteers (though with some reluctance), and chose for a new home on the 17th February 1861 one of our National regiments – the Highland Light Infantry – then stationed at Sealkote in the Punjaub, 1100 miles from where I now was.

At this time I met an old soldier on his way home, a native of Glenvale, who knew me at once, although ten years had passed since we had wandered together o'er the Scottish hills and glens. He had finished his ten years' service – most of it hard fighting in the Crimea and India – having fought in the ranks of the 55th Regiment in the battles of Alma and Inkermann, and when the Indian Mutiny broke out, astonishing the Christian world with its terrible deeds of blood and violence, Robert Bain transferred his services to India, and In the ranks of the Gordon Highlanders fought with that courage and coolness which distinguished the soldiers of his country. I believe he is once more in Glenvale contentedly labouring at the same occupation as caused me to become a soldier.

Railways being by no means so common in India as at home, I had to join my new regiment by marching, which took me five months to accomplish and during, that time I had passed through most of the principal cities on the route, including the holy one of Benares, and Allahabad, Cawnpore, Delhi, and Lahore. One can easily conceive with what avidity a few spare moments or an occasional half-day at any of the prominent places of the Mutiny was used to visit the scenes of carnage, and with how reverent and tearful an eye we gazed on the bloody well of Cawnpore. Some parts of India are very beautiful, though few songsters enliven its landscape with sweet sounds of music, and her mountains are silent and still, their solitude being broken only by the mighty roar of some- wild denizen of the forest in search of his prey. Still, the long march through this land of barbaric pearl and gold often caused me to long for a wander once more through the green fields and lanes of bonnie Scotland, where one can hear the "wee birdies singing frae ilka green tree" one harmonious Song of praise to God. In my opinion, no good-thinking being can view the beauties of nature unmoved, for what happiness arises within one's bosom when gazing on fair and lovely scenery, viewing the smiling landscape, roaming beside the rippling burn, or climbing the heathery hills. The scenery of Scotland is calm, sweet, and domestic; but in India it is the grand, the terrible, the sublime. Here we have mighty rivers rolling over beds of golden sand and mountains kissing the sky. Here, too, we have thunder and lightning, rain and sand storms awfully sublime. He must, indeed, feel little of devotion within his breast who can witness an Indian thunderstorm without being convinced of a "great First Cause," and that an Almighty God "reigneth in heaven and amongst the inhabitants of the earth." Why, the very brutes of the jungle, whose ferocity is beyond bounds and their nature untameable by the hand of man, at its first approach seek their most hidden lairs, and crouch and tremble with abject terror; and shall man, endowed with a reasoning soul, remain callous and indifferent, without a particle of holy awe arising within him as he stands before the voice of his Maker, and while these very animals are practically telling him "the hand that made us is divine."

I reached my new regiment in Sealkote on the 1st June 1861, and was posted to letter G. Company (Capt. Parker), the Colour-Sergeant of which was a native of Dunfermline. He had been in Glenvale in his civilian days, and knew a great number of the inhabitants of that important village, so that I was proud to find one in that far distant land with whom I could recall, as it were, the scenes and acquaintances of bye-gone days. I found, further, that almost every one of the regiment was a Scotchman – many of them being natives of "the Kingdom," so that old recollections came floating fast through my mind while once more surrounded by the constant sound of my own native tongue. Almost every man, too, who had five or seven years' service could boast of the possession of three war medals, the regiment having been in the Crimea, and ordered out to India on the out-break of the Mutiny, to form part of the field force there, and also to garrison Gwalior.

I had again to settle down thoroughly to the work of a soldier, and use my spare moments replenishing my mind with information from books or surroundings, for every British regiment in India is possessed of a good library – a blessing which cannot be too highly appreciated by the private soldier. The books are carefully selected and well calculated to inform and improve the mind, although too many young soldiers consider the bacchanalian song and the sparkling glass as possessing more charms to the heart than all the books in the world. Their cry generally is, "We have plenty of time; let us ply the bowl and carol the song, and thus be glad and rejoice in the spring- time of our days. We are yet young, and the world is bright and blooming before us; why should we curb our youthful pleasures? Time enough when we pass the noon-day of life to turn composed and sedate." And so, too, many young soldiers allow the brightest time of their life to escape from their grasp, thinking little of the present and far less of the great hereafter. Yet in this great age of books there is no soldier that has not the opportunity to improve and enrich his mind, and make himself acquainted with the world's history. Shame it is for any young man in this highly cultivated age to pass through the world and. become none the wiser of all the beauties and wonders surrounding him on every side, No man has more time for this purpose than the British soldier; besides which he has the advantage of travelling in foreign climes, which his limited means and occupation in civil life would not permit; and thus he can make himself acquainted with the habits, manners, and customs of the various peoples in the different parts of the civilised world.

For myself, I have felt more pleasure in my barrack room poring over the almost inspired pages of a Milton, a Cowper, or a Thomson, than I would amidst the attractions of all the gin palaces in the world. Still I must admit I often felt a sense of loneliness creeping over me when- ever my thoughts would revert to home, which they often did. I had voluntarily left the land of my birth for the life of a soldier. I had crossed o'er the boundless ocean and was destined to traverse, perhaps for many years, the plains of sunny Ind, perhaps never more to know a home – a home lightened with a mother's smile or cheered by a dear father's voice. Home, sweet home, calm and serene, never can I forget thy hallowed re-collections! What endearing associations are intertwined around that sacred and beloved spot. Often on a foreign shore the word Home has cheered my lonely heart; often have I looked back through the dim vistas of time, and beheld the beloved countenance of a fond parent hanging o'er me with an indescribable smile. Who has not felt the influence of home exerting a pleasing effect on the mind, although a harsh and unfeeling world may have well-nigh, with its cares and troubles, obliterated the pious counsels of a parental fireside. In our calm moments of reflection there will rush through the chambers of our memory some kind word long since breathed in our ears by a loving mother – awakening the recollections of bright and happy days.

I also began to find out here that India was not nearly so severe on the British soldier as we are generally led to believe at home, as the duties are not nearly so heavy, and all the fatiguing work is performed by the natives. Indeed, there were very few privates but who were able to keep their own bat-man, cook, barber, &c., as a few pice was all the expense for these. Many also possessed a horse of their own, while nearly all were owners of dogs, monkeys, parrots, or some sort of pet, a plot of garden-ground, or a gun of their own, so that there was no want of amusement. In fact, it was only those who revelled in the canteen, imbibed the killing drink of the country, or were too indolent to indulge in out-of-door exercise that had cause to complain of the effects of an Indian climate.

This was considered a very favourable station for a regiment, and ours remained in it close upon two years, being then under the command of Col. (now Major-General) W. Hope, C.B., after which, in December 1862, it marched to Nowshera, a station 200 miles distant from Sealkote, and 27 from Peshawar, my own company in the meantime being detached to a fortress on the Indus called Fort Attock, where we were until re-joining head-quarters in June 1863.

CHAPTER IV

Baptism of Fire – Attack and Defeat of Savages on the North Western Frontier – Tardy Recognition by Government

At the conclusion of last chapter we had joined head-quarters of the Regiment at Nowshera in June, where we remained until the 14th October, when, in accordance with instructions received, we marched to Nawakilla, in the Yusufzai country, leaving all sick men and invalids behind at Nowshera. The force which was assembled at Nawakilla for service in the hill country was under the command of Brigadier-General Sir Neville Chamberlain, K.C.B. The object of the expedition was to destroy Mulka, on the Mahaban Mountain, the stronghold of certain Hindoostanee fanatics, generally known as the "Sitana" fanatics, who infested our frontiers, and were incessantly attacking the villages in our territory. Mulka is just beyond the English frontier, and in the territory of the Indoons. The force marched in two divisions; the first, entirely composed of native troops, marched on the 18th; the second, composed of European troops, marched on the 20th. The Umbeylah Pass was seized without difficulty, but, owing to the bad road, the march, although a comparatively short one, lasted nearly 24 hours, and several days passed before all the guns and baggage were brought up. On the 21st the regiment encamped near the village of Umbeylah. On the 26th 150 men of our Regiment, under Major Parker, were engaged in repelling an attack from the enemy, on which occasion one private was killed and five were wounded. Privates William Clapperton and George Stewart were recommended for the medal for service in the field on this occasion. On the 30th the enemy made another attack on the pickets, but were repulsed. The regiment had three privates wounded on this occasion. On the 6th November a party of the regiment was attacked by the enemy, having been sent too far to the front, and not properly supported. Lieut. Dougall, Ensign C.B. Murray of the 79th (then attached to the regiment), one sergeant, and three privates were killed, and four privates were wounded. Captain Mounsey and Lieut. Davidson, the latter of the Indian Army, but attached to us, were specially mentioned for their gallantry on this occasion. On the 18th the whole force changed positions to higher ground, and was immediately attacked by the enemy, who was not repulsed before night. On this occasion Captain C. T. Smith, Lieut. Gore Jones, the latter of the 79th, doing duty with our regiment, and four privates were killed, and one sergeant, and four privates wounded. Major Parker being especially mentioned for his services. On the 19th Captain Aldridge and one private were killed, while another private was wounded. On the 20th, the enemy having succeeded in driving out the 101st Fusiliers from the "Craig Picket," by a sudden and unexpected attack, we were ordered up to retake it.

The "Craig picket" was situated at the top of a very rocky hill, which rendered the operation doubly difficult. Led by Colonel Hope, who was severely wounded, and supported by two native corps, we, in spite of the natural obstacles and the determined resistance of the enemy, re-took it at the point of the bayonet, and this day, in commemoration thereof, is still reckoned a jubilee day amongst us. The loss, however, was no less than seven privates' killed, one field officer, two sergeants, three corporals, and nineteen privates wounded. Another private was killed on the 27th.

On the 15th December, Major-General Garvock, commanding the Peshawur division, had succeeded Sir N. Chamberlain in the command of the whole force. The latter also had been wounded in the attack of the 20th, and having received strong reinforcements, he attacked and defeated the enemy at all points, but the regiment being on picket duty, we were not engaged on this occasion. Shortly after this the Bonyers asked for and obtained terms of peace, but not before we had burned several of their villages lying nearest our frontier, so as to leave them no nest to congregate in for some time to come.

Such, then, was my first – and as yet only – taste of the "baptism of fire," and never till my dying day can I efface its scenes from my mind. This was none of those fierce engagements with countless numbers, such as in the Peninsular, the Crimean, or in any of those later fields which were conducted by civilised nations opposing each other, and having, all the appliances of modern warfare brought into use. We had to contend against a stealthy, treacherous enemy of pure savages, to whom the laws of common humanity were unknown. Far from having the smallest drop of the milk of human kindness towards the wounded, our very dead became a prize to them like carrion to the vultures, and the scenes of mutilation that were enacted upon the bodies of our poor comrades whom we were sometimes compelled to leave upon the field, were disgusting in the extreme, and far too horrible to describe. The thought of this caused us to dread much more the fracture of a limb from some stray bullet than if it were to reach the most vital part and thus terminate our existence.

Often, as I have already said, had I read and pondered over the glorious deeds performed by my countrymen upon the field of battle, and longed to share in their well-merited honours, now that I had become a soldier; but when the stern reality was placed before me, and I had to meet such a foe face to face, I must confess I felt an indescribable thrill pass through me, and again when my front rank man rolled over a corpse and I had to step up into his place to keep the "thin red line" unbroken, all finer feelings gave way as I saw at once at what cost "Duty must be done," and how true was the exclamation of the Psalmist when he said –

"Come see what desolations war has wrought."

Savages though our foes were, they had a warlike fashion of their own in meeting us, as if the spirit of Cain was still rampant in the earth, and it was no child's play they gave us when we met them. Night and day it was a continual watch for them creeping, snake-like, in overpowering numbers through the tangled grass or brushwood, or stationing themselves behind some loose boulder in close proximity to us, whence they would rush, like a storm of locusts, with wild unearthly yells upon our positions, brandishing their weapons and seemingly courting death rather than avoiding danger.

Glad therefore were we, one and all, when we learned we had subjected our cruel enemy, and that peaceful arrangements had been completed; but our total loss proves our victory was not gained without a good deal of blood being shed – our own regiment's casualties during the campaign standing as follows: – Killed, five officers (including Lieuts. Dougall and Jones of the 79th Highlanders), 1 sergeant, and 17 privates; wounded, 1 officer, 2 sergeants, and 42 privates.

Though we still hear of troublous tribes about the North-Western Frontier, this campaign was the means of quieting these Bonyers, who have kept within bounds ever since; yet, thanks to the tardiness of our Government, our services in it were long in receiving the recognition they so justly deserved. It was close upon ten years afterwards ere the medal granted for it was served out to us. Different corps who had been in short campaigns subsequent to us, and with but trifling if any loss, had honours and rewards heaped upon them before us.

On the 4th January 1864 we marched to Peshawur, which place we reached next day, and on the 21st were inspected by His Excellency, Sir Hugh Rose (now Lord Strathnairn), K.C.B. Commander-in-Chief, who complimented us highly on the prowess displayed in the late engagements. Here we remained performing the usual duties the whole year, in the latter part of which the route for our proceeding down-country home was received with much enthusiasm. Each was more anxious than another to start "Westward Ho!"

CHAPTER V

March Across Country to Calcutta – Voyage Home and Arrival in Edinburgh

On the 14th December 1864 we commenced our march for home, and one can easily conceive the happiness felt by all when the welcome intelligence appeared in regimental orders, for in a few months more we would be back in the dear old land, gazing on the well-remembered scenes of former days.

> 'Tis sweet to see one's native land
> After many wandering years.
> And grasp the kind, familiar hand
> Of parents smiling through their tears.'

Prior to our departure, special general and divisional orders appeared eulogising the regiment, the following being a copy of the letter: –

"Rawul Pindee, 1st November 1864."

"The 71st Highland Light Infantry being about to leave the Peshawur Division en route to England, the Major-General desires to offer them his best wishes on the occasion. He has known the regiment or a number of years. He was very intimately associated with it in the Mediterranean, and his interest in it is now materially increased in no small degree by its having served under him in the field, and done its part, and done it well, in obtaining for him those honours which Her Majesty has been, pleased to confer. The Major-

General had not assumed command of the Yusafzai
Field Force when the Seventy-First recaptured the
Craig Picket, but he well knows it was a most gallant
exploit. Sir John Garvock, K.C.B., begs Colonel Hope,
C.B., and the officers, non-commissioned officers, and
soldiers of the Highland Light Infantry to believe
that although they will be soon no longer under
his command, he will continue to take the liveliest
interest in their career, and he now wishes them a
speedy and prosperous voyage."

The regiment was also inspected at this time, and medals for
"distinguished conduct in the field" were presented to Sergeant-
Major Blackwood, Privates W. Malcolm, W. M 'Donald, W.
Clapperton, and J. Ramsay, and the "Victoria Cross" to Private
G. Stewart, the whole of whom were highly complimented by
the General for their bravery. The Sergeant-Major also received
an annuity of £15, but had shortly thereafter to be invalided
on account of wounds, and presently occupies the honourable
position of one of Her Majesty's Yeomen of the Guard.

Our route was by marching from Peshawur to Delhi, and
from thence to Calcutta by rail. We crossed the river Indus at
Fort Attock by a large bridge of boats. The river here is very
rapid, and the country barren and wild, swarming with every
sort of wild animal. The daily march generally extended to from
ten to twelve miles, our camping ground being always spots
selected for that purpose which had been used by regiments
going and coming for many years previous. At Rawul Pindee
we encamped for a whole week, and, in accordance with custom,
volunteers were here allowed to draft themselves to any of the
other regiments in the Bengal Presidency. Two hundred of my
comrades accepted the offer, but I this time preferred to re-visit
Scotia. We crossed the Ihulum by a bridge of boats as at Attock,
and also the Chennah at Goojerat, which is more than three
miles broad there, and encamped outside the beautiful city of
Lahore, which is full of elegant and substantial buildings, while

the surrounding country is delightfully interspersed with wood, hill, and dale. Here I saw no beggars, and yet India is full of them, for from the time you touch the soil of Calcutta until you again quit the country you are everlastingly assailed with the incessant cry, "Backsheesh, backsheesh. Sahib!"

Our next halt was at Umritsur – a large and important town with a population of 128,000 inhabitants – and the next town of any consideration was Lodiama, situated on the banks of the Sutlej. The American Church has a mission planted here for the conversion of the natives, but what progress they have made, or are making, I am unable to say. They seemed very solicitous for the spiritual welfare of the British soldiers, by offering us their Bibles for sale at the low price of one anna (three halfpence). However, after being four years in the country, I do not recollect of ever coming across a thorough native Christian. It is true I came in contact with many who were said to possess the qualifications of the so-called British Christian, but these qualifications appeared to me to consist in their being able to speak a little English, drink Indian rum, and intersperse a few good British oaths in their conversation.

We reached Delhi on Kew Year's day 1865 and encamped outside the walls of that ancient city. It is very large, and is situated on the right bank of the river Jumna, the population numbering upwards of 160,000. We had our New Year's dinner on the plains where, but a few years previous, the deadly cannon were spreading death and destruction amongst the mutinous inhabitants of the city. The Jumna being only about three-quarters of a mile broad here, there is a stationary bridge of boats which we crossed and thereafter got the train direct to Chinsurahs, but the speed of the locomotives in that part of India can bear no comparison to those at home. As on the march, we encamped by day and as evening approached went whirring on our way again through the Indian jungles, no doubt often astonishing the tigers and jackals inhabiting them. We remained at Chinsurahs ten days previous to embarkation at Calcutta, the distance between them being only 24 miles, and the former a large military station, but on the 4th February the right wing (under Col. Hope, C.B.), got on board the hired transport

"Mauritius," and the left (under Major Gore), in a few days afterwards in that of the "Albert Victor."

I belonged to the former vessel, and we had a very pleasant voyage notwithstanding a few stormy days previous to sighting the Cape. We anchored in Table Bay for four days, and a number were permitted to go ashore and visit Cape Town, which was at the time garrisoned by the 10th regiment. I was one of the favoured few granted this indulgence, but, as I could see nothing of importance to attract my attention, after drinking a couple of glasses of "Cape smoke," a sort of whisky, I returned to my vessel. This was the only land we saw during the voyage (with the exception of Fayal, seven days' sail from Plymouth.) We had a newspaper started on board to beguile the time. A talented young fellow of the name of Edington was selected for its "Editor," to whom communications from all parts of the ship were sent during the week, and on the Saturday evenings the journal was read aloud to inform the whole of what had transpired in our little home since its previous issue.

We lost three men by death daring the voyage. Poor fellows! they were destined to find a watery grave just on the eve of reaching that Scottish home where fond parents were anxiously awaiting their return. We reached Plymouth harbour on the 29th of May, and went into barracks then for a few days until we got orders to proceed to Scotland.

These received, we again embarked this time in H.M. troop ship "Urgent," which conveyed us to Granton, our destination being Edinburgh Castle. Imagine the delightful feelings with which we again beheld the coast of our dear native land. Words would fail me to describe them. While rounding Berwick Law many was the anxious glance I cast over to the tranquil plains of Fife – that sweet wee "kingdom" which contained all I held dear in this world. Seven years had passed and gone since I, a young fair-haired boy, had left its distant hills for the active life of a soldier, yet they had not cooled my martial enthusiasm, for though the opportunity of again becoming a civilian was at this time afforded me, the attractions of the army still prevented my leaving the ranks where I had been

"A puir but honest sodger."

The dis-embarkation of the 71st created no small commotion at the pier of Granton, for many of its members belonged to, or about, Edinburgh, so that fathers, mothers, brothers, and sisters, crowded there anxious to again get a sight of, and press to their bosoms, sons and brothers who had been so long in the great land. (Five days afterwards, in the old castle of Edinburgh, I had the unfeigned pleasure of pressing my aged mother to my bosom. Poor body! At first she hardly knew her bronzed-faced son, but I had not the least difficulty in tracing the well-remembered features of former years. I at once knew the music of that dear tongue which was wont to instil into my soul the principles of love and self-respect, long years ere I thought of becoming a wanderer in foreign lands, or to mingle in the soul-stirring strife of modem warfare.)

Each was more enthusiastic than another to show their "love of country" on their first stepping on shore, and one high-spirited young fellow (Jamie MacTavish), who was an ardent admirer of everything belonging to Scotland, actually knelt down and kissed his mother earth after planting his feet on the soil of Scotia's classic stand. After the regiment was formed on the pier, previous to marching to Edinburgh, I said to young Mac:-

"Come noo, Jamie, let's hae that nice sang aboot landing in Scotland again."

"Well," says Jamie, "I intended no to sing that sang afore I reached my sister's fireside in the bonnie toon o' Stirling, but I heard the Cornel telling the band sergeant that the band was tae play ' Scotland yet ' on the road tae the Castle. Sae whan the band halts I'se sing ye my wee sang as we tread alang."

However, owing to other bands from the town and Jock's Lodge having come to meet us and give us music, we did not get Jamie's sang until after he had been divested of knapsacks, belts, &c, and had adjourned to the canteen. He possessed a charming voice, and sang in a sweet plaintive strain the following song, believed to have been composed by himself:

IS THIS BONNIE SCOTLAND AGAIN?

Lang years ha'e gane bye, sin' I left my dear hame
An' the freen's o' my early days;
But noo I'm at hame, an' nae mair will I roam
Awa' frae my sweet native braes.
Though ance on the blood-stained field I did lie,
Surrounded by comrades slain;
It's noo, thank God, I am able to cry.
Is this bonnie Scotland again?

Is this dear Scotia, the land o' my birth?
The land which did heroes produce;
Wi' ecstatic feelin's I noo kiss the earth
That ga'e birth tae Wallace an' Bruce.
Oh! deem me not weak, although I su'd shed
A tear on my bright native plain;
For noo my heart rises towards my head-
Is this bonnie Scotland again?

This is the land whar a fond mither smiled
Upon her Innocent boy;
This is the land whar a dear father styled
Me his pet, his comfort an' Joy.
But noo they repose in the auld kirk-yard,
Awa' o'er yon bonny green plain;
How happy I'd be, had they but been spared
To see me in Scotland again.

CHAPTER VI

Experiences in Edinburgh – The Guardroom – Walking Sentry at The Castle and at Holyrood Palace

The 71st received an exceedingly warm reception from the inhabitants of Edinburgh, while the Scotsman devoted no less than five columns of its sheet to detail the brilliant deeds achieved by the regiment on many a bloody battle-field. A few days after being settled down furloughs were granted to all those who had returned from India. Two hundred went off at a time, thus giving us all an opportunity of re-visiting the scenes of our youth, ere duty should once more call us to some distant land. The summer of 1865 was indeed a pleasant one to us dwellers in the Castle, as cheap excursion trains were almost daily arriving with multitudes from different parts of the country. Consequently the Castle was often crowded with "honest lads and bonnie lasses," each enquiring after "oor Jock, Tam, Jim, or Pete." This together with the temptations and charms of Auld Reekie proved too much for the wavering resolutions of many of us red-coats, the result being that many of us neglected to answer our names at Tattoo Roll Call. In this position I found myself twice during my short tour of duty there, and returning one morning after one of these occasions to the Castle I met an old friend (Mankey Bouffe) in a similar predicament wending his way homewards as merry as a lark.

"Weel, my old boy" says Mankey, "absent like mysel'. Hoo can we manage tae get a wet afore we gang intae the Castle."

"Hoo long is't since yer last drunk, Mankey."

"Eighteen months."

"Oh! you're sure tae be admonished the morn."

"Aye, oor guid Cornel is dealing very leniently towards us refractory sodgers, but I was absent last nicht an' got admonished the day already, sae I canna expect a chance the morn. But it's a puir heart that disna rejoice sometimes.

> I was absent last nicht an' I'm absent again,
> I've lost my shako in the wind an' the rain;
> I'll get a court martial the morn, I know,
> When up afore the Cornel pair Mankey maun go.
>
> I tore my new tunic in Mill's Court yestreen,
> An' lost my blue bannet in fechtin' wi' Jean;
> An' my bonnie war medal for service abroad
> Is popped i' the Coogate wi' Larry O'Dod.

What dae ye think o' that for a sang? That entirely flings oor regimental poet intae the shade."

"Weel," said I, "there's a'e thing strongly re- commends it tae my heart, an' that's its truthfulness," for at this time our friend Mankey was minus his head dress, while his tunic showed plainly he could fight in other places as well as the Pass of Umbeyla.

"I ha'e nae desire," says Mankey again, "tae gang intae the Castle afore I get a glass o' spirits. Sergeant Weston is for the regimental guard the day, I believe, sae I'll hae nae chance o' getting a smell after he gets me within his clutches."

"Weel, Mankey, in a little time Raeburn's'll be open, when we'll ha'e an opportunity o' drinking a health tae the bonnie lassies o' Edinburgh."

"I'm getting tired o' Edinburgh; I wish we got the route for some ither station, ane that would present less temptation tae the sodger; for it being my native toon, an' my auld companions sae numerous, I ha'e a hard time o't tae keep free o' the commanding officer's table."

"Nothing easier, Mankey. Just turn your back on the gay blandishments of Edinburgh. Resolve to keep inside the Castle instead of nightly singing o'er the sparkling glass, and you'll soon see yourself in the respectable position you occupied in India as a non-commissioned officer. I know, my dear Mankey, that the temptations of all our large cities are anything but favourable to a soldier; and while we are stationed at home, whether it be in Edinburgh, Dublin, or London, we will have the very same presented before our eyes."

"True, my old sodger; but let a red-coat be seen but ance on the public streets in a state o' intoxication, and he's considered no fit tae associate wi' the civil portion o' the community."

"What nonsense ye speak, Mankey. Are you not just after leaving a social bacchanalian band of brothers down the street there?"

"Yes, I left *them* happy enough, but they've nae commanding officer tae confront and hear the doom pronounced o' seven days in the cells an' ten confined tae barracks, for appearing drunk on the streets."

"No, but they can get fined in ten shillings, besides running the risk of losing their employment."

"I grant a' that; but yet the folks o' this country ha'e a strange way o' showing their respect for the defenders o' their country."

"Mankey, I'm proud o' the coat that I wear. I am prouder still of the distinguished regiment of which I am but a very humble member."

"Halt there, my callan. I yield tae nae man in admiration o' the great an' mighty warlike deeds that ha'e been accomplished by the Hielan' licht Infantry. But tae be ca'd a loafer by an ignorant clod-hopper is maist mair than the spirit o' Mankey Bouffe can bear."

"Such characters you ought to shun and treat with contempt. The British soldier who respects himself will be upheld by all good and honest men; and why be down-hearted, Mankey, we are but young soldiers yet. Although you have already fought in two campaigns, you might yet have to meet another foe on the plains of Europe. In all probability we'll have to wander in foreign lands again, and as we have chosen the army as our home let us make it as happy and as comfortable as we can. The 71st shall be our home for many years to come."

Mankey and I having by this time cleared the cobwebs from our throats, had to wend our way to barracks, where the sergeant of the guard provided us with quarters anything but congenial to our feelings, and where Mankey diverted the whole guard by singing to the air of " The Campbells are coming,"

THE SEVENTY AN' ONE

From the Grenadier Guards to the Hundred and Nine,
Distinguished regiments, that form the line;
I challenge ye a' to show me if you can,
A braver corps than the Seventy an' One.

Chorus
> Then hurrah! hurrah! for our country an' Queen,
> We're ready to fight when a foe's to be seen;
> Oor gallant corps, boys, stand second to none—
> Let's shout high the deeds o' the Seventy an' One.

Go search its old records, they prominently tell
Hoo the Glasco' heroes baith fought an' fell;
The Crimean plains an' wide Hindoostan',
Resound wi' the deeds o' the Seventy an' One.

On many a sanguinary red field in Spain,
The Seventy an' One did bright laurels gain;
On the slopes o' Vittoria the gallant Cadogan
Fell gloriously leading the Seventy an' One.

But time w'uld fail me, dear boys, to tell
The deeds o' the corps we a' love so well;
Wha carried the day at Seringapatam?
History exclaims 'twas the Seventy an' One.

In the year eighteen hundred an' sixty-three.
The Seventy-One were where the gallant s'uld be,

In storming the Craig Picket. Wha led the van?
'Twas Colonel Hope wi' his Seventy an' One.

Noo let us, brave comrades, high fill up the glass.
In memory o' those wha fell in the Pass;
Although they are sleeping in Hati-mor-dan,
Their memory is green in the Seventy an' One.

"Weel, Mankey," said Jamie Campbell from a corner of the guard-bed, "only sing that sang when you go before the Cornel the morn, an' he'll mak' ye a lance-corporal instead o' gie'n ye a court martial for losing yer shako."

"By the bye, Mankey, I heard you singing last night in a public-house in Rose Street among some Edinburgh Volunteers," chimed in Johnny Soutar, a young private in the guard-room.

"Weel, what o' that? We of the army feel proud o' oor gallant Volunteers. Should this country ever be involved in a European war, the Volunteers, in the absence o' the army, are weel able to defend the hearths and homes o' oor dear native land."

"An' hoo can man dae better.
Than in facing fearfu' odds—
For the ashes of his fathers,
And the altars of his gods?"

"Mankey's inclined to be very poetical to-night; he must have imbibed a considerable quantity of Rutherford's stout last night," says Andrew Thomson, who was a prisoner in the guard-room for neglecting to take his dinner.

A military guard-room is rather comical place, and the wit and humour sometimes displayed there would be precious to such military writers as Grant or Lever.

Many of my old friends, who occasionally visited Edinburgh during my sojourn there were surprised to find me only a private in the ranks, but I asked them to bear in mind that we had a great number of young ladies in Great Britain competent to adorn - the highest positions in society, and that, though a few were required to form the Peerage, one was considered quite sufficient to rule the gigantic possessions of the British Empire; so our sergeant-major, with a very few sergeants and corporals, were all that were required for a regiment. In subsequent years I was promoted to the corporal's rank, but never felt myself comfortable or happy, as stern duty often compelled me to have duties to discharge that were anything but pleasant to my mind. At this time, however, the non-commission officers of the 71st were a lot of able, intelligent men, well posted up in their duties, doubtless, through their teacher being one of the smartest adjutants in the British army. We hear much at present of a better class of recruits for the army, and no doubt educational ability in a non-commissioned officer is all very well; but if he is deficient of a thorough knowledge of human nature, and of how men who are under the restraints of martial law should be governed, he can never attain to real success in the profession of which he has voluntarily become a member.

On the 20th October we lost, by death, Lieut. - Colonel A. C. Parker, one of the most distinguished and promising officers of the army. He had served for 23 years in the 71st, and had fought with it throughout the Crimean and Central Indian campaigns, and received his Lieut. -Colonelcy in the Pass of Umbeyla for gallant conduct in the field. He belonged to a fine old English family, his great-grandfather being Admiral Sir Hyde Parker, who earned such a distinguished reputation as a naval leader during the last century. The Colonel's early death cast a deep gloom over the whole regiment (although he was a very strict disciplinarian), for he was greatly respected by all ranks. His body was laid in the Grange Cemetery, his funeral being one of the largest military ones ever seen in Edinburgh.

My first post as sentry in the Castle was over old "Mons Meg," and I thought the view from that elevated position a most magnificent one, commanding a glorious stretch of the surrounding country. I could see my native hills in the "Kingdom of Fife "rearing their majestic heads towards a lovely Scottish sky; the winding Forth rolling on its way to the mighty ocean; fields ripe for the sickle on every side; and the city of archi- tectural beauty and social culture lying at my feet. Language of mine is unable to describe "Modem Athens." I have seen some of the most splendid cities in the world – London, Dublin, Benares, Lahore, and Calcutta – but to my mind's eye they sink into insignificance when compared with the romantic city of Sir Walter Scott. While gazing on the charming scenes of my native land from the ancient Castle, I could easily understand the spirit which prompted the exclamation –

> "Where is the coward that would not dare
> To fight for such a land?"

I was always happy when it came to my turn to mount guard over the old Palace of Holyrood, for while on my lonely post at silent midnight my imagination would inhabit again its tenantless rooms, and I would carry me away back to the time when living men and fair women were won't to make its venerable walls re-echo with sounds of mirth and gaiety –

> What lovely females have been seen
> Inside thy walls in former days;
> Here reigned our beauteous Scottish Queen,
> The theme of many a poet's lays;
> Oh, for a pen to write thy praise
> Like Scotland's Burns.

> Yes, I have seen old Holyrood,
> Where Mary lived in days of yore,
> And where her cowardly husband stood
> While Rizzio's blood bestained the floor.
> Round her walls for many an hour
> I've mused on days now past and gone.
> When Scotland owned a Stuart power,
> Before a stranger filled the throne.

But we soldiers have no continuing city. We are like the tribe of the wandering foot and weary heart – here to-day and away to-morrow; from town to town, fort to fort. After eight pleasant months in bonnie Scotland we proceeded to Aldershot Camp, where we arrived on the 19th Feb. 1866, and formed part of the 3d Brigade under Major-General Sir B. Russell, K.C.B.

Farewell, Scotia, land of my fathers, I must again leave thee for other scenes and other lands. Farewell, thou bright romantic land of love and song; I hie me to other climes, but carry with me that undying love which every true Scotsman cherishes for the land of Wallace and Bruce. Land of historical associations, land of warriors' graves and martyrs' urns, land of heathery hills and wimpling streams, farewell to thee and the bright scenes of my youthful days; but when far from the hills where I wandered "In life's morning march when my bosom was young," many a weary sigh will I breathe towards thee. Duty may call me to mingle again in the deadly strife of battle fields; I may find a grave where no countryman can shed a tear over it; but while the Scottish blood warms my veins, here's a heart that will never prove false to thee.

> Farewell to Scotland's pleasant fields and
> forests clad in green,
> Her winding vales and flowery dales, where happy
> I ha'e been;
> Noo my heart is sad an' lonely, I let the tears doon fa',
> To leave dear friends behind me in Caledonia.

CHAPTER VII

Cork – The Irish Girls – Wounded in the Heart – Visit to a Roman Catholic Chapel

I'm off to Queenstown early Sn the morning,
I'm off to Queenstown before the break of day;
Give my respects to all the pretty English girls —
I'm off to Queenstown a little time to stay.

I was stationed with my regiment at Aldershot during the summer months of 1866; everything was quiet and peaceable at that large and important camp. We had our routine of guards and pickets to perform, and a weekly divisional field day in the Long Valley, which latter was always graced with the presence of the aristocratic beauty of England's daughters. When free from martial duty, many of us enjoyed ourselves in wandering over the hop-clad plains of Kent, admiring the beauties of smiling nature, or enjoying the 'chaff' of the bar-maid in the gin palaces.

In November 1866 we got a sadden order to hold ourselves in readiness to proceed to Ireland. I was entranced with the thought of beholding that magnificent country, of which I had read so mach. I pictured in my imagination the pleasures and enjoyment I would have wandering through that lovely land, where every hill and vale is immortalised in undying song. I felt extremely happy at the prospect of beholding the birth-land of Edmund Burke, the distinguished philosopher, orator, and statesman. I had read the works of Grattan, Curran, Moore, Lever, and Lover, and I had heard something about the great agitator and repealer, Daniel O'Connell. Consequently I longed to see the mountains of Kerry, where the great political opponent of Peel was born.

My regiment disembarked at Queenstown on 11th November

after forty-eight hours' sailing from Portsmouth. When Ireland burst upon my view, I was highly delighted with the general appearance of the green island. We got but a partial view of the beautiful city called Cork, as we marched through only some of her streets on our way to Fermoy Station, but I could see that Cork possessed some very beautiful public buildings, and the glorious river Lee, which flows through the town, gives a very picturesque aspect to Cork. I once heard a story about a rustic Irishman who had paid a visit to this city. On being asked how he liked the appearance of Cork, he exclaimed, "Bedad, it would be a beautiful place, if it was removed out to the country."

On arriving at Fermoy Station I witnessed a most painful and heartrending scene, the departure of emigrants for the distant wilds of America. It was a sorrowful sight to see grey-haired parents with the tears flowing down their withered cheeks taking an affectionate farewell of their dear sons and daughters, perhaps never more to meet around the old cabin door again.

In the centre of Patrick Street stands the monument of Father Mathew, the great temperance advocate; but from the number of public houses which abound in Cork I don't think temperance principles have made much progress amongst her citizens. I could see men and even women reeling through the streets under the influence of intoxication. But still I consider the Irish people more temperate than either the English or Scotch, and for this especially they deserve credit. Ireland with all her squalid poverty keeps her maidens comparatively pure from the social evils so prevalent in the adjoining isle. Scotland can produce more illegitimacy in one month than Ireland can do in a year, and one reason I think is that while many of the ministers of the Scotch Church – at least in my young days – paid no attention to the domestic education of her daughters, the Roman clergy, on the other hand, are most solicitous for the domestic as well as the spiritual welfare of their young women. Of course, I admit that owing to the imprudent and too early marriages in Ireland, you have a great many poor children brought into the world without food to feed them. That is a great blot on the Emerald Isle.

Fermoy is a picturesque town, beautifully situated upon the banks of the Blackwater, one of the most rich and fertilising streams in Ireland. On the banks of this romantic river stand many of those round towers so famous in Irish story. There are also some delightful cottages on both sides of Blackwater. Fermoy was founded by an enterprising Scotchman named Anderson, whose descendants are still wealthy inhabitants of the town. It contains some elegantly constructed buildings. The Roman Catholic College is well worthy of a visit from those who love to view venerable ivy-covered buildings. On the south side of the town lies a beautiful amphitheatre of hills, from which you have a splendid view of the surrounding country; away in the far north you behold the gigantic Galtee Mountains in Tipperary towering in majestic grandeur up to heaven, while the green fields and rural scenery along the Blackwater form a prospect delightful to behold.

Four miles from Fermoy stands Castle Hyde, the noble residence of Lord Fermoy, at the time of which I write Lord-Lieutenant of County Cork. The sequestered walks around this noble castle are truly picturesque. Nature seems to have furnished here a lovely paradise for moonlight, music, love, and poetry. Sweet lovers in such a nook could

> Breathe the tender tale
> Beneath the milk-white thorn
> That scents the evening gale.

Fermoy abounds with not a few bewitching girls, and many a sly look they give to the red coats. The Irish girls appear to be fonder of the military than the civil portion of mankind. But with respect to the stability of their love, I cannot say much in their favour. I have known them to change their affections with wonderful quickness when a more imposing or persuasive wooer would lay himself imploringly at their feet. If a private soldier is paying his endearing addresses to an Irish girl, she gives him up whenever a sergeant presents himself for matrimonial honours. A sergeant, however ugly, has no difficulty in procuring a handsome wife in Ireland, while a young recruit would have a formidable' task to secure the same. I do not mean to insinuate that there are no exceptions to this rule; but in all garrison towns where I have been rank and high pay possessed more charms to the loving eyes of the fair sex than the most perfect features of manly beauty.

After, staying sometime in Fermoy, my company, was sent to Tallow, a town in County Waterford. We were sent to assist the Civil Power during the election of a Knight of the Shire to serve in Parliament. Now, whether Ireland is badly governed or not, it is not my province to say. I have been present at General Elections in England and Scotland, but never did I witness such a display of military and political enthusiasm like what I saw on this occasion in Ireland. The candidate who holds the recognised opinions of the priesthood is generally the successful Member.

The people of Tallow were extremely kind to us. Our services, fortunately for us, were not required, so we had little to do. The 12th Lancers, who were sent to Dungarven on the same duty did not fare so well as we did. They were compelled to charge the unmanageable mob in self-defence, when three persons were killed, Captain Kelly, harbour master, Waterford, being one of the victims. My company remained seven days in Tallow.

The country around Tallow presents to the eye of the traveller a dreary, desolate aspect, so we began to weary for our quarters at Fermoy. We were in billets, and the most comfortable of billets are never very agreeable lodgings for a soldier. Soldiers know very well that civilians don't care about their company, and would see them far enough before occupying the best rooms in their houses. I was billeted with three more of my Company upon a Mr Keehoe, a publican. When we received our daily pay (one shilling per diem) we generally spent it on drink, instead of procuring the proper necessaries of life. Consequently many of us were anxious to return to Fermoy, where we would have the pleasure of regaling ourselves with good kail, beef, and potatoes, luxuries which we did not enjoy during our sojourn in Tallow.

Before leaving this town I received a deep wound in the heart, which put the strings of my affections in beautiful confusion. This fair one was the daughter of a tailor, and although she did not possess many of those prepossessing charms which are the distinguishing features of female beauty, she was a sweet, amiable girl, and passionately fond of poetry. One thing I believe that drew me towards her was that she happened to be the daughter of a tailor. My first early love in Scotland was the daughter of a tailor, and although I have wandered through many strange countries since those sweet golden days, seen many beautiful faces, and mixed with strange people, the image of that sweet girl yet rises above them all, awakening my recollections of happy, joyous days now flown for ever. Oh! reader, if we could but enjoy the golden opportunities of life's young morn again with the same experience we possess now, would we not steer our bark in a different channel, and sail more calmly down the stream of time?

The Irish, I found, had not a little of the mother wit for which they are famous the world ever. I made a remark to an intelligent Irishman in Tallow about the want of gas in the town, to which he immediately replied, "Sure, an' what do we require with gas in the large town of *Tallow*?"

The streets of Tallow are wide, but extremely dirty, the houses are irregularly built, and the spirit of poverty seems to pervade the whole town. The ground on which the town is built belongs to the Duke of Devonshire but that distinguished nobleman, like many more of his order in Ireland, draws his rents from a hard-working peasantry, without troubling himself about the condition and happiness of his tenantry.

The Catholic Chapel is a large venerable building. I am fond of old churches. They are a tangible connecting link between the present and the past. What associations cluster around an old Parish Church, wherein repose the sainted dust of many generations. Daring my short stay in Tallow I went once to the Catholic Chapel. I was deeply impressed with the beautiful service although a part of it was unintelligible to me, being conducted in the Latin language. I enjoyed the profitable sermon, which was a plain, simple exhortation to the immense congregation to live peaceably with all men, and to keep themselves unspotted from the world. I was rather surprised to see so much holy earnestness characterising the good priest, and the humble worshippers so devout, after what I had often heard from the lips of Protestant clergymen as to the Roman clergy being a money-seeking, self-serving class of men. Nothing is more common in Scotland than a course of lectures on Popery by minsters whose duty is to promote the world's happiness. In declaiming against the Church of Rome, the Protestant clergy, I think, commit a great error. Thousands of young Protestants after leaving home meet with all classes of men, and when they meet with Catholics with equal intelligence to themselves and possessed of the broad liberal principles of charity and love, they are very apt to have their own Church lowered in their estimation.

Many of the most distinguished men both of ancient and modem times, belonged to the Church of Rome. It can lay claim to its Drydens, Popes, Moores, Currans, and O'Connells, and many thousands more who have secured an imperishable name in the world for all the virtues that adorn and exalt mankind. I yield to no man in admiration of my own Church. I was born a Presbyterian, and in that faith I hope to die; bat I have known so many kind friends and intimate acquaintances belonging to the Church of Rome that I can never bring myself to look with hostile feelings upon that ancient and venerable communion.

CHAPTER VIII

A Gallant Captain – The Fenian Outbreak – The Irish Lasses

I left Tallow on the last day of the year 1866. It was a cold, gloomy, snowy day indeed. When I arrived at Fermoy I felt very tired after a twelve miles' march with a heavy kit on my back. The roads were slushy and hard to march upon; but soldiers are the most uncomplaining men in the world. We were cheerful under all circumstances. While on the road from Tallow to Fermoy we enlivened our pilgrimage with songs, stories, &c. We halted at a small village half-way between Tallow and Fermoy, where the only public-house in the place was left minus a pint of porter. Our much esteemed and respected captain, Charles Howard, Esq., gave to each man under his command a pint of porter, which raised him a considerable distance in our estimation. The captain was respected by every man in the troop for his many endearing qualities. He belonged to none of your obscure plebeian families. He was a real aristocrat; such a one as the British soldier loves to be commanded by.

The country between Tallow and Fermoy is desolate and barren. The houses which we passed on the road were mere hovels, and were very smoky in consequence of the fire being in the centre of the house. His highness the pig, too, might be seen occupying a corner in the peasant's humble cottage. But notwithstanding the wretchedness of their domiciles, the people appear quite contented and happy. The Irish peasant; is naturally of a cheerful disposition; and I never met one who did not have a "God bless you" on his lips when merely passing him on the road.

I arrived in Fermoy on Hogmanay night at 5 P.M.; and when I got comfortably seated around a cheerful fire in the canteen along with my companions in arms, I felt happier than a new crowned king. My weary feet and hardships were all forgotten. It is a poor heart that does not rejoice sometimes, and I would blame neither soldier nor civilian for taking a glass of spirits to cheer his heart while contending with the bitter blasts of life's stormy sea. I have spent Hogmanay in various parts of the world, and I never met the Scotchman yet that did not enjoy his glass upon that festive occasion, coupled with the singing of the songs of home and fatherland. In Highland regiments the soldiers do not go in general to bed until New Year's morning. When the clock strikes twelve, the band plays up the familiar air of "Auld Lang-syne." Then what cheering, shouting, and hurrahing takes place in the barrack-square. The band and pipes play at intervals our national tunes, while the soldiers begin the Scottish custom of exchanging glasses, and pledging each other's health.

Our commanding-officer on such occasions is usually very indulgent and considerate. He will neither confine nor punish, unless we are incapable of taking care of ourselves, and then the guard-house, as a matter of course, must become the home of every drank, unmanageable soldier.

New Year's day passes away in Ireland like any other day. Christmas is the great festival, in which everyone is dressed in his or her best attire, and all attend chapel during the day, but at night they conduct themselves like a victorious nation commemorating a great battle, such as Waterloo or Trafalgar, instead of observing with becoming holiness of life the great day on which the Saviour of the world was born.

I spent January and the two following months in the usual way of military life – drilling, acting as guards and pickets, and performing other multifarious duties inseparable from a large garrison. My evenings off duty were divided between "books and woman's looks." I may mention here that the Fermoy girls were very fond of the Highlanders. Some twenty of them selected husbands from my regiment, while a few others, I believe, clandestinely married.

We were enjoying ourselves in Fermoy pleasantly and happily until the memorable 5th of March 1867, when the intelligence flew like wildfire through Ireland that the Fenians had risen in thousands at last, and were determined to free their country from the Saxon yoke, and annihilate the British army, or drive it from the Emerald Isle.

Report fearfully exaggerated their strength. General O'Connor was marching on the city of Cork with twenty thousand men, and General Burke was concentrating a large force on Limerick Junction, while Colonel O'Brien had taken possession of Mallow. Such were the reports that came to Fermoy on that dismal, snowy, March morning. There were only three companies of my regiment in Fermoy; the others were out on detachment duty. So we all expected to be cut up and put in barrels, and sent to America, as specimens of the brave British army. Those who favoured the Fenians did everything in their power to create false alarm. We know that the rails had been torn up at Limerick Junction, and that the telegraph wires were broken in various places between Dublin and Cork, but we never dreamt that the British army was to be swept from the Emerald sod and give place to a new order of Government.

Really this Fenian affair, after all, was a silly movement. To think that a few school boys, lawyer's clerks, and counter-loupers, were able to overthrow the British power in Ireland! The very idea was preposterous. Yet the movement assumed large proportions in my imagination. I had pictured to myself a brilliant array of armed men who were determined to try the strength of the British lion upon an honourable field of fight. But when they confined themselves to incendiary proceedings, to murder, and secret assassination, they did not show themselves humane patriots, but despicable rebels.

Ireland should now become a contented country. That she has been long subject to wrong, no intelligent man can deny; but the disestablishment of the Protestant Church, and giving the farmer a proper hold of his land, should help very much to calm and pacify the Irish. Was Scotland a contented nation when King James tried to force Episcopacy down her people's throats? No. Scotland resisted to the blood against Episcopalian encroachments, and ceased not till she got a form of ecclesiastical government in accordance with her own feelings. Now this favoured Church in Ireland, which was only countenanced by a few English settlers and aristocratic families, was a standing insult to the universal faith of the country. This Church of the few had no love nor sympathy for the Church of the many. I have worshipped in large Episcopalian Churches in Ireland where I have counted the worshippers in tens, while the Catholic Chapel in the same parish was crowded by an attentive, devoted, but poor congregation. By all means let the Protestant Church flourish in Ireland, but let it do so upon the strength and purity of her own doctrines and not live on the money which belongs to a hard-working Catholic peasantry.

However, I am no politician, and will never have the distinguished honour of standing in Parliament to redress Ireland's wrongs. I shall therefore say no more about her manifold grievances.

My opinion of Fenianism is simply this – The ill-starred movement had its rise and progress in America. On the disbandment of the American army, after the civil war, many Irishmen who had held subordinate rank in that army found themselves without employment. Perhaps they were unable to distinguish themselves on the battle fields of that mighty Continent, and probably they thought it would be fine fun to come over to Ireland and organise a rebellion, thinking by that means to earn that immortality which the American war denied them.

The leaders of the Irish Fenians were Americans, every one of them. If not born in Ireland they were the descendants of Irishmen who had left the Emerald shores for America, carrying with them undying hatred of the British rule in Ireland along with them. But there is a certain class of men in every country who would not feel content under their country's laws, although they were framed within the portals of heaven. Oh! poor Fenian leaders. In a few years your names will be forgotten, if even now they are remembered. Your grand ambition is to be known to posterity as the brave emancipators of Erin from British power. You would like to have your names enrolled on the pages of history along with a Tell, a Wallace, and a Washington, but Ireland shall be flourishing, free, glorious, and intelligent, when the name of Fenianism will be buried in oblivion. The great promoter of sedition in Ireland was the inflammatory newspapers which were spread in tens of thousands over the country, such as the Irishman, Nation, Shamrock, and others of a similar stamp. The peasantry eagerly believed every word written by the editors of these papers, in which the most glaring falsehoods were daily circulated against the British Government.

In dealing with Fenianism the Government exercised extreme caution in all their proceedings. Had they suspended a few editors by the neck as an example to those who were less to blame in detestable conspiracies, they would have done a good thing for Ireland.

Be that as it may, we had hard duties to perform while chasing the Fenians. Great battles have been fought and won on the Continent of Europe with less fatigue and hardship on the part of the victors than we had to endure daring the few months that Ireland was in a state of rebellious fermentation. Still we were only chasing an imaginary enemy. While we were marching at the still hour of night in pursuit of the foe, I suppose the rebels were enjoying the comforts of a warm bed.

If Fenianism had its gloomy aspect, it had also a cheerful one. It gave to us the opportunity of marching into quiet country villages, where red coats were hitherto unknown. What the men may have thought of our appearance amongst them, I cannot say; but the girls – dear creatures – welcomed our presence amongst them with demonstrative joy. We enjoyed many pleasant hours in snug little parlours with the charming Irish lassies. I verily believe those Irish maidens did their utmost to support and encourage Fenianism (not that they were rebelliously inclined towards her Britannic Majesty), but only that they might have their streets paraded by handsome young soldiers. Seeing that the Fenians would not give us an engagement, we felt very thankful to the girls, who were willing to give us an engagement for the natural period of our lives. Indeed, many an old maid who had resigned all hopes of ever tasting the sweets of domestic happiness, put on her most endearing smiles, that she might win the heart of some old soldier, and many of them were successful in their love endeavours. Many a lovely girl in Ireland would have wasted her sweetness on the desert air, if the Fenians had not thus indirectly provided them with husbands.

After war was over with the Fenians, and peace restored, my company was sent to Mitchelstown to relieve a company of the 6th Regiment, who had rendered themselves obnoxious to the Mitchelstownians in connection with Fenianism. My company left Fermoy on the 29th of May 1867.

CHAPTER IX

Mitchelstown – Helen O'Keefe – Promotion

It was a calm, fine morning when my company entered Mitchelstown. Joy seemed spread over the beautiful landscape as the golden rays of the morning sun fell in soft splendour on the Galtee Hills.

A feature of Mitchelstown is the number and beauty of her fair sex. The rustic girls in Ireland are, I think, more graceful and majestic in their carriage (because more natural) than either the English or Scotch; and I am free to confess that an Irish country girl has made more impression upon my heart than the most elegant, gay, and witty girls I ever met elsewhere. In every town and village I found some sweet Desdemona to put my affections in beautiful confusion.

There was one young lady in particular in Mitchelstown, Miss Helen O'Keeffe, who won the admiration of every soldier in the barracks by the exquisite symmetry of her form. Her beauty was irresistible. Her large, lustrous, expressive eyes were fringed with glossy lashes, a fine ruddy glow shone on her beautiful cheek, and raven hair braided and adorned her pure sweet brow. All these physical charms were heightened and intensified by her bewitching smile. It was impossible to remain long in her company without feeling the warmth of pure affection for such a lovely creature. The beauty of her mind, which was well stored with useful knowledge, corresponded with her comely presence, and made her a most delightful companion. The sweet hours of happy and instructive conversation which I enjoyed with that fair daughter of Ireland will be cherished by me like a delicious dream of the past. Farewell, sweet Helen O'Keeffe, may you find all the happiness in this world which your goodness deserves. Meanwhile let me lilt this farewell ditty in your praise: -

ELLEN O'KEEFFE.

Alas we must sever, dear maiden, for ever,
While tears like a river now flow from my eyes;
Since I saw thy sweet face in thine own native place,
My heart has been nought bat a fountain of sighs.

Wherever I roam now, far from thy sweet home now,
Nothing shall come now bat sorrow and grief;
Where'er I may wander, 'mong beauty and grandeur,
On thee I must ponder, sweet Ellen O'Keeffe.

Then art brighter by far than the pore morning star.
And may sorrow ne'er mar thy passage through life;
May angels defend thee and blessings attend thee.
And husband befriend thee when thon art a wife.

I must soon roam again far beyond the dark main.
While my tears are all vain, thou young rosy thief;
Ah! a sweet thief thou art, thou hast stolen my heart.
And in sorrow we part, sweet Ellen O'Keeffe.

Mitchelstown is chiefly remarkable for its romantic situation. The buildings are in a rather dilapidated condition; the streets wide and commodious, but extremely dirty. The town, however, contains two good hotels, besides a number of second-class shops. Its public-houses number over fifty, and a bookseller's shop is not to be found in the whole town. This state of things says little for the intellectual improvement of the Mitchelstownians. The Galtee Mountains, the highest in the interior of Ireland, are situated about three miles from the town, while the little village of Ballygreen, immortalised in song, lies within five miles of Mitchelstown. Marshallstown and Kilbennie are two nice looking villages, all within an hour's walk from Mitchelstown. It was near Marshallstown where the Fenian Crowley was killed. Poor misguided rebel, he fought with a bravery worthy of a better cause. Although surrounded by the military on every side, his indomitable spirit would not yield till a bullet laid him weltering in the Funchian River.

Kingston Castle, one of the most elegant of modern structures in Ireland, stands in the immediate neighbourhood of Mitchelstown. But the Earl is an absentee, like many more of his order in Ireland. If men of his wealth and influence were to spend the money at home, which they draw from a hard-working peasantry, there would be less cause for discontent among the rural population. The Irish people are waiting with tolerable patience for happier times. I have seen strong healthy men working in Ireland for six shillings a-week, while his fellowmen can earn eighteen in Britain. Of course, it is a great misfortune for nearly all Ireland outside of Ulster that she has no manufactures – only the land to depend on.

Through Kingston domain flows the river Funchian, which affords excellent sport to the angler; many a sweet summer gloamin' I have wandered along the banks of that lovely stream, admiring the beauty of the tranquil scene. In the vicinity of the town there is a spring well which is much visited by tourists in summer. It is held in great repute by the natives of Ireland for its healing properties – the blind, the lame, and all who are afflicted with divers diseases, come to its health-giving waters. It is called Saint Fainin's Well after an Irish saint. Nothing irritates the feelings of the people more than to disbelieve in the potency of its healing powers. I heard a story from the lips of a young lady about an old woman who once committed great sacrilege by washing her clothes in the Well. The holy saint was so enraged at this unpardonable indignity that he came in the night-time and removed the Well from its original situation, which was on the opposite side of the town, to where it now stands, and so carefully did he remove the trees, shrubs, &c., which surrounded it that no one could tell the change had it not been on the other side of the town. So runs the story which is implicitly believed by everyone in Mitchelstown.

During my stay in Mitchelstown I made frequent excursions to the Galtee Hills. To climb these mountains and behold the surrounding country is a great pleasure. Give to me the

> Mighty mountain, purple breasted,
> Peck clouds cleaving, snowy crested.

During my sojourn in Mitchelstown I sometimes went to the Catholic Church, not so much, perhaps, for the purpose of worshipping as to see the pretty girls going to and from the church. Now, dear reader, you may consider me a very irreligious person to make such a confession; but in the beginning of these remarks I plainly stated that I intended to speak the truth. Now, gentle reader, be thou as candid and acknowledge the truth. Many a time have you not gone to church with more love in your head than religion in your heart?

The Rev. Father O'Brien, parish priest of Mitchelstown, was a good, kind. Christian clergyman, but if it came to his knowledge that any of us redcoats had had a clandestine meeting with any Mitchelstown beauty, her name was called out in the chapel the following Sunday, and her conduct denounced in no measured terms. But Father O'Brien is a clergyman of the old school, and, I daresay, entertains strange notions about military morality. I can tell him, however, or any gentleman that wears his cloth, that soldiers are not the abandoned wretches which we are sometimes called. I have known the service to make honest men of civil rogues; but out of the great number of men who annually leave the army we hear of few of them turning out scoundrels and vagabonds.

The Irish have a good deal of theology in their mental composition. I have mixed among the common working people of Ireland, and I have had friendly discussions with them upon scientific and religious subjects; but I am bound to say I do not remember of ever hearing an Irishman give expression to atheistical opinions, such as I have heard in the large cities and towns of Great Britain. An Irishman will swear, fight, and drink, still he strongly believes in the doctrines taught by his Church. An Irishman, however exhilarating his spirits may be, never forgets his God, at least after his own way. Just pass an Irishman on the road. His first salutation is, "Good day" (as the case may be), and "Glory be to God," &c. Hume, Voltaire, and Paine are names unknown among the peasantry of Ireland. Long may they remain ignorant of that system of infidelity which has long tried to overthrow the moral government of God and to hold man irresponsible for his belief.

Being on parade with my company after returning to Fermoy, Colonel Hope, C.B., our distinguished commanding officer, informed us that he had received a letter from Neil Brown, Esq., the resident magistrate of Mitchelstown, apprising him that our conduct and behaviour in Mitchelstown had been most exemplary, and that the Highlanders had won the respect and esteem of all classes of the community. We felt extremely gratified at this pleasant intelligence, because some of the papers were loud in their expressions of disapprobation at the conduct of the military in other parts of Ireland. On returning to Fermoy I only stayed a few days there when I was promoted to the rank of corporal in Captain Lewis' company, at that time stationed at Ballincollig, a small village romantically situated four miles from Cork. I felt so reluctant to leave my old company that I had requested permission from my commanding officer to resign the rank of lance corporal, but my request was not granted; so I had just to leave the company in which I had spent several pleasant years and join a company in which I was a comparative stranger. I had to undertake duties of which I had little practical knowledge, and I was leaving a captain and pay- sergeant both of whom were distinguished by many amiable and soldierly qualities. They were both deservedly respected and esteemed by the men of their company, while the men themselves were everything that could be desired. No wonder, then, that I felt a little sorrowful in parting with my old companions in arms.

On joining the Company, I received a warm reception from the men. I found my new Captain, Robert Lewis, Esq., condescending and considerate to all under his command, and the pay-sergeant just the proper man for his position. John Summers possessed the essential requisites for the discharge of the multifarious duties incumbent upon a colour-sergeant; besides he kept his proper position in the company. He was just, impartial, and had a sound discriminating judgment. The men of the Company I soon learned to like; they were jolly social fellows, and lived in great harmony with one another. Indeed I loved I Company so well, that when I had the opportunity of returning to C. Company I preferred to remain in I. Company.

I arrived in Ballincollig on the evening of 28th October 1867. It was a lovely glorious night; the bright moon hung like a golden lamp in the midst of the heavens, bathing the majestic landscape with a glory indescribable, while the wimpling waters of the river Lee were heard in the distance, playing sweet music to the silence of tranquil nature.

> How lovely the enchanting scene
> Appeared that night to me,
> When I beheld the flowery banks
> Of lovely flowing Lee.

My leisure time was mainly occupied in exploring old towers and castles which abound in the vicinity of Ballincollig. One old time-worn castle I admired very much, once the residence of Brien Baro, King of Munster. The hand of time, however, had made sad havoc with its towers and battlements; but still:

Its majestic ruins are glorious in decay.

My stay in Ballincollig was of short duration. After remaining six weeks there my company was re-called to Fermoy. I left the little village without a lingering regret. I had formed no friendships among her people, and Cupid had stuck none of his darts in my heart.

CHAPTER X

In Love – Soldiers' Wives – Taking a Prisoner to Cork – A Most Unfortunate "Spree," With Its Humiliating Consequences

When we returned to Fermoy it was the depth of winter, and the desolating blast was howling o'er the plain, making fields and forests bare. Snow was lying on the ground; the days were short, and the nights long. We had in consequence few drills to perform, and time hung heavy on our hands. The studious and thoughtful found employment for the intellect in our large library, the social and gay had their amusements in the canteen, while the lover of feminine beauty found his sweetest pleasures amongst the happy girls of which Fermoy possesses not a few. I belonged to the latter class. My evenings, when off duty, were invariably spent among the lassies. The result was that I fell in love – deeply, fearfully and desperately in love. The object of my affection was a tall graceful sweet romantic girl. She was what I poetically designated her, "the sweet flower of Fermoy." I had often fallen in love before, but it was all moonshine compared with this. The glorious summer of my manhood was a thing of the past, the fresh early feelings of life's young morn were withered and dried up, and still I fell in love. I exerted all the strength of my poetical powers to celebrate in song the charms of my inamorata. Still her love was cold and phlegmatic in comparison with mine. Had our affections been reciprocal, I would have been a happy man, bat the course of true love never did run smooth. I was like a great many more men in the world - fond of the courting part of love but I entertained different feelings with respect to matrimony. Courtship is bliss, but matrimony often turns out a blister. The Irish girls abominate protracted courtships, and while I was writing love poetry and assailing her ears with amorous affections, I should have been deeply engaged in matrimonial speculations. Domestic happiness may be very enjoyable in civil life, but after mature consideration I don't think that the domestic element should be so largely infused into the army. On the admission of females into the army. Government should be careful in giving instructions to commanding officers to institute a strict investigation respecting at least the moral character of those who are about to become married women in the army. A minister's certificate of character is not often much to depend on. I do not mean to say that soldiers' wives are the off-scouring of civil society. I have known and do know soldiers' wives who are patterns of virtue. Such women I reverence with all my heart; but when I hear a woman opening her mouth and belching forth the most obscene expressions I am covered with shame.

> I do not for a moment say
> That soldiers' wives are all the same;
> The sun's not purer at noon - day
> Than some sweet wives that I could name.
> But, Lord, they're few and far between.
> Like tufts of grass on desert plain;
> I would not marry some I've seen
> For all the wealth that's in the main.

I may mention here that during my rambling! through Ireland I had a most disinterested friend and companion in the person of George Bock, one of the most manly and independent soldiers I ever met with in the British army. My dear friend and valued companion will, I trust, pardon this slight expression of affectionate remembrance, and forgive me for introducing his name here. Dear George, we have climbed the pine-clad hills of India, and wandered by Indus's rushing river; and when duty calls us to foreign lands again, we will cast many a pleasant look back to old Ireland and her bright-eyed daughters.

We enjoyed much happiness in Ireland this winter. Fenianism 'had entirely collapsed. The American element of Fenianism had left the country, and nothing existed to give indications that the malcontents were still fomenting rebellion. We, no doubt, heard of a few Fenian orators on the other side of the Atlantic, who were speaking high sounding words about the invasion of Ireland, the annexation of Canada, and the expulsion of the British from the American Continent. But while such braggadocios were airing their ostentatious language before American dupes, Ireland was enjoying the quiet and rest of peace. The peasantry were working diligently and perseveringly, while well cultivated fields everywhere bore testimony to the arduous nature of their labours. This detestable conspiracy was foreign in its origin. Once the immigration of its leaders into Ireland was checked, Fenianism died a natural death. Ireland's quietness this winter was extremely pleasing to us. We had no night marches to perform; and our duty was regular and easy, which brought me to this conclusion, that Fermoy was a very pleasant town to soldier in.

We spent the New Year 1868 similar to its predecessor – drinking, dancing, and keeping up the customs of Auld Scotland. At this time, I received a letter from my brother, a sergeant in H.M. 92d Highlanders. They had just left Dublin for Cork, and he was anxious that I should pay him a visit previous to his embarkation for India. We had only met once during the past ten years of our military life, and then it was only a brief shake of the hand and a long, affectionate parting. Oh, how many brothers and sisters have parted with the sentiment of those beautiful words of the Irish poet hanging upon their lips:

> "Oh, well may we know, when this short life is gone.
> To meet in a world of permanent bliss,
> A friendly grasp of the hand hastening on
> Is all we enjoy of each other in this."

Well, I could not but embrace this opportunity of seeing my brother. "Accordingly I got two days' leave from my commanding officer, and went by the next morning train to Cork. On my arrival, my big brother received me with every demonstration of brotherly affection, while my good sister was very solicitous in her endeavours to render my visit happy and comfortable, and my little nephew, Harry, before I was ten minutes in the house, was pulling my whiskers (I beg pardon, reader, I am not permitted to wear whiskers, I meant to say my hair) in a way anything but pleasant, and calling me by the endearing appellation of "Uncle." After seeing my brother so happy in his married life I was not altogether pleased with bachelor ways, and I thought there might be some happiness in domestic life after all.

My brother was fresh from Scotland, where he had been on a visit to our aged parents – perhaps his last meeting with them on earth. They are now old and stricken in years, and he was about to sail for India's sunny clime, a land which in all probability would be his home for many years to come. He had many things to tell me about home and fatherland, and of meeting and parting with friends, much of which was very touching and all of it interesting. Although I am five years his senior, my brother counselled me against the sins and temptations peculiar to a military life with wisdom and knowledge becoming a Grecian philosopher, and winded up his well-meant exhortations with something about matrimonial alliance, domestic happiness, &c.

My brother and his wife accompanied me to the railway station. We took an affectionate farewell with each other, hoping to meet in the land of our birth, when our military wanderings were done. We shook hands warmly and parted – they to their quarters in Cork Barracks, while I went by the evening train sad and lonely, to my regiment at Fermoy.

During my two hours' ride between Cork and Fermoy I gave myself up to melancholy reflections. I took a retrospective view of the unclouded past. I thought on the sunny days of childhood, when that fair-haired brother wandered with me over the hills and glens of bonnie Scotia. I pondered o'er the golden hours when we chased the butterfly along the banks of our native streams. I thought on the changes and vicissitudes of our lives since those sweet, happy days when we gamboled in frolicsome glee around the parental hearth. No clouds sat upon our souls. No cares disturbed the peace of our minds in those happy days. Oh, reader, we all know what childhood's days were – one long unclouded summer day!

Such were my reflections. I was sorry in parting with a dear brother whom I might never meet on earth again.

> "We grew in beauty side by side,
> We filled one home with glee;
> But now we're scatter'd far and wide
> By mount, by stream, and sea! - *Hemans,*

When I arrived at Fermoy station my old friend and companion, George Rock, was waiting to accompany me to town, where I soon got happy and merry. Sitting o'er the intoxicating glass my melancholy reflections passed away like the morning cloud and the early dew. The cares and trials of life were all forgotten, all anxious cares were banished from my memory.

> "I sat glorious
> O'er a' the ills o' life victorious."

After enjoying two social hours I wended my way to barracks. Next morning I was corporal for canteen duty, which is a very unpleasant duty to perform. I may explain the nature of this duty to my civilian readers. A non-commissioned officer is detailed daily by the sergeant-major, whose duty it is to see that no defaulter enters the canteen for the purpose of procuring drink, and if the corporal allows one defaulter to get one pint of malt liquor he runs the risk of being reported to his superiors by some officious parasite, because every regiment contains a few of such characters, who glory to build up a name upon the fallen fortunes of their military contemporaries.

Now comes the grand crushing point in my military history. I have endeavoured to be faithful in these wanderings, and I intend to let the reader know everything concerning the calamity which shortly befell me.

On the 26th day of January 1868 I was called before Sergeant-Major Alexander Barr, who told me that I would have to parade in front of the regimental guard-room the following morning, and escort a prisoner to Cork military prison. After giving me orders relative to that important duty, I marched next morning to Cork.

On arriving there I handed over my prisoner to the prison authorities, which was all right. But that same evening I went out to the beautiful city and got intoxicated. Being in this condition I foolishly absented myself four days from my regiment, indulging in riotous living, over which I desire to cast the veil of oblivion. When I came to my sober senses I felt a little of the prodigal's shame and repentance. I would arise and go to my regiment; but the thought of confronting my commanding-officer in my present condition filled my mind with bitter and remorseful meditations. I will never forget that morning when I emerged from my degraded den. The morning was cold, gloomy, and black, which accorded well with the melancholy state of my feelings. I stood on the streets of Cork hopeless, helpless, and almost penniless. I longed, like David of old, for the wings of the morning that I might flee away and be at rest. But many a soldier besides me, I encouraged myself by thinking, had been in similar circumstances. I had killed no man. I had committed no disgraceful crime. Why, then, should I be afraid to face my regiment? Though dark despair surrounded me on every side, I plucked up courage, determined to wend my way to Fermoy, and present myself before my commanding-officer. But although I had traversed most of Cork's streets during my previous visits, I was entirely bewildered this time. On leaving the city I took a wrong direction, and instead of finding myself, as I expected, near Fermoy, I was within two miles of Macroon, a town some twenty miles west from Cork. Gentle reader, conceive my astonishment when a policeman, whom I accosted by the way, told me that I was nearly forty miles from Fermoy. Here was I in a proper dilemma. Forty miles from my regiment in a cold January morning, while the only friend near me was a sixpenny bit in my pocket. My misery was complete; my despair was perfect. Tom Hood's melancholy and pathetic lines came rushing to my memory –

"Mad from life's history,
Glad to death's mystery.
Swift to be hurled
Any place, any place, out of the -"

Out of Macroon by all means. It is wonderful what the human heart can endure when burdened with the cares of life. I tried to be as cheerful as the circumstances of my position would admit. I sat down by an old roofless house by the wayside and refreshed myself with a smoke from the peace-yielding pipe. Oh, sweet, comforting pipe, thou cheerest the heart of the humble peasant as well as that of the mighty philosopher. Gentle reader, if thou art a smoker, thou knowest what a great consoler the smoke of a pipe is when vexed and disturbed with the ills of life. Notwithstanding my melancholy condition I actually felt supremely happy and comfortable while enjoying my pipe that cold, dismal night. I dreamed my- self in a dream, but not a dream of fair women like Alfred Tennyson. I dreamed that I was in Fermoy, with nothing to mar the peace of my mind. But, like Alexander Selkirk in his foreign island,

"Recollection soon rushed me back to despair." Alas, poor Pindar! you have been in some strange scenes in your lifetime, but nothing ever like this.

After reflecting on my gloomy condition, I saw no other alternative but to retrace my steps back to Cork, where I arrived about eight o'clock in the morning. Here I had marched upwards of thirty miles since the previous night, and still I was no nearer Fermoy. I was afraid to pass through the streets of Cork during the day for fear of the police, who might apprehend me for a deserter from H.M. 71st Regiment. So I concealed myself in a haystack during the day. When the shades of evening had gathered around my path I emerged from my hiding-place and crossed the river

Lee, leaving Cork two miles behind me ere I drew breath. I had still threepence left out of my sixpence, with which I got a pint of porter and a pennyworth of bread, which refreshed me very much. The nearer Fermoy the happier I was getting. I was in desperate exultation to see Fermoy, although I knew well that I would be severely punished for my unsoldierly conduct.

I got into Fermoy the same night I left Cork at 10.80, when I went to a dear friend's house and got something to refresh me after my weary journey. I then went to my barracks, where I was received as a prisoner by Colour-Sergeant Murray. My court martial and imprisonment will form the substance of next chapter.

CHAPTER XI

Cork – Last Visit

Next morning I was taken before Colonel McDonnell, the commanding officer of my regiment. He simply read over my crime, and informed me that I would have an opportunity of clearing myself before a court-martial. I could not have said one word in vindication of my conduct. I was removed under an escort back to my barrack room, where I had to remain for five days until they received an order from Cork, sanctioning my court-martial. The next day, word having come from Cork, seven officers sat in judgment on poor Pindar, viz.: – one colonel, two captains, and four subalterns. After entering the court-martial room, the president read over the charge preferred against me, which was as follows:

> "For conduct unbecoming the character of a non-commissioned officer, and to the prejudice of good order and military discipline, in having at Cork, on or about the twenty-ninth day of January 1868, when on escort duty, absented himself without leave from tattoo, and until the evening of the first day of February 1868, when he returned to his quarters at Fermoy.
>
> **Signed**, "I. I. McDonnell, Lieut. -Colonel, "Commanding 71st Highland Light Infantry."

I had nothing to say calculated to extenuate my conduct in their eyes. Consequently I pled guilty to the charge preferred against me. I had now five days longer to wait in anxiety and suspense before I knew the result of my court-martial, which had to be sent to Cork for confirmation and approval by the General commanding the Cork division. But lo, on the sixth morning after my trial, I

had to confront my regiment and hear my doom pronounced
in unmistakable language by Lieutenant and Adjutant Wilson.
I was inclined to feel a little nervous, when Mr Wilson read in
a clear tone of voice the opinion of the Court, which was to the
following effect: –

> "The Court is of opinion that No. —, Corporal John
> Pindar, is guilty of the charge preferred against him,
> but taking into consideration his previous very good
> character, and the absence of former convictions,
> now sentence him to be reduced to the rank and
> pay of a private soldier, and further to undergo an
> imprisonment with hard labour for a period of fifty-
> six days. Approved and confirmed.
>
> "George Campbell, Major-General,
> "Commanding Cork Division."

Ah, me! The morning after my sentence was read I was marched to
Cork Prison in the same manner as I had taken my own prisoner
a few days before. Indeed, I was the first prisoner which the
prison authorities had received since I handed over my own. I
had brought myself to my present position by my own foolishness,
so the best philosophy which I could exercise now was to resign
myself to my inevitable fate I had little difficulty in conforming
to the rules and discipline of the prison. No fault was found with
me during my imprisonment. I was promoted to the second-class
for being, I suppose, able to command my tongue. The infernal
silent system which is imposed on all prisoners is enough to
drive a poor victim insane, while the harsh language employed
by some of the ignorant and uncultivated warders towards a
poor prisoner requires a sublime philosophy to endure. During
the fifty- six days in which I was confined within its gloomy
walls, I felt like Giant Despair in the dungeon. My life was one
complete round of unmitigated misery, but oh, what a glorious
day was the 2nd of April 1868. It was indeed a joyful day to me,
when I emerged from my gloomy cell to breathe the pure, free

air of heaven. When I went into prison, Winter was monarch of all I surveyed; but now hope-inspiring and health-invigorating Spring was bursting upon the world with her odoriferous flowers and sweet songsters. The joyous lark was carolling forth his hymn of praise from the meridian sky, while the murmuring music of the wimpling streams and the sweet rustling of the waving trees filled and ravished my soul with inexpressible delight and pleasure, making me almost forget my late dreary incarceration. When I joined my regiment it was waiting orders to proceed to Dublin. So in a few days after, I took farewell of County Cork, the scene to me of many ups and downs, pleasures and sorrows.

> Where'er I roam in future years,
> Oh, I'll remember well
> Cork county and her pretty dears,
> Likewise my prison cell.

CHAPTER XII

Dublin

On the 28th day of April 1868 my distinguished regiment entered the capital of Erin, and took up its quarters in Richmond Barracks, along with Her Majesty's 72d Highlanders. After we had our packs taken off, each company of the 72d took a company of my regiment and regaled it with bread, ale, and cheese, a refreshment which proved very acceptable to us after our long dusty march. It likewise showed a very friendly feeling, and that blood is thicker than water. The few months that I was quartered in Dublin I was very happy. I had much to delight and interest me in wandering through the city of Wellington and Moore; and though we had a considerable distance to march to and from our different guards in town, duty was regular and easy, while the field-days in the Phoenix Park were always pleasant. The Park is very spacious and beautiful. For me it was a real Eden of delight to wander in the summer evenings among its blooming flowers and green trees.

Dublin contains some splendid buildings, but it wants the picturesque beauty which characterises the romantic city of Walter Scott. The river Liffey is a dark, muddy stream, and is of little importance. But the honour of having Dublin upon her banks gives her a title to hold np her head among the riven of the world. Ships of large burden cannot enter the month of the Liffey, but must discharge their cargoes at Kingston, a town on the south side of Dublin Bay. Sackville Street is considered the most elegant in Dublin. It is remarkable for its great width, but for cleanliness it cannot be compared with Princes Street in Edinburgh. It is, indeed, very dirty. The old; Parliament House is an elegant but sombre-looking building; but who could gaze upon its venerable walls without being reminded of the great eloquent spirits of the old Irish Parliament. Ireland may well feel proud of her Grattans, her Tones, her Floods, and Currans, but I was sorry to see no national monument to the memory of the immortal Daniel O'Connell – the only man who spent his life in the cause of the Irish people. College Green, however, is well studded with statues of Ireland's famous men. Goldsmith, Moore, and Burke have statues in prominent places in front of the College, while Orange Billy occupies- a conspicuous position in the centre of the street. Dublin, though not a commercial town like Belfast, has a considerable trade, and an air of activity and industry pervades the whole place. In the centre of Phoenix Park stands the Vice-Regal Lodge, the summer residence of the Lord-Lieutenant of Ireland. It is a beautiful palace surrounded by beautiful scenery. Its situation, with its lovely green hedges and ponds en- livened with little golden fish, is very pretty.

But my pleasant ramblings in and around Dublin were brought to a speedy termination. After Fenianism had been extirpated from the land we reasonably expected to enjoy peace and rest for a season. No such luck, however. We must march again, although, not to watch Fenians but an opposite faction altogether – the Orangemen, a society of men in the north of Ireland who cost the Imperial purse thousands of pounds every 12th of July (the anniversary of the Battle of the Boyne), to pay for the maintenance of peace in this part of Ireland. Last year we were hunting Fenians up among the mountains of Cork and Kerry, and now we must go to the north of Ireland to watch men whose loyalty to our beloved Queen has never been questioned. Strange country are thou, oh! lovely Erin. When will thy generous-hearted sons learn sense, and banish that bigoted intolerant spirit which animates so large a portion of your sons? If only you could allow charity and goodwill to prevail amongst you, your magnificent and happy country, I verily believe, would soon blossom and rejoice like the rose

On the tenth day of July 1868, two companies of my regiment were despatched to the county of Tyrone. Our destination was the town of Dungannon, where we were to maintain the public peace until the Orange demonstrations were over. My company was one of those selected for this duty. The companies left Dublin by the morning train, under the command of Captain R. Lewis, and arrived in Dungannon at 3.30 in the afternoon, after seven hours' travelling by train.

The north of Ireland does not present such a pleasing aspect to the eye of the traveller as the south does. The ground is in many parts marshy and barren, while the hills are tame compared with those in the south. But the towns here are more lively and industrious than most of the southern communities. Many of the towns in the north are large, and rapidly increasing in wealth and prosperity. Drogheda, Dundalk, Newry, and Portadown, through which I passed, are all large flourishing commercial places. Drogheda is a place of great historical celebrity, and is situated upon the river Boyne, where James Stuart was defeated in battle by his son-in-law, William Prince of Orange.

In passing from the south of Ireland to the north you feel as if you were entering another country. The people dress and speak with a different accent from those in the south. The north partakes more of the character of Scotland. The inhabitants are largely of the Presbyterian persuasion, but the Church of Rome also occupies an influential position, which is easily seen from the great number of her elegant chapels. The young women are extremely handsome, their faces being very prepossessing; but their extravagance in dress is only equalled by the factory girls in Scotland. Nothing looks more unbecoming than to see a young woman dressing beyond her means and spending her all in external display.

> "A weel dressed lass, I will confess,
> Is pleasant to the e'e;
> But without some better qualities,
> She's no a lass for me." – *Burns,*

Dungannon is a large, well-built town – the first of importance in the county of Tyrone. It stands upon an eminence, and commands a good view of the surrounding country. The town contains two large linen factories, which give employment to the trim lassies who flocked round us in sections when we marched up the principal street. The Captain having procured billets for the men under his charge, we got liberty to roam the town and see the lions; but the most delightful place at Dungannon is a splendid park, belonging to the Earl of Ranfurly, abounding in green trees and grassy lawns. In all parts of Ireland where I have been, I have seen nothing to admire so much as the parks of the aristocracy, and the public have free admission to them at all hours of the day. Such a privilege is a great boon to the working-classes, who can there wander and enjoy a sweet relaxation from their daily labour. The I2th of July being a holiday in the north of Ireland, the public works were hushed and silent. The girls were dressed in their gayest attire with a profusion of orange ribbons encircling their necks. The public-houses were ringing with hilarity and glee, and King William, I am sure, had his memory drunk a thousand times in a thousand different ways. Passing along the streets I could hear the Orange boys in the gin palaces drinking to the memory of their hero in the following language, "Here's to the pious and immortal memory of King William, Prince of Orange." I can see no harm in drinking to the memory of King William any more then drinking the health of His Holiness the Pope, but when opposite factions in the country indulged in such unrestrained abuse of one another as they do here, even going the length of committing murder in their sectarian faction fights, the Government should deny them the liberty of these demonstrations.

The people of Dungannon and Dunochgmore, however, conducted themselves in a quiet and orderly manner. I did not see so much as even a plebeian street fight, but in other parts of the north of Ireland there were great rows, and in the *melee* human life was lost.

On the afternoon of the 12th of July my company was sent to Dunochgmore, a village about two miles from Dungannon. Here our services were fortunately not required. So we spent the afternoon among the rustic beauties of the village. Mr Lyle, the resident magistrate, gave us permission to dance in one of his fields, and we had plenty of music from our piper, who discoursed his martial strains to the light fantastic toe.

Of all the nations in the world, Ireland, I think, stands foremost in dancing – old men and women, young men and maidens, all take delight in this harmless amusement. But the country people don't dance in sulphureous crowded halls – the grass plain is their floor, the genial sun or the silvery moon is their candle, and the canopy of heaven the roof of their ball-room. We returned to our billets in Dungannon the same evening at 11:30.

I was very fortunate in procuring a good billet. My landlady, Mrs Megill, was the sister of the Catholic Archbishop of Armagh. She was extremely kind and condescending to the six soldiers who were domiciled in her house, anticipating our every want, and making us very comfortable indeed. Mrs Megill had an adopted daughter whose parentage was a mystery to the people of Dungannon. The story goes that one beautiful morning in the month of May 1850 Dr Dickson, parish priest of Dungannon, went into his chapel for the purpose of offering up his morning prayer to God. While in the exercise of his religions devotions he heard a child's plaintive cry. Proceeding to where the voice came from he beheld a young infant lying in one of the chapel pews. No one in the place knew how the little thing came there. Every effort was made to discover its parents, but without avail. Dr Dickson baptized the child Mary after the Virgin, and May after the month in which she was found. And at the time of which I write Mary May was a blooming young girl of sweet eighteen.

> "To see her is to love her, and to love but her for ever.
> For nature made her what she is, and never made
>   another." –   *Burns*

We left county Tyrone on the 16th of July, and repaired to head-quarters at Dublin, returning to our regiment without injury to either limb or person. During our stay in Dungannon our boys had made some impression upon the hearts of the girls. After joining my regiment I could see letters bearing the Dungannon post-mark very often in the hands of the postman.

When we arrived in Dublin the regiment was under orders for the Curragh of Kildare. So in a few days afterwards I was drilling under Lord Strathnairn upon the plains of the Curragh.

The Curragh camp at Kildare is to Ireland what Aldershot is to England. Troops from all parts of Ireland concentrate in the summer months in the Curragh for brigade and divisional movements. The Curragh of Kildare is one immense plain, and is a capital place for manoeuvring a large body of troops. Instead of the long dusty valley of Aldershot, there is a beautiful grassy bed bespangled with many a sweet daisy and fragrant flower. Our field days on the Curragh were very pleasant ones and generally under the command of Sir Hugh Rose. Many distinguished persons from England were often present to witness the movements under such a commander as the hero of Central India. Then we had many of Ireland's daughters gracing our field days with their enchanting presence, and with their beaming eyes smiling upon us.

The scenery around the Curragh is flat and un- interesting; but the land is well cultivated, and the farmers in the county of Kildare are said to be wealthy.

Donnelly's Hole, at the east end of the camp, is a beautiful romantic place. It was here where Donnelly and Cooper attacked each other like infuriated tigers. But the sweet flowery dell in which they fought appears more suitable for lovers' gentle whisperings than the display of brute force.

The Curragh Races, which take place annually, create a good deal of amusement for the soldiers in the camp. The thousands of showmen which frequent the races with all sorts of sports make the course a lively place. The town of Kildare, once a community of considerable importance, is situated three miles from the camp, and is now a very dilapidated looking town. ''Norah, the Pride of Kildare,'' no longer graces it with her fascinating presence. The town is chiefly inhabited by a few old men and women, who seem to earn a living by vending water cresses, milk, and butter amongst the soldiers.

The Curragh is a good place to soldier in during the summer, but it is extremely dull in the winter season. There is no gas in the camp, and candle affords but a poor light in the long winter evenings. Every regiment in the camp is supplied with a good library and recreation room, which is a great boon to those who love to frequent such places.

We left the Curragh on the 17th day of October 1868, and embarked at Kingston' for Gibraltar, after being exactly three years and five months home from India.

CHAPTER XIII

Embarking and Sailing for Gibraltar – Description of the Rock and Military Arrangements

Arrived at Kingston on 17th October 1868, we embarked on H.M. troopship "Simoom." Being on ship's rations, we left camp without breakfast, expecting to find it and dinner in one dish as soon as we were embarked, as two men of each company were sent along with the married people the day previous – one of them a cook – but, to our great surprise, through some one's bungling, the beef was not allowed to be drawn until our train was in sight. We weighed anchor about 2.10 p.m., and were soon out of "Sweet Dublin Bay" and steaming down the coast of Ireland; but we roamed on board like ravenous wolves for nearly three hours before we managed to get a dinner of fresh beef – hard as iron – biscuits, and thin soup. It was, however, greedily devoured, and in about an hour we were served out with our porter and our tobacco – a great many of the restrictions on smoking being relaxed. As darkness began to creep over us we were served out with hammocks, but finding mine improperly strapped up I took the ground for safety with my blanket wrapt around me. I found this better than I had done the preceding night, as, owing to our beds and bedding having been taken in from us previously, we were left with nothing but the bed-irons to lie upon.

As soon as rouse sounded (6 A.M.) next morning I betook myself to deck and found neither land nor sail in sight – nothing but sickness on every side – each one seemingly worse than his neighbour, and the whole of the women *hors de combat,* but I was as brisk as anyone was fit to be myself. This was as beautiful a day as I ever beheld, and yet the ship pitched and rolled fearfully, although I have often seen my own Forth much more angry than the wide ocean then was. At 10 A.M. we were formed four deep on the poop for church parade, where one of our captains read the lessons for the day, but only about ten minutes had passed when we were dismissed – not over three-score, I daresay, having heard a word, and few even of these understanding the Episcopalian service, as most of us had been brought up in the simple Presbyterian form of worship. We were piped to dinner at noon, but precious few put in an appearance, all preferring to lie on deck like a flock of sheep, with scarcely a passage to be found amongst them.

At rouse sounding on the 20th I got on deck, after a good comfortable night's rest, and found the coast of Spain in sight – Capes Ortegal and Finisterre. Great amusement was afforded all on board to witness the leaping and diving of a great shoal of porpoises that had gathered around us as we skimmed along, hugging the shore. Being on watch at 9 a.m., and close to the quarter-deck, I had a fine opportunity of hearing the captain of the vessel read the service (which he did daily to his own men) in a most reverential tone, for he seemed a kind, God-fearing man, and was very attentive to his crew. The scene was impressive, with a marked difference from the one we had on Sabbath, and must have brought serious reflections to many present. At noon we had a splendid dinner of preserved mutton, with boiled rice and soft bread. We got the latter four days a week. We were enjoying our voyage very much, as there was scarcely a breath of wind, and it reminded me of a pleasure trip up our own Scottish rivers. We were at this time also signalling to a large steamer about four or five miles distant, which many of us took to be a war vessel. During the afternoon they raised the fore and main top-gallant masts to make us look nice going into Gibraltar; but nice or not nice I did not relish very much seeing the poor fellows perched on the very top with scarcely anything to hold on by, and the ship rolling very heavily with the ground swell. What an enchanting scene I had at 6 P.M., as, seated on the fore deck, the vessel gliding along smoothly, I beheld the sea like a lake, scarcely a cloud in the sky, in fact nothing but blue over-head, and one of the most beautiful sunsets ever I witnessed. It was truly a glorious sight, and with the band playing in the poop and wafting sweet music over the vessel, one's thoughts were raised from earth to heaven – so enchanting was the scene.

By mid-day on the 22nd I found we had a good view of both the Spanish and African coasts, with the Straits quite plain in front, and at 2 p.m. we began to enter them; but I was surprised to find them much narrower than I expected. The coasts on both sides are very bleak, rocky, and dangerous looking. At 4 p.m. we passed Tangiers on the African coast, and then the huge mass which was to be our home for some years spread itself before us; and the largest shoal of porpoises I had yet seen were the first to welcome us to the Mediterranean. An hour afterwards we were slowly gliding in towards the New Mole, but all, except those on watch, were kept below to be out of the sailors' road. About 6. 30 they allowed us on deck, and what a scene burst upon our view. It was just after sunset, with a beautiful crescent moon shining brilliantly; we were close in to the pier, and the huge mass of rock rose straight above us. The side we lay next (the west) was of a sloping nature, and the town lay at the bottom of the north-west comer.

Next morning (the 23rd) we were all on the move as early as four o'clock to get out the baggage, and a hazardous job it was to disembark it on a narrow pier in a very dark morning, but it was ultimately managed, and the officers' baggage and the married people were packed off by nine, after which about one-half of the regiment indulged in a good bathe at the end of the pier. We disembarked at 1 P.M., and had a long march through the whole town. This was a most wearisome job, being a continual up-hill down-dale walk until we reached the North Front, where we were encamped in double tents, with eight in each, until the 29th. The 74th, being in barracks in town, were ready to receive us with open arms, but as our camping ground was outside the gates of the fortress, and these shut every evening at sunset, it was entirely out of our power to have a jollification with them in their barracks. To make amends, however, they had an abundant supply of porter, biscuits, and Stilton cheese awaiting us, so that the tea (without bread) served out to us about five o'clock received only a very scant amount of attention, every one being too much taken up with their new quarters and their old acquaintances in the 74th. This North Front on which we were encamped is a piece of level sandy ground forming an isthmus between the Rock and Spain. The only buildings erected thereon are – A pretty large iron-foundry, belonging to an English firm of the name of Hayes & Son; a few boat-building sheds; the wash-house for cleaning the military bedding, &c.; and the garrison slaughter-houses. Here also are the garrison and Jewish cemeteries, together with a pretty large vegetable garden, while at the back of the latter are the ball-firing ranges (facing east), and on the ground composing these the weekly "field days " are held when the weather is favourable. The main road from Spain, running close past the tents, was in a perfect turmoil of traffic from morning gun-fire till retreat, mules and donkeys laden with all kinds of merchandise, but principally fruit, huddling and jostling each other in their anxiety to be first inside the fortress, and one could not help wondering where purchasers could be found for such quantities as daily passed us. Fruit was sold to us too at a mere nothing, as many as 6 or 8 good sweet oranges being purchased for a penny; a large bunch of grapes for the same money, and a water melon of the size of a reasonable cheese for twopence. This piece of ground must have been, at sometime or another, quietly taken from the Spaniards to form a recreation ground for the inhabitants of Gibraltar, as a good carriage drive surrounds it, and the grasping nature of the British Government would not allow them to stop here; but a piece of ground further north, of about half a mile in breadth and stretching from beach to beach east and west, must needs be called " neutral ground," and so neither of the countries' own, but we could see the Spanish soldiers from the neighbouring town of Lena at exercise upon it, though since then further restrictions have been placed upon it, so that neither their troops nor ours can use it for any purpose whatever. Our sentries on the lines could also see theirs walking on their posts on the opposite side of this ground; but, in the present peaceful attitude of the two nations, their principal duty is an outlook for smugglers, of whom there is no lack. We could also see the hills of Spain rising in the distance, where the charcoal burners' fire shone brightly through the dark night, with the "Queen of Spain's chair" towering high above them all; but across this neutral ground no private soldier of the British army is permitted to set his foot or to touch the soil where the Spanish champion

> "Bowed his crested head
> And tamed his heart of fire."

Non-commissioned officers are granted this indulgence, and when the bull fights at San Roque or Algiceras take place it is greatly taken advantage of by them, but the roving propensities of the private or his incapability to take care of himself when beyond the control of military discipline renders him unsafe to be trusted there. It is stated that the privilege was granted them also until somewhere about the time of the Crimean war, when some militia regiment then stationed there committed so much outrage, disgracing themselves and their country that the indulgence was withdrawn, but I cannot see that this ought to be deemed sufficient cause for "visiting the sins of their fathers" upon the soldiers of the present day. Without any disrespect towards the non-commissioned officers of the British Army, I must here honestly state that for intelligence, sobriety, and zeal for the service, there are many in the ranks equal if not superior to the great body of the non-commissioned. Clergymen, physicians, and lawyers have even served as privates in the ranks, and I myself have had for a comrade one who in his better days held Her Majesty's commission as an officer in her army. Anxious as I often was, therefore, to be able to say I had been in that land where so many of my brave countrymen found a grave in the beginning of this century, this restriction prevented me, and

I had to content myself with hunting up the historic corners of the Rock itself, and yet after a stay of 4 1/2 years there I am compelled to say that I feel confident I was never able to trace all the nooks and crannies in it.

We remained under canvas until the 29th, when the 2-15th having taken up our quarters on board the "Simoom" for passage home, we got into the Europa and Buena 'Vista Barracks, situated pretty high up in the south-west corner, and considered the most healthy; but we would never have believed such a stretch of road could be found in so small a place, and we were tired enough by the time we reached our destination. Still we were doubly thankful to once more have a firm roof over our heads, and a good comfortable bed to rest our weary limbs upon. In our march through town, I was greatly taken with the appearance of its inhabitants, as the motley group reminded me of the streets of Calcutta-Jews, Greeks, Turks, Armenians, Arabs, French, Spaniards. In fact every nation of the earth except China and Japan seemed to have representatives here arrayed in all the fantastic dresses of their own countries. The women, too, wear no covering for the head save a veil which surprised me much seeing the sun was so hot.

Gibraltar, I need not say, is a place of great natural as well as artificial strength. The guns now mounted on the different batteries surrounding it are quite able to keep any fleet out of the bay.

> Oh! famous Gib, historic Rock,
> While thy big guns look o'er the main,
> Thou canst withstand the combined shook
> Of Russia, Austria, France, and Spain.
>
> Harmless is the power of Spain
> To injure thy exalted brow;
> Erect thy head in proud disdain
> For thou art impregnable now.

Where is the nation that would dare
To 'siege a giant rock like thee?
Thou'd blow its armies in the air.
And sink its fleets beneath the sea.

The buildings on the Rock have but little pretensions to architectural beauty, the only ones aiming at that being the English Cathedral and a Roman Catholic Church in the south district. The houses generally are built of brick, mere shells, and like all Eastern towns flat-roofed with tanks built in each to collect and retain their water supply. This used to be their only source, but during our stay an abundant spring was discovered at the North Front, and a huge engine for pumping this flow therefrom and forcing it into the town was erected by English workmen. The opening ceremony of the works caused quite a stir, so that now at very small cost the inhabitants have little to fear from a drought or scarcity. The Scotch Church is a small modest-looking building which was erected in 1854-the Rev. Andrew Sutherland, at one time minister of Free St Andrew's, Dunfermline, being its first pastor. He died there in 1867, and was buried in the North Front Cemetery, a beautiful monument being erected over his last resting-place, and a marble tablet on the east wall of the church, by his sorrowing congregation.

The Rev. John Coventry is the present incumbent, and is a gentleman who takes great interest in the moral and spiritual improvement of the Presbyterian soldiers to whom he officiates as chaplain. I believe he was at one time Free Church minister of Yetholm, on the Borders, and was wont to preach to our regiment when they were in Malta in 1856-57, prior to their going out to India to take part in quelling the mutiny.

I never entered that little church but the thoughts of better days, long past, would rush across my mind; those happy and innocent ones when, on the calm Sabbath morn, I wended my way to the Free Kirk o' bonnie Glen vale. I have been in numerous places of worship since then, where I have beheld forms of worship more imposing and gorgeous, but the simple faith of a

Presbyterian creed has far more charms for me than the organ's solemn peal or the gaudy paintings and thousand candles blazing on a Roman Catholic altar. The simple song of praise and the pure words of the Most High as heard in a Scottish kirk must ever awaken pleasant recollections in the breasts of Scotland's wandering sons. As a Scotchman I am proud of my country; I love her flowery meads and heathery hills. The very murmur of her wimpling rills is as sweet music as ever assailed mine ear. And not only is her scenery sublime and beautiful, her sons are brave and gallant, and have often made a glorious stand in the cause of civil and religious liberty. Every Scotchman must feel proud of his country's noble history, its rich traditions, and romantic poetry, and his heart must warm with sympathetic affection towards the land that gave him birth. We have no cause to be ashamed of our glorious Presbyterian Church. It has been principally through her teaching that her sons have risen to such positions of respectability, honour, and trust throughout the world. The same faithful preaching, the same holy earnestness, characterises the Scottish clergy in every land. Whether on the banks of Heathen Rivers, or midst the ruins of Hindoo temples, the Scottish minister can make us feel the hallowing influences of a Scottish Sabbath at home.

CHAPTER XIV

New Year's Night

After being located in barracks we had to settle down to the different duties incumbent upon as in our post which we found to be no sinecure. They were far more weighty than those that had been imposed upon us during- our brief sojourn at home. The gentlemen composing the staff of that garrison are thoroughly acquainted with their duties, and while performing their own, see that what has to be done by those under them is done to the very letter. In the midst of all, however, a holiday comes round, like an oasis in the desert, to brighten our lot. One of these was New Year's Day 1869. What pleasant recollections of auld lang syne are awakened in the breasts of Scotia's sons when their annual /holiday comes round. If fate has marked one of them to be a wanderer on a distant shore, he is up and off on the wings of imagination to the dear old hearth where in fancy he sees his aged parents seated round the festive board; where his young bright-eyed sister rests in her little chair; or he hears a kind father or a loving mother yearning over their absent one, while his vacant chair is set in its wonted place. But what family hearth is complete? Death steps in and snatches a beloved one away; another takes to a seafaring life and makes the wide ocean his home, while a third mayhap seeks a grave with nought but "his martial cloak around him." Still it comes natural for a Scotchman to rejoice and be glad on New Year's Day, and no matter what part of the world he may be located in, he loves to keep alive the time-honoured custom of wishing his neighbours "mony o' them." That too often on this day Scotchmen indulge rather freely in drink, I am bound to confess; yet their conduct on these occasions will compare favourably with that of their brethren of the sister islands at their Christmas festivities, while they have no religious obligations binding them in its observance such as the others have in theirs. They can enjoy themselves without being chargeable with hypocrisy, for it looks rather inconsistent in an observer of Christmas to attend his Church services in the morning, joining in the angels' anthem, and then wind up the day hip, hip, hurrahing, amongst a lot of "jolly good fellows."

In true Scotch style, who should be my "first Foot" that New Year's morning but my old friend Mankey Bouffe, who came reeling into my room with a bottle in his hand, and singing the following verse of an old Scotch song –

> "I've aye been fou' sin' the year cam' in,
> I've aye been fou' sin' the year cam' in;
> The doctor cam' in wi' a bottle o' gin,
> I've aye been fou' sin' the year cam' in."

"Noo, come, my old boy," says Mankey, "an' drink a flowing bumper tae auld Scotland an' the dear frien's we a' lo'e sae weel. Mony an absent ane '11 be mentioned at a thoosan' firesides this mornin', an' altho' oor seats are vacant at hame we ken brawly that parental lips are whusperin' oor names in accents o' affection an love – '

> 'Round a cheery, bright fireside
> Our aged parents will preside.
> Far frae their sons a' scattered wide
> On life's rough main,
> Imploring heaven's power to guide
> Us hame again.'

"After dinner-time we intend tae ha'e a little Scotch spree. We're to meet in Jamie Dum-dums, an' surely you'll ha'e nae objection tae join us, as we only inten' singin' a wheen auld Scotch sangs, tae keep us in min' that we're a' Scotch men frae the lan' o' the mountain an' the flood. Ye ken a' the fellows wha'll be there - Bauldy Forsyth, Sandy Ross, an' Pate Tamson. Auld Bauldy is tae be chairman, sae if he disna gie's a sang we may expect a speech frae him. Wull ye come?"

"Of course," replied I; "do you really think I could refuse to participate in the enjoyment of such worthy fellows."

"Weel, twa o'clocks the oor; we'll expect tae see ye there punctual tae time," said Mankey, as he hurried off to some other acquaintance, singing

"Here's tae the year that's awa',
We'll drink in strong an' in sma',
   Wi' Jamie Dum dum we'll hae plenty o' fun
As we drink tae the year that's awa."

When I got tae "Jamie Dum-dum's" (which, by the way, was the wine-house nearest our barracks, the proprietor thereof being so nick-named), I found my auld cronies already assembled. Bauldy Forsyth was selected as chairman, and his witty expressions and comical retorts kept us all in a genial, cheery mood. Forsyth was a bit of an orator, and at times could make a few pithy remarks on the principal topics of the day. In replying to his election as our chairman he said: –

"Well, my dear friends, I beg leave to return you my sincere thanks for the distinguished honour you have conferred upon me by asking me to preside over you on this particular occasion. This is the twenty-second New Year's-day that I have spent in the British army; and allow me to tell you, if I had my days to live over again I would select the army for a home, for my past years in it have been pleasant and happy, and if I have occasionally got myself into trouble I have no one to blame. Like all the other sections of the human family we cannot lay claim to infallibility; and we, who are bound by the strong, stern chain of military law, may even get ourselves into serious trouble through our being too liberal in our sentiments. But here at present, my fellow soldiers, we are free from the ties of martial discipline, and are met to enjoy ourselves as best we can at this festive season of the year. On this day, in all parts of the world, the sons of auld

Scotland are in thought looking back to the dear old land where
they were wont to gather round the parental hearth and sing
those endearing songs of Caledonia which a Scotchman never
forgets. Before another New Year comes round, Old Bauldy, as
you love to call me, with God's help, will have returned to the
ranks of civil life, where he will have to make a new home. Those
who gave me birth now rest in their lonely mools on the banks
of my own beloved Clyde. There are few soldiers but have an
inclination to re-visit the home of their childhood, especially
if any length of years have passed away since they trod their
native hills and listened to the music of a fond mother's voice,
but when I return to the scenes of my youth,

> 'I might stand forsaken wi' the tear in my e'e,
> To think there is none wha remembers o' me.'

The well-remembered features of former years are buried in the
dust; early companions are scattered up and down the world, and
many friends of my early days are sleeping in the valley of death
on yonder Crimean and Indian plains. Oh! my dear friends, I feel
a tinge of sadness creep over my soul as memory calls up one by
one the lively companions of life's smiling morn. I shall never
have the honour of presiding at your annual gathering again.
In a few months the 71st will cease to be Auld Bauldy's home;
but remember, dear companions in arms, wherever Providence
may cast my lot in civil life, I will cherish a warm remembrance
of the distinguished Regiment wherein I have dwelt for two-
and-twenty years. Now, fill your glasses and drink a health to
Scotland's bonnie lasses. Although we are all old bachelors here,
we still cherish an undying love for the fair maids o' Caledonia.
We are not to blame for the small amount of the domestic element
infused into the army. Of course we cannot all have wives in it,
so we must just live in anticipation of getting a bonnie and a
good one after our wanderings are over."

The toast being enthusiastically responded to, our Chairman
again said – "Now, my lads, I have another toast to propose.

That is, 'May honour and success ever attend the arms of the 71st Highland Light Infantry.' Since the embodiment of the Regiment, its reputation for gallantry and chivalrous deeds in the field stand second to none in the British Army. And now, after you do due honour to this toast, I will use my prerogative, and call upon our friend, Sandy Boss, for a song, as he is the next oldest soldier; but remember nothing but Scottish songs must be sang in our hearing to-night."

"Mr Chairman," says Sandy, "I was just thinkin' ye wad be wantin' a bit sang frae me, sae I ha'e composed a few lines for the occasion; still ye maun promise to o'erlook ony imperfections o' my verses, an' I ha'e nae objections tae let ye hear

THE LAND O' LANGSYNE

Sweet isle o' the ocean, my soul clings to thee
Wi' the purest devotion whare'er I may be;
Tho' noo I maun wander in lands o'er the sea—
My dear fatherland is the licht o' my e'e.

In dreams I revisit the auld cottage door;
The wee village schule an' the bricht scenes o' yore;
An' though I'm wearin' fast doon life's decline
My heart's awa hame tae the land o' langsyne.

I linger wi' joy o'er the days that are gane—
The bonnie bricht days in my sweet Scottish hame;
Tho' here I ha'e beauty an' grandeur sublime.
My thochts are awa tae the land o' langsyne.

Oh! hasten the day whan I'll hameward return
To wander ance mair on the banks o' Cree Burn;
Though noo in the land o' the monkey an' vine,
My heart warms still tae the land o' langsyne.

Bright hame o' my faithers, tho' noo far awa,
Lang may the dear thistle wave stately an' braw;

The sun he will cease on my Scotch pow tae shine
Whan my heart turns cauld tae the land o' langsyne."

"Well done, Sandy, you've done your part to perfection. Though many long years have passed away since you gambolled in infancy upon the flowery banks of the Tweed, with a true Scotchman's heart you fondly cling to the beloved hills and streams o' auld langsyne. Now, Mankey Bouffe, I think you are entitled to give us the next song – something in a cheery strain.

"A' richt, Bauldy, but I doot much if ony sang o' mine wud be properly appreciated in an assembly like the present. Sublime sentiments an' profoun' thochts are rather beyond the intellectual comprehension o' auld sodgers like you. Hooever, if I can in ony way contribute towards yer happiness by singin' a sang I'se sing ye a dizzen."

"Mankey, your language is neither parliamentary nor complimentary to your friends assembled here, but I'll admonish you on condition that you sing to us that good old Scotch song, Callum O'Glen."

"Rax across the toddy, for my lips are as dry as Mr Dossy's sermons. Noo here's a sang that ocht tae thrill the heart o' every Scotchman. Listen tae this: –

'Auld Scotch whisky sweetly gangs doon
Wi' sugar an' candy in Cammilton toon—'"

"Halt, Mankey Bouffe, halt. Dress back; you're oot o' the time entirely. If these are the sublime sentiments you spoke about I can thoroughly understand them."

"Weel, Mr Chairman, if sugar an' candy is offensive tae my compatriots I'se cheenge it tae something mair elevating in its tendency –

"My mither made a mutch for me.
She thocht I was a dandy;
An' sent me o'er the Hielan' Hills
Tae see my uncle Sandy.

There was a man, they ca'd 'im Tam,

His name was Alexander;
He catch'd a paddock by the tail.
An' fried it on the brander.' "

"In the name of goodness, Mankey, what songs do you call these?"
"Good nursery rhymes."
"But you've no children here to divert."
"Sodgers are maistly fond o' children, an' nane mair sae than oor worthy chairman, sae I'm at a loss tae understan' his antipathy against thae noble an' soul-inspirin' rhymes. I can look back through the lang span o' thirty years an' see my beloved mither danglin' my wee sister Mary, an' singin'

"Dance little baby, dance up high.
Never mind, baby, mother is bye;
Crow an' caper, caper and crow.
There, little baby, there you go-
Up to the ceiling, down to the ground.
Backward and forward, round and round.

There's a rhyme for ye; ye'll seek Tennyson in vain for sic anither."
"I like that, Mankey. Anything that brings to our memory the joyous days of our unclouded youth will always exert a pleasing influence on the mind of a soldier. It was only your sugar and candy affair I objected to."
" Since ye're pleased, I'm content; sae I'll gie ye an original sang Calculated tae fling Sandy Boss's land o' langsyne in tae the shade – joost a few lines I hae penned in honour o' oor worthy host, Jamie Dum-dum. Noo ye can a' help me tae sing this Spanish sang tae a Scotch air –

Should auld acquaintance be forgot.
An' bowls o' sparklin' rum;
Bring in anither reekin' pot.
My bonnie Jamie Dum.

For this is New Years day, ye ken.
We're bent on sport an' fun;

Perhaps we ne'er may meet again
Wi' bonnie Jamie Dum.

Then fill yer glasses ane an' a',
An' drink till half- past nine;
A health tae Jamie's lassies braw,
I wush that ane was mine.

But I'll conclude my little wag,
I'll sing nae mair tae you;
I feel my head is gettin' wrang
I'll soon be mair than fou."

At this stage of the proceedings, seeing Mankey's closing words of his song were too literally true, with a little persuasion we got him to agree to take the road home, when

"He left us glorious,
O'er a' the ills o' life victorious."

And we could hear his cheery voice, as he wended his way towards Europa, singing –

"I was drunk last nicht, I'm drunk the nicht too,
An' I've lost the ball o' my auld shako"

CHAPTER XV

New Year's Night Continued – Military Duty in Gibraltar – How the Rock Came into British Possession

After we had got Mankey on his way home, and still having sometime to call our own ere the bugle sound would summon us to quarters, we resumed our seats and continued the evening's enjoyment, recapitulating the stormy scenes we had passed through during our military career, and calling up the traits and characteristics of many an old comrade long since called to give in his account, at the same time wondering where and how many of them were still fighting the battle of life; for I am here forced to confess that there are but few soldiers who keep alive their name in the Regiment they have left by corresponding with old comrades still serving. True, many of them do write as soon as settled down in civil life, giving what information they can as to the condition of trade, and how they have succeeded in obtaining employment; but when this has taken place they seem to consider they have done their duty and wiped off any debt of gratitude they may have owed a comrade of many years' standing.

Time wore on apace, and we could see the hour for parting fast approaching, when Bauldy said: – "Now, my lads, let's pledge one bumper more to the Land o' Langsyne. I have been extremely well pleased with Sandy's song, for it shows that a man without education or the means to mingle amidst cultivated society can be a poet. I think it was Lord Macau lay who wrote that 'before a man can become a great poet in an enlightened and literary society, he must first become a little child and unlearn much of that knowledge, which has, perhaps, constituted hitherto his chief title to superiority.' Now, before we go, I'll recite, for I can't sing, to you my farewell to the 71st Highland Light Infantry, as but a short time now must elapse ere I am domiciled in the Land o' Langsyne; but time or distance shall never obliterate from my memory the happy years I have spent amongst you all."

Auld Bauldy was greatly respected in the Regiment for his many soldierly qualities. His kindness in assisting a comrade soldier in hours of trouble' made him a favourite, and when the gallant old man left, many an earnest wish and sincere prayer followed him to his native land, where, I understand, he is still hale and hearty, and working hard for an honest livelihood, and only too proud to meet his old comrades, as they one by one are following him fast to civil life.

BAULDY FORSYTH'S FAREWELL TO HIS REGIMENT

Fareweel, My brave regiment, my heart's fou o' sorrow
To part wi' the number I've worn sae lang;
But I canna forget the famed deeds o' glory
Recorded in history, an' immortal in sang.

I've fought wi' yer sons on the plains o' the Crimea,
An' under Sir Hugh Rose on India's wide plain;
Forgi'e me, dear frien's, if my e'en should be rainy
When leaving a corps I may ne'er see again.

I'm proud to ha'e been in the Pass o' Umbeyla,
An' shared in that arduous an' bloody campaign;
When Colonel Hope – that distinguished brave hero-
Did lead us tae victory, tae honour an' fame.

Fareweel, brave companions, sae gallant an' true,
Emulate your forefathers, wha bravely fought
On the fields o' Corunna an' famed Waterloo;
Maintain at a' hazards the proud name you've got.

Companions in arms! I hameward return
Tae the scenes o' my youth after years twenty-two;
But cherished remembrance will keep my heart warm.
When I think on the bricht days enjoyed wi' you.

Brave Seventy-First, when wi' age I am hoary,
Perhaps you'll be fechting in some distant clime,
Reaping fresh laurels on fields grim an' gory,
While I can dae naething but think o' langsyne.

Fareweel, companions, nae mair shall the rattle
O' rifle, an' cannon, 'neath an Indian sun,
Arouse me ance mair tae gae forth tae battle —
I've grounded my airms, my life's battles are won!

"Now, my lads, the hands o' the clock are pointing to the hour of
tattoo, and I hope you are all satisfied with our night's enjoyment.
Let us return to barracks sober and correct, for the most of us
are for guard tomorrow. I know my friend Pate Tamson here is
for the "Devil's Tower," while I maun march to the "Old North
Front" myself, along wi' Briny M'Mahon an' Dosey Crawford.
Only one glass more, then, as this is my last New Year in the
army; so fill them up high and drink –

'Here's to our noble land o' glory.
Conquered yet no man ere saw;
Here's long life to Queen Victoria,
Wha in safety rules us a'.'"

Having drained our bumpers with all the honours, we proceeded
towards barracks leisurely rehearsing to each other how satisfied
we were with our night's enjoyment – the only tinge of sadness
we felt being the knowledge that our New Years' sprees with
Bauldy were over. We managed to be in and answer our names
in good time, and found the great majority of the Regiment had
not yet began to think of winding up the day's jollity, while not
a few were reeling –

"From gaiety that fills the bones with pains,
  The mouth with blasphemy, the heart with woe."

Another thing that was keeping them in high dudgeon was that
a field day was in orders for the next day, and that was thought
by some to be taking an undue advantage, considering that we
of the Scotch Regiments had taken up the duties of our brethren
belonging to the English ones to enable them to enjoy themselves
as best they could on Christmas and Boxing days; and though they
had returned the compliment to us on this day, still the field day
did not afford the least opportunity of " getting to rights" after
the day's joviality. The consequence was that a few were confined
for being "drunk on parade! – the least drop taken reviving the
quantity imbibed previously! – while others remained absent
rather than incur the risk of the weightier crime. These field days
were no joke, and were the bane of our existence in Gibraltar,
being, with scarcely an exception, held on the Saturdays – a
day the soldier generally counts his own after the usual weekly
cleaning out. However, field duty on Saturday was considered
the most suitable, as Regiments took all guard duties in rotation
for the whole garrison, unless on Saturdays when each furnished
its quota for these duties in accordance with the number of men
they had employed with the Royal Engineers during the week,
thus permitting each regiment to appear on parade. As I have
already said field parades were always held on the North Front,
so that the march from the barracks we occupied to attend them
and back was considered amply sufficient for a parade itself,
but when we add to that that all movements had to take place
amongst soft sand, in some places knee deep, and the ground
at disposal being but of limited dimensions, they were looked
upon with anything but favour, duty being preferable to them
at any time, and he was considered a lucky dog who dropped
into doing something that kept him out of them. Still, were these
parades not to take place occasionally we would have little use
for a General and his staff in command, for he must do something

for his pay, even though it should be the means of adding fuel to the soldier's too ready habit of grumbling.

One of these field days, however, occurred here over which there was no grumbling. It will be remembered I mentioned in a former chapter that we had long to wait before we received anything in the shape of honour or recompense for the Umbeyla campaign, but it came at last in the shape of a medal and clasp. On the 11th March 1871 on a parade of the whole garrison, the Governor (General Sir William Fenwick Williams, Bart, of Kars, G.C.B.) presented these to all entitled to them, at the same time eulogising the regiment for its conduct in the campaign in a speech replete with incentives to military ardour such as might be expected from the lips of so gallant a soldier.. To show that many still remained in the regiment who passed through that campaign I may state the number distributed was 194.

I have spent a few New Years in the service since then with merry comrades, and enjoyed myself to the utmost; but never has the band played "the auld year oot an' the new ane in" but that one in Jamie Dum-dum's comes rushing across my memory, and I think I can still behold the genial merry face, and hear the happy tones of the voice of auld Bauldy Forsyth.

We had Gibraltar as a home for four years and a half; and during that time I spent not a few happy days, but none more so than the one just mentioned; and the day I parted at the pier with auld Bauldy was about the saddest one I spent of them all. Our duties were a regular routine from 1st January till 31st December, the only complaint – and it was a general one – being that duty prevented us having but very few days we could call our own. When we arrived there the garrison consisted of five regiments of Infantry, a brigade of Artillery, and three companies of Engineers; but during our stay its strength was reduced by one regiment of Infantry, thus causing us to feel it heavier than ever; but I understand they have had again to resort to the old strength. Of course, it must be understood that in a garrison such as Gibraltar there is a great number of men employed on what is, in soldiers' parley, called the staff – such as orderlies to staff officers, telegraph and other clerks, bakers in the commissariat and tradesmen with the engineers – thereby greatly reducing the number available for duty. The role week by week, was that each regiment took all the fatigues in garrison one day; furnished close on 200 men for labouring work with the Engineers; another and the one following took, as I have said in a preceding chapter, the whole guards in garrison except regimental ones; and when I say that no less than 220 men were required for such not including those furnished by the Artillery and Engineers, it can easily be seen the complaint was well-grounded, as it was but rarely we could exceed four or five nights in bed, and if not on any of these duties there was generally two, if not three, parades to face; but, on the other hand, there were but few allurements to entice anyone abroad, as no such thing as a good walk could be attained, unless round the North Front, or a theatrical performance was got up by the amateurs of some of the regiments; hence the only fall back was to listen to some would-be professional singing in a wine house, as you sipped away at their "black wine" from a quart pot, the contents of which could be purchased at sixpence or eightpence, not including, of course, the headaches, which were the sure consequences succeeding these concerts.

Gibraltar is, as most people already know, a little world in itself, and governed by military law; and it may not prove uninteresting to recount here how it came into our possession, and the several attempts that have been made to deprive us of it.

During the war of the Spanish Succession, Britain aided Charles, Archduke of Austria, both by land and sea^ and one result of that effort is our possession of the town and promontory of Gibraltar. The rock is one of a pair called the Pillars of Hercules, one of which is upon the African Coast and this on the Spanish, and called the Culpe, and rises above the sea to a height of between 1400 and 1500 feet. Its greatest length is three miles north and south, and its greatest breadth three-quarters of a mile. Every accessible part of it is defended by batteries, many of which are "casemated," that is made bomb-proof, and so well are they arranged that the fortress is deemed impregnable. On the western slope of the hill the town is built, and contains about 15,000 inhabitants. But it is not from its physical peculiarities that Gibraltar is so interesting to us; it is because it was once the pride of the Spaniards, and is now the boast of Britain – notwithstanding so many vigorous and prolonged sieges – and will doubtless so remain so long as Britain can maintain a sufficiency of ships at sea to prevision and garrison it.

In 1704 Admiral Sir George Rooke was sent with the squadron under his command to land Charles at Lisbon, which he did, and afterwards sailed to attack Barcelona. Having failed in his attempt he consequently returned to the entrance of the Mediterranean Sea, where he was reinforced by Sir Cloudsley Shovel. On the 17th of July a Council of War was held on board the Admiral's ship as to what should.be done, when it was mentioned that Gibraltar was then weakly garrisoned by the Spaniards, and, if vigorously assaulted, would no doubt surrender to the first attack. The whole fleet therefore sailed for Gibraltar, and arrived in the bay on the 21st. Immediately 2000 marines were landed on the sandy isthmus, mentioned in a former chapter, in order to cut off all communication with the interior, and the Spanish

Governor was summoned to surrender. This, though he had only 150 men of a garrison, he refused to do, and declared he would fight to the last. Next day, therefore, the fleet was ordered to take up position to batter the works, but the wind blew so hard it was impossible to do so until the morning of the 23rd, when the ships were laid with their broadsides to the works. Admiral Rooke gave the signal and a brisk cannonade was opened, which lasted six hours, with such effect as to drive the Spaniards from their guns on the South Mole Head. As soon as the Admiral saw this he ordered all the boats in the fleet to be let down, the men armed, and an assault made. Capts. Hicks and Jumper, being nearest, landed first, and, though few in number, the gallant tars sprang up the ascent, heedless of the springing of a mine which killed two lieutenants and forty men, and in little or no time cleared the platforms and maintained possession of it till Captain Whitaker and the rest of the men arrived. On being thus reinforced, the whole body threw themselves upon a redoubt (now called the Eight Gun Battery) between the Mole and the town, carrying it by storm and driving the Spaniards before them. Next day the Spanish Governor surrendered, and our gallant tars marched in and took possession. The Prince of Hesse Darmstadt, who was present, hoisted the Austrian flag and proclaimed the fortress to be the possession of Charles; but Admiral Rooke very quietly hauled it down and hoisted the standard of England, and declared that the British took and meant to keep it. Thus, on the 24th July 1704, Gibraltar fell into the hands of the British.

CHAPTER XVI

First Siege of Gibraltar

I have said that many attempts have been made by the Spaniards to recover this important fortress, the first of these being made three months after the British took possession. Then the combined French and Spanish army appeared on the neutral ground purposely to besiege the place. So determined were the Spaniards to regain possession of it that 500 volunteers swore by the Holy Sacrament that they would win it back or perish in the attempt. Having taken this oath and engaged a goat-herd to guide them, they prepared at dead of night to scale the rock. They managed before dawn to conceal themselves in St Michael's Cave, which lies half-way between Windmill Point and the signal station. Here they remained till night again fell, when they succeeded in scaling the wall and penetrating to Windmill Hill, where they took the guard by surprise, fell upon and put every man of them to death. But an alarm had been given, and a party marched from the garrison to aid the guard. A fierce contest ensued, the Spaniards were totally defeated, and 150 driven at the point of the bayonet over the Rock, thus meeting a miserable death. The remainder were taken prisoners, and amongst the number were a colonel and 30 commissioned officers. This attempt having failed, a cannonade was tried, and a breach effected in one of the towers in the lower wall; but an attempt to carry the place by storm was defeated by the garrison, who inflicted heavy loss on the besiegers. Shortly after the garrison was provisioned and reinforced from England, and the enemy contented themselves with entrenching on the neutral ground, thus converting the siege into a blockade. The loss of the French and Spaniards was computed at 10,000, while that of the garrison was only 400. In 1713 Spain yielded up Gibraltar to England by treaty.

Second Siege, 1720

Of course the Spaniards had not yielded up Gibraltar with pleasure; nor was their king any better pleased, indeed he is known to have said he would willingly do much to pull out the thorn in his foot – meaning he wished the British anywhere but in Gibraltar. Accordingly in 1720 an attempt was made to take the place by surprise, which, however, came to nothing, as the garrison had become aware of it and were prepared to resist. In 1727 Gibraltar was again besieged by no less than 20,000 troops. At that time the garrison happened to be strong enough, with sufficient supplies, to resist until reinforced from England. The reinforcements arrived just in the nick of time, and brought the number in the garrison up to 6000. The besiegers threw great quantities of bombs into the place, which, however, did very little damage; and the siege was raised after having lasted four months, during which the garrison lost 300 and the enemy 3000. About this time George I. of England would willingly have given up Gibraltar to Philip of Spain, but the people and Parliament raised such an outcry that he was fain to give up the proposed arrangements. The dangers to which Gibraltar was exposed were not alone attacks from a foe without the walls, but also from mutineers within. Then, as now, regiments abroad were relieved by regiments from home, but the reliefs then were more uncertain, and the service abroad consequently was sometimes protracted to very great length. This was the cause, in 1760, of a mutiny in the garrison. Two regiments who had been long on the rock became discontented at their confinement and arduous duties, and formed a conspiracy to put their officers to death and seize the place; but what they intended to do with it no one knew. As usually happens in most conspiracies, they could not keep their tongues from wagging. There were spies and informers amongst them, and their plans were soon known to the authorities, who immediately caused the ringleaders to be arrested, tried, and shot for mutiny. This prompt and energetic conduct put an end to the mutiny, which went no further, and the discontented regiments were shortly thereafter relieved. From this until 1779 Gibraltar suffered no molestation, but in that year was commenced the last, most determined, and most prolonged siege it ever sustained. For three years, seven months, and twelve days was it invested, and during that long time prodigies of valour were performed daily both by besieged and besiegers.

Third Siege

In 1775 England became involved in a war with its American subjects, which lasted till 1783, and is now known as the American War of Independence, and which terminated in the declaration by England of the independence of the American Colonies. In 1778 the French entered into the contest, and sent a fleet to assist the Americans. At the same time war was raging in the East and West Indies – dependencies of Great Britain – and while she was so busily engaged in so many different quarters, Spain threw herself into the contest, fancying that England would have then plenty to do elsewhere without attending much to Gibraltar. The Spanish Government did not attempt to conceal that anxiety to recover Gibraltar was the cause of the war, and every nerve was strained in order to be successful. Gibraltar at that time, as well as at present, derived most of its supplies from the opposite seaports of Tetuan, Tangiers, and Laroche, on the coast of Africa, belonging to the Emperor of Morocco. The Spaniards solicited the Emperor to allow them to arm these ports, that is to hire their use, and this the Emperor did. It may then be easily supposed that in such a state of affairs Gibraltar was no longer supplied from these ports and had to depend solely on what it could receive from England. Immediately on the before-mentioned arrangements having been made, Gibraltar was invested by an. army of 40,000 troops, 50 sail of the line, frigates, gun-boats, and floating batteries almost innumerable. For twelve months the gallant garrison, under General Elliot, had to sustain the full brunt of the contest. Provisions began to grow scarce, and they were reduced to eat nettles, grass, and in fact anything they could get, when, to their great joy, Admiral Sir George Rodney (who had been despatched from England for that purpose), came to their relief with a large fleet. Rodney, soon after setting out, fell in with a Spanish convoy of fifteen merchantmen laden with wheat, flour, and just such other provisions as Gibraltar stood in need of. These he chased, captured, and took with him. He also met, chased, and took eleven ships of the line belonging to Spain off St Vincent, after which he sailed for and relieved Gibraltar. Sailing for the West Indies immediately after, for another twelve months the garrison were left to their own resources, and assuredly would have been starved out had it not been for the caution of Elliot, who issued the provisions but sparingly, and even forbade the use of hair-powder as he considered it a shameful waste of flour (hair- powder was then used in the army). In the beginning of 1781 another fleet under Admiral Darby was sent to the relief of the garrison. The Spanish fleet was found quietly at anchor in Cadiz Bay, and the Admiral sent on the provision ships, while he stayed to watch the Spaniards. They were not molested, and Gibraltar was once more placed in a position to resist. By this time the Spaniards had erected enormous batteries carrying 170 of the heaviest guns of the time; constructed numerous vessels intended to be fire and bomb proof, and poured a continuous shower of iron into the place. Day and night the cannonade and bombardment continued, and Elliot answered, but when he came to consider that during three months his loss had been 1 officer and 52 men killed, and 7 officers and 253 men wounded, and that it had cost the Spaniards 10,000 lbs. of powder and 7500 shot to do this, he slackened his own fire to save his ammunition, and seemed to be little troubled by the continuous but aimless fire of his opponents. Gradually the fire slackened on both sides till quiet fell upon the Rock. The Spaniards were engaged adding to their works, and when they had perfected them Elliot thought it high time to do something; so on the night of the 27th November

1781, after the moon set, a strong detachment left the garrison in three columns, and stole along in silence so great that they reached the works without being detected. The attack was so well planned that all three columns were faced at one and the same time and together assaulted the whole front of the enemy's works. The Spaniards were taken by surprise and gave way on all sides and the works were taken. No time was lost. Mortars and guns were spiked; the batteries torn down; the traversing platforms, mortar-beds, and gun-carriages overthrown, and what would burn was given to the flame while the magazines were blown up one after another. Meanwhile, the Spanish army stood gazing on the wholesale destruction and never attempted to move in defence of their works. The whole time occupied in thus destroying, what took the Spaniards many months to erect, was not more than two hours, while scarcely an accident happened to the detachment, and the enemy's loss was very trifling. The Spanish army having met with success in the island of Minorca in 1782, the Spanish king and nation were full of joyful anticipations that Gibraltar would soon fall into their hands, but they knew if they only stood gazing at the place it would not of itself condescend to drop into their mouths, so they made every preparation for its recovery. No less than 1200 pieces of heavy ordnance were brought before it, and the quantity of powder and shot was something tremendous, gunpowder alone being said to have amounted to 83,000 barrels. 40 gunboats, as many bomb vessels, and 50 sail of the line were mustered to the attack. Ten great ships were formed into floating batteries, constructed so as to be bomb proof and beyond the danger of fire, being covered with a heavy roof of rope overspread with (supposed to be) wool, while throughout the inside in all directions were water pipes to extinguish fire. 40,000 men and all the best engineers from France, Italy, Germany, and Switzerland were sought for and brought to aid in the great task. Elliot was not idle within, though he knew little of the resources of the enemy. He distributed furnaces and grates for red-heating shot, and calmly awaited the course of events. But before the enemy were ready Elliot got tired of waiting and determined to provoke an attack, so, observing that the batteries on the land lines were nearly ready, he opened fire upon them about seven in the morning of the 8th September 1782, which he continued throughout the day with far greater effect than he had dared to hope for, for by ten o'clock two batteries were on fire and a considerable part of the trenches and parapets were destroyed. This provoked the Spaniards to retaliate next day by opening fire first with a battery of 64 guns, succeeded by a flight of 60 shells and a general discharge of 186 guns, all from the land side. While this was going on the Spanish fleet passed slowly in front of the works, firing as they went on the batteries till they passed Europa Point, when they formed in line and continued their fire, but it was returned so spiritedly that they were obliged to retire and repair damages. Day by day more guns were brought to bear, the mortar boats were now added to the assailants, and the floating batteries were towed to their stations. It was calculated that at this time 4000 shot were thrown daily against the rock, and so completely was it hemmed in by this circle of fire that it was fully anticipated that the garrison would fall into confusion; and so assured of success was the Spanish King that when he woke in the morning he always asked "Is Gibraltar ours?" and when he was told it was not, answered, "Well, it must soon be," and turned over for another snooze. Nothing of importance occurred until the 12th, when the French and Spanish fleets sailed into the bay. While the garrison were watching the ships a flag on the signal station signalled the approach of a fleet, and all concluded it was the British fleet in pursuit, but their hopes fell when the flag suddenly disappeared. It was afterwards found out that what they took to be a flag was an eagle, which had perched for a few minutes on the flagstaff, but this the garrison took to be a signal of good fortune. On the 13th a grand attack was made. The land batteries issued forth a perfect storm of shot and shell. The ships of war and floating batteries vomited forth torrents of missiles of every description against the place, while the surrounding hills were crowded with spectators as if all Spain had turned out to see the fall of the fortress. So terrific and sublime was the scene that neither pen nor pencil can give an abject idea of it. Suffice it to say, that 400 of the heaviest artillery were at work at the same moment. Nor were the garrison idle. A prodigious shower of red hot shell and curracoes filled the air without intermission and astonished the enemy, who could not believe that it was possible for Elliot to have a sufficiency of furnaces within the small space at his command to heat the large number of shot he fired against them; but he had caused bonfires to be lit, and the shot, &c., heated in them. I may here state that they jocularly called the shot heated in the bonfires "roasted potatoes." For several hours the floating batteries were found to be as intended; fire and bomb-proof, the heaviest shot bounding off their tops, and 32 lb. shot failing to penetrate their hulls. Several times they were set on fire, but the water pipes were so well laid, and the screws so active in their use that the fires were speedily put out. These ships caused the garrison so much annoyance that at last all their efforts were directed against them. At last, about two o'clock, the Spanish admiral's ship was seen to have caught fire, and one of the floating batteries began to smoke on the side next the Rock. This caused some confusion amongst the enemy, and their fire slackened till it almost ceased about eight o'clock, but the garrison still pelted the Spaniards with their "roasted potatoes," and that so effectually as to set one battering ship on fire completely. About midnight another soon began to blaze, and shortly after six more, giving the garrison sufficient light to direct their shot with deadly precision. About three o'clock Brigadier Curtis, in command of the Marine Brigade, manned the gunboats at Europa Point, and took the battering ships in flank. Almost immediately one blew up, and Curtis captured two launches filled with men rescued from the burning ships. Hearing from them that numbers were still left on board, he manfully dashed to their aid, and while engaged in this humane task a ship blew up close to his boat and killed the coxswain. He now deemed it prudent to return, as little good could be done, and the danger was great. Eight more of the battering ships blew up next day, and the British burned the 10th, thus depriving the besiegers of the very means they most depended on for success. Nearly 400 were saved by the British from the burning vessels, yet it is estimated that at least 1500 more perished either by fire or water. The garrison suffered very little when the amount of fire directed against them is considered, seeing their loss in killed was only 3 officers and 65 men, and wounded 12 officers and 388 men. This attack having been foiled, little more was done to molest Gibraltar, though now and then the garrison got an alert, and it was shortly after provisioned and reinforced to the extent of 1600 men by Lord Howe, who caused the Spanish fleet to retire after a smart though short skirmish. The land force did little to maintain the blockade, but made themselves very busy in trying to tear down and undermine the Rock beneath the Devil's Tower, but their works were soon made too hot to hold them. On the 6th February 1783, the Duke de Crillon, commanding, informed Elliot that war had ceased, and withdrew his army. Thus this long siege of over three and a half years ended; and, though the loss of the enemy has never been ascertained, the total loss in killed and wounded to the garrison was only 1231. For his services Elliot was decorated with the Order of the Bath. Gibraltar has never since been invested, and but for a slight disturbance amongst the troops in garrison, has remained peacefully in our possession. In the next chapter we will take a glance at it as it is at present, and must then hurry off to another of our possessions.

CHAPTER XVII

The Fortress of Gibraltar – Farewell to the Rock

I have already said we were never permitted to quit the Rock "on pleasure bent," so that, with the exception of the town or North Front, a walk to any distance could not be got; still some even attempted the climb to the signal station on the summit, for the view therefrom amply repaid the trouble – a radius of some 60 or 70 miles being exposed to the view. The town itself, which nestles at the foot in the north-west corner, is not ornamental. It consists of one long street, with a number of small, narrow alleys running into it. At one end is the Alameda, a nicely laid out promenade with beautiful shrubbery and flowers. Each man has built his house with the knowledge that if there were a siege it would probably be blown to pieces. The natives, though a mixed race, have mostly English blood in their veins. There are exceedingly few things which they will not do for money; and they are living examples of the melancholy fact that the proverb about honesty being the best policy is not universally followed. They live and thrive upon very questionable practices. In Constantinople the Mahometans of Stamboul are far more honest than the Christians of Pera; and here the Moors, who come over and established themselves are far more honest than the natives, who are called "scorpions." But Gibraltar is remarkable as a fortress, and not as a school of morals. Vast sums of money have been spent to make it impregnable, and they have not been thrown away. Level with the sea are the water batteries, driven into the solid rock, and above these are galleries rising one above the other, in which there are cannon, which may be fired with hardly any risk of being struck. The portholes give the rock the appearance of a warren of mammoth rabbits. Most of the guns in position while we were there were 36-pounders, but cannon of enormous calibre were being sent out from England to replace them. Those which had arrived were 18 tons, for one can no longer reckon in pounds, and 40-tonners are yet expected.

"Gibraltar," says a local proverb, "is heaven for 'scorpions' and hell for donkeys." Of course, the authorities at home have not thought fit to send out a small traction engine, so these enormous masses of metal have to be dragged to their places up the rude paths of the rock by mules and asses.

Notwithstanding the natural and artificial strength of the Rock the authorities do not go to sleep, but day after day, and night after night, everything goes on as though half-a-dozen determined men might take it by a *coup de main*. No foreigner is allowed to enter the gates without a permit, which has to be renewed every month. Even the peasants who bring in vegetables are obliged to obtain one of these permits. At sunset a gun is fired, when the drawbridges are raised and the gates shut, and they remain closed to everyone, officer or civilian, until the morning gun, which announces sunrise, is fired. At nine o'clock all soldiers, without special leave, are obliged to be in their barracks; and after midnight the inhabitants are arrested if they are found out of their houses. Sentinels are everywhere, guarding apparently nothing. Drums beat, fifes and bagpipes play at all hours; troops march, counter march, and drill from morning to night. The officers endeavour to vary the monotony of their existence by making excursions into Africa and Spain. They also keep up a pack of hounds, and have some very good runs during the winter. Scarcely a day passes without two or three steamers putting in to land or ship cargo or coal. The guards are "trooped" on the Alameda twice a week, and one of the bands play in the evenings there, when the inhabitants turn out to promenade or sit on chairs to listen to them. On these occasions one can see that the young women of Gibraltar are extremely handsome, but greatly given to extravagance in dress, for I have seen more pretty faces there than I ever saw in London or Edinburgh. I do not mean by this to say that England cannot boast of charming girls; but there is a kind of artistic excellence about the girls of Gibraltar not to' be found amongst any other. The celebrated novelist, Lever, says "a Spanish woman, with a skin like an old drum head and the lower jaw of an old baboon, will actually get herself up to look better than many a pretty girl of our country." The fascination of a Spanish girl lies in the brilliancy of her love-speaking eyes. I cannot understand what can make girls possessing such attractions voluntarily abandon the pleasures of the world and enter the gloomy abode of a loveless convent as so many of them do. The softening influence of woman's love is lost when she leaves her proper sphere in the world, and we require all her sympathy and smiles in a world like this without her burying her beauty in a living tomb.

In the clefts of the rock are to be found a few monkeys. They are the only wild ones in Europe and having been there from time immemorial they are reverenced as much as their brothers in the sacred groves of Benares. Most stringent orders are issued against injuring them.

Much sentimental twaddle is periodically written about giving up Gibraltar to the Spaniards on the ground of its being a portion of Spain. We require it now more than at any previous period, because sailing vessels are gradually being superseded by steamers for carrying purposes, and we must have coaling stations. In point of fact, what we want is not to reduce the number of these stations, but to increase them by adding to their number one in the vicinity of Egypt. As for the noble Spaniard being indignant at our holding the Rock, the noble Spaniard cares little about it. Few Spaniards even know – so great is their ignorance – that there is such a place as Gibraltar, though the Governor of Algiceras is still styled by them as the Governor of Algiciras and Gibraltar. This climax of absurdity, however, was reached some years ago, when it was seriously suggested that we should exchange it for Ceuta. Now Ceuta is a Spanish penal station in Africa, not in the Strait, and of no particular natural strength. It has, too, an exceedingly bad harbour. The Moors have always protested against the Spanish occupation and this protest they carry into effect by the simple expedient of shooting every Spaniard who strays outside the lines. On moral grounds, therefore, we should have no more right to Ceuta than we have to Gibraltar. It would be robbing Peter to make a present to Paul, and losing very considerably by the transaction. To put Ceuta in a proper condition of defence would cost millions, and those millions would have to come out of the British tax payers' pockets.

The inhabitants of Gibraltar are mostly Roman Catholic. They have little sanctimonious sourness about them. If they attend their mass in the morning they consider they have done well, and become worshippers of Dr Greenfield for the remainder of the day. This propensity of theirs caused but little trace of a holy Sabbath day to be found, and I often sighed –

> Oh! for a sound o' a Sabbath bell
> On the calm, sweet summer's gale,
> The same as I heard in years gone bye
> In the sweet toon o' Glenvale.

After attending Divine service on the last Sunday I was in Gibraltar I climbed up for a last view and sat upon the highest peak on the Rock. It was a beautiful day; the sun shone with refulgent glory on the brow of the old grey hill, while the town lay slumbering in peace and quietness at the bottom. I had a magnificent view of the hills of Spain, and the cool pure breeze wandered over earth and ocean, while the voice of children playing down the slope sent through my heart a thrill of cordial delight and pleasure. Oh! what a glorious world we would have if that tyrannical spirit which delights in the oppression of poor humanity was only banished from amongst the sons of men.

I then looked on the great Mediterranean Sea; but my thoughts wandered back to the days when I was an under-ground worker. I thought of the tens of thousands of Briton's sons who are shut out from the beauties of nature working deep down in their sunless den excavating the precious material which propels the mighty leviathians across the trackless ocean. I might have be inclined to forget the din, the noise, and smoke of unpoetical coal-pits, accustomed as I have been for the last 12 years to traverse rural and primitive lands; still I can sympathise with my hard-working countrymen away in the dear old land. I would, however, prefer to live at the flood-gates of eastern day than amongst the eternal roar of machinery and steam. I love to roam along the beach of an orient land –

> "Nourishing a youth sublime
> With the fairy tales of science
> And the long results of time."

The Regiment was exceedingly healthy while stationed in Gibraltar, having only had 12 deaths daring the four and a half years, and two of these were the result of accident. The Regiment was also highly respected by the inhabitants, who expressed great regret at losing us, as the following quotation from the *Gibraltar Chronicle* – the only paper published there – at the time of our departure, will show: –

> "The Seventy-First Highland Light Infantry embarked for Malta on the 24bh April 1873. It is always a painful matter to say 'Farewell' to old friends, and the task becomes doubly difficult when these old friends are held in such popular estimation as are all ranks of this gallant regiment in the minds of every one with whom they have been brought into contact here. From the first to the last there has been only the most cordial good- will between them and the inhabitants, and the regrets and good wishes of all will follow them to their new quarters. We take leave of them with the greatest regret, as gallant soldiers and good fellows, and when we say good-bye we wish in our hearts that it may be, and that very speedily, *"au revoir."'*

We received a few drafts from the depot while there to fill up the blanks caused by those leaving with their time up, and as they dropped off in twos or threes painful leave-takings were the order of the day, and none more so than when it came to the turn of Sergeant-Major Barr and Sergeant-Instructor of Musketry Mitchell, who were both highly respected, and left us about a year before our departure to Malta. After so long A stay there I must say I felt rather sorrowful at leaving, the people having been so kind to us, and we had almost become a part of themselves, so to speak, but to show our gratitude for their kindness we took a few of their bonnie lasses along with us.

Farewell, dear old Rock; I may never climb thy rugged side again, but in after years I will often think on the bright and joyous days I enjoyed on thee.

> Four years and six months I have seen
>   Since landing on thy aged brow,
> And bright and happy ones they've been,
>   But dear old Rock, I leave thee now.
> Yet I shall cast a look behind.
>   And think on days enjoyed here;
> I've found thy sons and daughters kind
>   I give you all I have – a tear.

CHAPTER XVIII

Arrival in Malta – Its "Lions"

And this is Malta? Don't you hear
The chapel bells already ringing.
And see the candles burning clear,
And grey-haired priests around them singing:
Although grim-featured superstition
Reigns o'er Malta's barren plain,
A holy, pious, pure petition,
Ne'er went up to heaven in vain.

On the 24th April 1873 we embarked on board H.M.S. "Tamar" for Malta. The incidents peculiar to sea voyages being all very much the same, I need not detain the reader by recounting our experience. I shall only say that we had more than an ordinary share of sickness, at least to begin with. Occasionally we had some fine views along the coast, including the ruins of Carthage – bringing to mind the fact that "thrones, principalities, powers, and dominions," all have their day, and may at last come to nought. When we entered the harbour at Malta we were received by many old friends, in the l-13th, 28th, and 74th regiments, the band of the latter playing "Auld Lang Syne", but we did not disembark till next day. Byron, in his leave-taking of Malta, says –

"Adieu, ye streets of La Vallette;
Adieu, sirocco, suns, and sweat;
Adieu, ye streets of steps and stairs,
How surly he who mounts you swears."

And truly he had good cause, as we afterwards found out, to call them "streets of steps and stairs." The houses seemed substantial, and being built of the clean white stone quarried from the island, with beautiful green painted verandahs, they appeared very picturesque, and at short intervals domes and spires of churches towered above the surrounding buildings. In the Grand Harbour (of which more anon), and which in a manner divides Vallette from the Three Cities, the most of the passenger traffic is carried on in boats (or dycos, as they are called). By using them you save a walk of some four or five miles round by the road. To see the number of boats continually crossing and re-crossing made one wonder where all the people that used them could come from, for they looked as if they were a swarm of mosquitoes sporting in the sunbeams on the surface of the water. When night began to throw her curtain over us, and lights peeped out one after another from the windows of the different houses, and the port holes of the vessels around us, it recalled to mind some of the panoramas which we loved so well to see in our youthful days.

As might well be expected the next morning was one, not only of stir, but also of anxiety, as we were unaware as to how we might succeed in our new quarters. We commenced by giving in our hammocks as early as 5 A.M., and then to clean ourselves with all possible speed. As we were not to disembark until after the hour for breakfast, and were in rations on shore, they were generous enough to inform us that we were to be given that meal on board, free, gratis, for nothing; but such an one, a dish of tea (boiling hot) without bread of any kind – fitting commencement for a day's hard work. Then all of us were ordered on deck with all our belongings at 7 A. m. to shift as best we could, but there we had to stay. Our rifles were served out to us at 7.45. Then we had muster parade in marching order at 8.15, after which there was no end of crushing and knocking about with our packs on until nine had come and gone, when a Government tug came alongside and kindly took us all on board (unless one company that was left to put out the baggage into barges), and we made our way to the shore with the band giving us "Rule Britannia," and "Auld Lang Syne" from the bridge. All the bands of the other regiments in the garrison were waiting us, and played us straight up to barracks, a benefit for us owing to the 28th having generously gone under canvas previous to our arrival to permit our entering the barracks. The distance we had to go was but trifling, as we were to occupy Floriana Barracks - -the same as was occupied by the regiment on their return from the Crimea in 1856; but as soon as we were told off to rooms time sufficient to throw off our knapsacks was barely afforded us, when we were away to the harbour again to get the baggage up, and, though it had the appearance of being a difficult job, yet by all working with a will it was all on shore shortly after three, and safely housed by retreat. However, it was past two ere we managed to get anything to eat, and even then nothing to brag of, but famished as we were anything was welcome. From what we could see our quarters were to be very comfortable, every convenience being at hand, only the barrack rooms were far too large, no less than forty-six living in each. We had any number of the 28th and 74th paying us visits during the day, but being so busy we had but little time to have much convention with them. A good few of the Regiment who had been in the Crimea had been in Malta before, but to the majority it was quite a new world, and I, for one, found it so, for the people were very different from any others I had been brought into contact with during my military career. The very sound of their language was harsh and un-poetical, and seemed as if it were some of the dead ones revived. The features in general too, especially of the male sex, were anything but pleasant or good-looking, yet I could see at a glance that many of the opposite sex were prepossessing in appearance and seemed to belong to a different or mixed tribe. I soon became reconciled to my new home and began to fall in with the ways of the place.

My duties in Malta were exactly similar to those in Gibraltar, the strength of the one garrison being the same as the other, only there was one company of engineers less in Malta, to make up for which we had their local corps the "Royal Malta Fencible Artillery," numbering in strength somewhere about 400. The regiments forming the garrison along with us on our arrival were the l-13th, l-18th, 28th, and 74th, all of which, with the exception of the second mentioned, were along with as in Gibraltar, so that we were, so to speak, at home with them. In nearly all parts of the world the British soldier's duties are the same – guards, picquets, fatigues, and incessant drills, following each other in rapid rotation. My first duty in Malta was to mount the main guard, one of the most important in the garrison, situated on one side of St George's Square, and directly opposite the Palace. It is in one sense the Governor's body-guard, the same as the Convent guard was in Gibraltar. It is also the principal guard on the Valletta side of the water, and is under the command of one and sometimes two officers. The Palace itself has but little claim to architectural beauty, being rather a plain, square building surrounded by balconies, with a large courtyard in the centre, the whole covering close upon an acre of ground; still the interior is superb, the court being tastefully laid out in flower plots, with several orange and other trees interspersed here and there. The Armoury and Council-room – where the Council of Government hold their sittings – are numbered among the "lions" of Malta. The former contains many specimens of arms and armour belonging to a remote age; a Pope's Bull to the Knights Templars of the sixteenth century; the identical bugle that sounded the celebrated retreat of Rhodes, and relics of the different grand Knights far too numerous to mention. The Council-room is a plain furnished but gorgeous apartment, the clean tapestried walls laying claim to being about the best of their kind extant.

The most important "lion," however, is the far famed St John's Church, A structure of huge dimensions built in the form of a cross, with two belfries rising above the main entrance in which huge "Bens" keep clattering from early morning till far on in the night day by day. Time having laid its hand rather heavy on the exterior the stranger has but little to draw him towards it, and is quite unprepared for the sight that bursts upon his gaze after he is once inside the door-way; in fact it almost baffles description. The floor is paved with small square blocks of different-coloured marbles; the walls hang round with large framed paintings; while the roof is squared off, and figures of the most prominent of the saints placed therein by the brushes of some of the most eminent painters of Italy. Statues also abound in niches and comers, while the principal altar is surrounded and surmounted by them, and its wealthy decorations quite dazzle the eyes of the beholder. It is also enclosed by gates of solid silver, said to have replaced gold ones carried away by the first Napoleon, and thrown into the

Grand Harbour, but somehow they have never managed to be picked up again as yet, although the Maltese would move heaven and earth for anything that could be converted into money. I have said the principal altar, for it must be borne in mind there are altars for all the different nations of the earth almost who boast of being the children of " Holy Mother Church," while near bye each is to be seen the confessional box, with a priest as its occupant well posted up in the language required. I never can forget the feelings that rose within me when I first entered that edifice; it was a sort of holy awe stealing over me, for the floor, the ceiling, and the pictures made me almost forget that I was still an inhabitant of this lower world, and I then thought of the contrast between that magnificent temple and our own simple Presbyterian kirks with their barrel-looking pulpits and cribbed seats; and yet the attendants in both churches are each in their own manner striving to worship the same great *Infinite Being*.

CHAPTER XIX

TheValletta Opera House – The Spacious Harbours of Malta – Two Imposing Catholic Processions

Malta is an island of about 60 miles in circumference, so that we had no need to complain here, as in Gibraltar, of the want of room for a walk. It comprises the city of Valletta, with Floriana just outside the principal entrance; Port Reale, or Royal Gate; and on the opposite side of the Grand Harbour, is what is termed the three cities, viz., Vittorosa, Isola, and Burmola; while further out are several villages of some consideration such as Zabbar, Zeitun, Birchicircara, and Civita Vecchia. The barracks we first occupied (Floriana) were, so to speak, in Valletta, or, as we generally say, on the Valletta side of the water. This city was first founded by La Vallette in the sixteenth century, and is now the principal one on the island. It is beautifully situated, rising with a pretty steep gradient from the north side where it forms the division of the entrance to the Grand and Quarantine Harbours, thus becoming the quay to both of these. Entering it from the country side you cross a draw-bridge thrown over the main ditch, some 70 or 80 feet deep, and are directly under the archways of Porte Reale, a beautiful structure with a statue of La Vallette and L' Isle Adam on either side. Proceeding but a short distance down Strada Reale (the principal thoroughfare), on the right hand side yon have the new Opera House, a building erected during the Governorship of General Sir Gaspard Le Marchant at a cost of between £50,000 and £60,000, which I can safely say is one of the most magnificent of its kind that I have ever been permitted to see. The walls outside are elaborately decorated with sculptured work representing some of the great composers and a variety of musical instruments, and its dimensions are in no way inferior to the largest Opera House in London. It was indeed the pride of the island, and seemed worthy of the expense that had been caused by its erection, but its beauty was doomed to destruction. About a month after our arrival, on a quiet Sabbath evening, the fire-bugle sounded the alarm, and as we each rushed out into the dark night the whole of the city seemed to be in flames, and we could scarcely credit our ears when told it was the Opera House on fire. All at once we were turned out, and neither water nor willing hands were awanting to do what could be done to save the building. The fire, however, had obtained too fast a hold, and in about a couple of hours from the first alarm all that was left of it was the four walls – a blackened mass. Had the military not been at hand it would be hard to say what the consequences might have been, as the inhabitants were quite terrified with horror, and flew, as if bereft of their senses, with what they stood in to all parts of the country fearful lest the magazines in the vicinity would be blown up. It stood thus for upwards of three years, but at last, through the energetic efforts of some of the members of the Government, though not without much and determined opposition, it is fast regaining its former appearance.

Next in importance to the Opera House is the Auberge de Provence, a large palatial residence used principally by the officers of the Army and Navy as a Club-House. In Valletta, which, as a town, is built in squares, there are several other imposing buildings. The Roman Catholic Churches I have already mentioned; and in addition to them there is the English Cathedral Church of St Paul with its beautiful spire. This building cost somewhere about £9000, and was the gift of Queen Adelaide. The great fault of the streets is their narrowness. For example: Strada Stretta, or Straight Street, which was so much admired by Sir Walter Scott while visiting the island shortly before his death, is only from 7 to 8 feet broad and over 900 yards in length, while the buildings are all from six to seven stories high.

The harbours of Malta are the great feature of the island. They are much about the same as regards length and breadth, but the Grand has several creeks more than the Quarantine, in which all the Navies in the world could ride safely at anchor. They run inland close upon two miles, and as far as 20 or 30 steamers, independent of the Fleet, may be seen within their bounds at one time, for the traffic now is much greater since the Suez Canal route was opened, while multitudes of small craft are continually arriving, principally with the products of the Island of Sicily and the northern coast of Africa.

In Malta, as in most Roman Catholic communities, there are a great many festival days, and on some of these days, imposing processions may be witnessed. I will endeavour to give a brief description of two of these, which I myself beheld. The first was that of St Paul, which is held in the month of February in celebration of the anniversary of that Apostle's landing on the island. On the night previous there is service in St Pauls Church, a modest enough looking edifice, but gorgeously decorated within, while the whole district under its sway is ablaze with illuminations, and the streets spanned by ornamental arches. Bands of music, too, are interspersed here and there playing far on into the silent watches of the night, and even the poorest vie with their more fortunate neighbours in hanging banners or tapestry from the windows of their dwellings. The service in church continues the whole of next day, and it being the time the opera is in full sway the most of the *artistes* engaged in it lend their assistance, so that the music both vocal and instrumental is of a very high class. About 4 p.m. the procession is formed, and pursues a circuitous course through the various principal streets of the city, much in the form of that of a military funeral Both sides of the roadway are taken up by those forming the procession with a couple of paces interval, while the centre is kept quite clear. First comes a banner of enormous dimensions with the letters I.H.S. and I.N.R.I. emblazoned thereon, followed by all the different holy crafts and guilds, each bearing their own devices and figures of the Saviour on the Cross in different sorts of workmanship, from plain wood to solid silver with diamond-headed nails. Then follow monks and priests of all orders, amongst them being boys in their teens and old men with grey hair, but all with the shaven crown. Next come several acholytes bearing a number of the jewels used in their worship, two of whom wave censers of incense, perfuming the whole atmosphere around. Following them, under a canopy of satin, is the principal clergyman, rich in jewellery, with an elaborately-finished cross in his hand, muttering his *aves*, and the priests chanting around him. Bringing up the rear is a mighty figure in wood, glaring in paint and gilding, of the great Apostle with an open book in his right hand, and his left outstretched over the heads of the multitude. The gigantic figure is borne aloft on the shoulders of eight sturdy men who rock and reel under the weight of their burden. Truly the first time I beheld this, the scene on Mars Hill at Athens, as described in the Acts of the Apostles, rushed vividly across the eye of my imagination, and I wondered within myself why the dry bones of Paul did not come forth from their grave and protest against such mockery. When I say that each of those not otherwise employed in the procession carried lighted candles of close upon four feet in length, and that the procession took close upon an hour and a half to pass a given point, one can have a slight conception of the expense of getting it up, to say nothing of the loss of income through the suspension of labour, not only to those joining it, but also to the gazing crowds around.

The other I refer to takes place in Vittorosa (one of the Three Cities) on Good Friday. Of course, throughout the Christian world this day is kept as a holiday, so that no difference exists here; and special services are conducted in all the churches. As the procession in this case, which starts about 5 p.m., is conducted in entirely the same form as the other, it may suffice to notice only the figures or images carried in it. The first that makes its appearance is that of our Saviour in, the Garden of Gethsemane enduring His bloody sweat amongst branches of real trees, while the angel is close bye with a silver cup, which he offers him to drink. The second is after our Lord has been taken before Pilate, who has sent him to be scourged, and the figure – entirely naked – stands bound by the wrists to a tree stump with the back so thoroughly lacerated that the flesh is entirely flayed to admit of the bones appearing, while the blood runs streaming down the legs. In the third we have our Lord seated with the purple robe thrown loosely over the shoulders, the crown of thorns piercing his brow, and the reed (made of solid silver) held sceptre-like in the right hand. The fourth shows Him labouring greatly on hands! and knees up Calvary's steep sides with a huge cross upon his back. The fifth represents the price of man's redemption in the shape of the blessed Saviour extended on the Cross with three weeping women at its base. The next is a spacious catafalque richly ornamented, the floor of which represents roughhewn rock, and on it laid the bleeding and wounded body; while the last is a huge cross empty, draped in mourning, and Mary kneeling at it with the sword piercing her heart. Now when I add that all these figures are life-size, it will be seen that I am not at all exaggerating when I say each requires from six to twelve able-bodied men to carry it, and yet though they have to bear their burden for four hours (resting a few minutes occasionally), long before the time of the procession arrives the Catholics out-bid each other for the honour of being a sharer in the work, money having to be given to the Church for the permission. In this one, also, I saw a few children scarcely able to walk, representing guardian angels with their tiny wings and halo of glory, while the poor little innocents required to be guarded themselves for fear of being trodden in the press. No doubt the figures are richly-executed pieces of workmanship, and are decked off in the most gaudy colours. Still I cannot help thinking (though I am strongly in favour of freedom of opinion in matters of religion) that this is scarcely the manner in which He, who entered Jerusalem meek and lowly, desires to be worshipped, preferring rather to see the heart bent in lowly adoration to Himself, than these uncovered heads and prostrate forms giving glory to His imaginary likeness hewn from a block of wood.

CHAPTER XX

Mankey Bouffe's Love Difficulty

Not long after settling down in Verdala Barracks, my old friend, Mankey Bouffe, came to me, and with charming innocence made me his confidante in a very tender matter.

"I want your advice," he said, "in an affair that has quite upset me. To make a long story short, I am deeply in love with one whom I shall ever regard as the 'Flower of Verdala,' and I want you to give me the benefit of your large experience, and tell me how I shall best secure such a sweet blossom!"

"Go boldly forward," said I, "and besiege the fortress at once. You know the old saying – 'Faint heart never won fair lady.' "

"True, true," replied he, "but she has a host of admirers beside me, some of them much younger than I am, though they never can surpass me in the strength of my affection and love I have for that sweet girl."

"Has she given you any encouragement? – any hopes of storming the citadel of her affections?"

"Well, I think I am not altogether disagreeable to her presence. But I'm afraid I shall never be able to call the Rosa Coochperwanie mine. She is a very intelligent girl; she can sing Burns' songs and quote Byron and Scott. I would have given the price of a Colonel's commission last night to have only had the pleasure of touching the points of her fingers. When leaving her mother's house I had the courage to come out with

'Maid of Athena, ere we part,'

and oh! how she made my blood thrill in my veins when, with the most captivating voice, she added –

'Give, oh! give me back my heart.'

I felt quite overpowered, but just as I turned to show her my feelings, in comes Tarry Lyons. She gave him a cordial smile, which extinguished my last glimmering lamp of hope. Do tell me, my trustworthy friend, what I am to do?

> 'My Amy mine no more;
> Oh! that dreary, dreary wilderness,
> The barren, barren shore.'

I'll die, like Lord Byron, in a foreign land with no wife to wipe the sweat from my brow. Break out, O, Russian War, that I may have a chance of burying my broken heart on some field of battle."

"Cheer up, man; when we leave Malta you'll forget all about Rosa Coochperwanie ... "

"Never;
'While there's leaves in the forest and foam on the river, Manky Bouffe shall cherish her memory for ever.'

You're a friend of hers, can you not say a kind word for me?"

"That would be dangerous ground to tread upon. In interceding for you I might put in a word on my own behalf, for I cannot lay claim to infallibility, and I am sensible of the great personal attractions of Miss Coochperwanie. If a strong^ handsome looking fellow such as you is powerless to move her heart I know not who can succeed in winning it."

"I have been writing poetry till I am tired, and have made her the subject of two of my effusions, and she told me I had stolen my ideas and love expressions from her favourite poet, Byron. Now, I shall submit both my songs for your critical inspection, and if you find anything Byronic about them I'll believe her to be a female Jeffrey; so I'll give you a verse from each that you may judge for yourself. Here's the first –

> When the bricht stars are peepin' doon
> I dream o' my sweet lammie,
> Awa' in auld Verdala toon –
> My Rosa Coochperwanie."

"Well, Mankey, I see nothing sublime about that; but I also guess at the same time that she must have felt rather proud to have her charms set to verse by such a gallant fellow as yourself. But why so melancholy over a girl who neither understands your feelings, disposition, country, nor religion? Wait till we return to bonnie Scotland, and if we cannot secure a sonsie Scotch lassie we may win the affections of some buxom widow. You remember the words of the old song –

> 'The widow can bake an' the widow can brew,
> The widow can sing an' the widow can sew.
> An' mony braw things the widow can do.
> Then hae at a widow, my laddie.'

When Miss Coochperwanie has so many *beaux* to her fiddle I think you ought to give her up. To me she appears a bit of a flirt. However, I don't think you're much heart-broken. If we go to Bermuda you'll forget all about her, for a change of scene has a powerful effect in curing wounded affections. Still, let me have a verse of that other song that celebrates the charms of your Rosa."

"Well, don't call me a fool if I should show symptoms of weakness in singing it to you. Here's the first verse –

> Sweet flower of Verdala, I'll never
> Forget a maiden like thee,
> Thy mind is so charming and clever,
> Thou'rt all the world to me."

"Very good, Mankey. You're a real poet, full of power, spirit, and fire. Had Burns and Tannahill been still in this lower world, they would have extended to you the hand of poetical friendship. Go on courting the muses, and your cares and sorrows will melt away like the morning dew. Leave this Coochperwanie to waste her sweetness on the desert air – at least so far as you're concerned. I daresay, after all, she'll be satisfied with a Maltese barber or tailor for a husband, instead of a gallant son of Mars like you."

"Your advice may be good – I don't doubt it – but oh! It's hard to relinquish such a sweet fascinating girl."

"I have been in love myself more than once, and let me tell you that, old soldier though I be, I cherish a profound respect and affection for bonnie lasses, whether Greeks, Maltese, or Moors. The language of Tennyson is applicable to me –

> 'I know it true whate'er befall,
> I feel it when I sorrow most,
> Tis better to have loved and lost
> Than never to have loved at all.'

Yes, Mankey, I can cast my mind's eye back over the last 25 years of my life, and see all the dear sweet girls who captured my affections long ere I thought of being a wanderer in foreign lands. I have lost them all, but the memory of those golden days of manhood's early morn remain with me as a delicious dream. My sun is now past its meridian; still the scrap of an old love letter, or a lock of hair, brings to my mind recollections of joyous days which no language of mine is capable of depicting."

"You speak with truth and sense, but I find it hard to tear my heart away from Rosa. I have a letter here with me that I wrote on Lower Castile Guard last night. Many strange thoughts passed through my mind while I was writing it, and I've come to the conclusion if Miss Coochperwanie can find amongst her host of admirers one more true in his love, or more sincere in affection than I am, she'll be the happiest wife in Malta."

"Really, I did not think Rosa was surrounded by such a martial band of lovers. Who are all the brave fellows who are wooing at her, pooing at her, but canna get her? Surely you've no objection to let me have their names. Are they six years' men? for, if so, they cannot, according to the general order, be allowed to marry before they have put in that service; so as all the 'Cardwell men' appear to be disgusted with our glorious British army, you have nothing to fear in that quarter. But time will cure your love;

you're in the Snider-hot stage at present. I'll wager you a pot of Jamie M'Lachlan's best ale that if you were back amongst the bonnie lasses of Auld Reekie, Malta and all her sun-burnt girls would never cost you a thought. Now I'm prepared to listen very attentively to your letter, and may it ease your mind and restore you to something like your former buoyancy of spirits. Who would have thought Mankey Bouffe, the life and soul of every social circle, would turn so sedate and melancholy?"

"Not so melancholy but lean enjoy a pundy of porter at the canteen yet. But as I'm for the Butcher's guard to-morrow I have little time to get my traps in order, so I'll read ye the last piece of either prose or poetry that the hand o' Mankey Bouffe will ever pen to the beauteous flower o' Verdala toon –

> Lower Castile Guard,
> 12 o'clock, midnight.

> My Adorable Coochperwanie, – My soul is grieved to think that you expressed an unfavourable opinion relative to the genuineness of the two songs I had the honour to present to you the other day. With great respect for your brilliant, and I might say critical, talents I beg to inform you that I never was (to my knowledge) guilty of stealing the printed thoughts of any of our modern poets to enable me to convey my sentiments to the fair sex. In my rhymes I only express the simple sentiments of a pure but uncultivated mind. I now part with you for ever, for I can never again trust myself in your enchanting presence, but sincerely hope you may find amongst your host of admirers one true heart to love you with sincere affection that your soul may be filled with perpetual sunshine and bliss, is the sincere prayer of forlorn

> MANKEY BOUFFE

Mankey enclosed this heart-stirring epistle and despatched it to his charmer, after which his mind appeared to be wonderfully at ease, his pent-up feelings having thus got vent, for in less than half-an-hour he was making the canteen ring with his favourite bacchanalian song of –

> "Auld Scotch whiskey sweetly gangs doon
> Wi' sugar an' candy in Camm'elton toon."

Poor fellow, Time is now laying his hand somewhat heavy on him, bat we cannot expect much other as he has served over twenty years, and the majority of these in foreign climes. I must here record that I have all along found him a generous friend and steadfast comrade, and I pray he may be long spared to lead a useful life in his favourite "Auld Reekie."

CHAPTER XXI

The Primitive State of Agriculture in Malta – A Royal Birth – The Catacombs of Citta Vecchia – St Paul's Bay: The Place Where the Apostle Landed

We occupied Verdala Barracks for six months, the duties on that side being much the same as on the other, although it has three regiments located there while the Valletta side has only two, for we had occasionally to give a share of the duty on it, crossing and re-crossing in boats. With the exception of the two prisons (civil and military), erected in 1864 or 1865 on Corradino heights, and the Royal Naval and Zabbar Hospitals, there are no buildings of any consequence in the Three Cities; and if Valletta is in want of sanitary measures the Three Cities are much more so – dirt and filth being predominant in all corners.

During the summer I took the advantage of several trips into the country, and I was indeed greatly surprised at the amount of vegetation I saw. The people are very ignorant, and seem to cling with a tenacity worthy of a better cause to the rites and customs of their rude forefathers, for they are truly a century behind the remainder of the civilised world. One would scarcely give it credit, and yet it is too true, that in a possession of England so close to the mother country as this is, the old rude plough drawn by oxen is all that is used. Many a time have I stood in the cool evening gazing with wonder at the countryman trudging his way home with his small wooden plough on his shoulder, while his steer, or perhaps a dried up milch cow, which had been ploughing the hole day through, steps along quietly at his heels.

At times I have seen' an ox and a mule yoked together in these ploughs, though it is but seldom such is the case, as the latter are too much employed in cart work. The mode of threshing here is a very ancient one too. The produce of the field is not cut as at home by scythe or sickle, but dragged up by the roots. It is then placed round a stake in the middle of a field, to which is fastened a solitary ox, which wends its way round and round until the grain is thoroughly loosened from the straw. The people here, however, seem either to be ignorant of, or heedless about, what the Decalogue says regarding the muzzling of the ox that treadeth out the corn, for the poor brutes must undergo that torture here. Their harness and carts are antique and uncouth also, the latter only being of sufficient size to take what at home would be termed a wheel-barrow load. The fields are mere patches, and all enclosed by dry-stone dykes four or five feet high – said to be for the purpose of keeping the soil from being washed away by the rain from its rocky bed, for you must know we have what we term a rainy season here, which, when it comes, is a not inapt specimen of a deluge. Fruit is not very plentifully grown; yet some of the oranges are most delicious. The most of the supply, however, is brought from Sicily; but vegetables of all lands are to be had in abundance, and the melon and pumpkins are often of enormous size. I have seen some of the latter that would weigh close upon fifty or sixty pounds. Potatoes in general are very good, and of them they always have two crops. Then, agriculturists throughout the world know to what extent the name of Maltese clover has risen.

Amongst the first places I visited was the famed gardens and palace of San Antonio, situated about four or five miles from Valletta, and used as a residence during the summer season by the Governor. This last winter it has been occupied by the Duke and Duchess of Edinburgh, and it was within its walls their youngest daughter was born – an event of which the Maltese are exceedingly proud, as they claim to be the first colonial possession that has had the honour of having a member of our Royal house born within its limits. We passed through the important village of Birchicarcara on our way out, and I was indeed surprised not only at its dimensions but also at the beauty and size of many of its houses; but I understand it is a sort of summer residence for the wealthier inhabitants of Valletta and the Three Cities. As I was not within the palace itself I cannot speak of the size or decorations of its apartments; but from an outward view it appears to be very commodious and is substantially built, with a turret tower from which the royal ensign waves when the palace is inhabited. The grounds, however, are beautifully laid out, and are interspersed here and there with ornamental fountains in full play, their basins also swarming with gold fish. It is, strictly speaking, a pure orange grove, and the fruit being in season at the time of my visit the trees were literally borne down to the ground, so bountiful was their harvest of fruit.

I also paid a visit to Citta Vecchia, one of the most delightful resorts of the inhabitants of the island. The whole garrison generally have a march out to it at the close of the marching-out season every year, and as they start at early morning they are encamped and dine on the glacis of the fort, their dinners being cooked on the ground. It is not very large, bat it was a place of note during the time of the Knights, and has a clean, picturesque appearance. It has a large fort (of course never used now as no troops are stationed there) which commands the country round, so that no enemy having gained a landing in the direction of St Paul's Bay or Gozo could dare to attempt to pass on its way towards Valletta with impunity. Inside the Fort is a large and beautiful sanitorium (or hospital), which is only occupied during the summer months, and to which the sick of the garrison, who may be recovering but slowly from some lingering disease, are sent for change. It can also boast of a very beautiful church, decorated in much the same style as St John's, but not of very large dimensions.

But the catacombs away deep down in the earth like those in Rome, though much smaller, form the chief attraction to the village. As I groped through them by the dim light of the candle, carried by my guide, and peered into this niche or that comer, my mind rushed back to the time when these dark cells were the habitations of living men and women doomed for the sake of their faith to seek such a dwelling; and I thought if the cold damp walls were only for one hour to be gifted with speech, how would my feelings be harrowed by the tales they would unfold. Then a silent prayer rose to my lips, blessing the Infinite Giver of all good that it had pleased Him to cast my lot in a Christian land, where I could worship Him under my own vine or fig tree, without the least trace of fear hanging over me.

The one trip I most enjoyed of the whole was a visit to the neighbouring island of Gozo just about the close of this summer. Shortly before it there took place some annual feast, which occupies three days, and to which on one or other of these days you would think every inhabitant of Malta, old and young, rushes, as some three or four steamers run cheap trips from early morn till late at night, as fast as steam can propel them. Many of the garrison take advantage of these to pay Gozo a visit, permission generally being given to do so then, but as I was anxious to see as much of it quietly as I possibly could, I preferred " biding my time." At last three of us agreed to make a start. Our drive was no less than eighteen miles through as beautifully cultivated ground as if we were amongst the groves of Italy, and every now and then we passed villas in all the different styles of architecture. The chief thing, however, that really attracted our attention was St Paul's Bay, where the great Apostle of the Gentiles was wrecked, and where after he had gathered a bundle of sticks and laid them on the fire, there came a viper out of it and fastened on his hand. The scene described in the Acts was now fairly before our very eyes, so much so that I have no hesitation in believing this to be the place therein mentioned for we have here from the shape of the rock and the position of a large rock, literally the two seas meeting. A locality of such note could not escape something like priestly consecration, and so a memorial chapel is erected in one of the clefts of the rock to which pilgrimages are often made; but our time would not admit of delaying to pay it a visit. We did not reach Marfa until rather past noon, bat were only a very few minutes in crossing the Strait (about three miles broad) as the wind was in our favour, and we rushed across as if by steam, then drove up to Rabato, the principal town or village, whichever you wish, fully three miles from the landing place. I was quite unprepared to see the vast difference in the cultivation of the two islands. Not an inch of this one, unless the roads, but what was bringing forth fruit, grain, or vegetables of some kind; but perhaps the nature of the inhabitants may be the cause, for they seem as much different from the Maltese as day is from night, especially in their habits. Here I found them clean and tidy; there they seem to vie with each other as to who will carry most dirt on their persons. Here everyone, from the child of tender years to the very blind with age, male and female, were employed, their nimble fingers busily knitting or working the far-famed lace, or else weaving coarse fabrics for home wear; there you find groups of loafers lounging at every comer, who would almost rather starve than work, or find their food in very questionable ways so long as it does not put them to much trouble. And during my six hours' stay I only met two beggars; in Malta their name is legion, and you are surrounded by them at all hours, whether walking, driving, or standing. They even follow you into the very places of business where you may desire to make purchases, and so much is the "blood thicker than "Water," that the Shopkeepers permit them to do so with impunity. Rabato has nothing to boast of in the shape of sight-seeing; but there is a moderate-sized good hotel, which, I expect, must thrive off visitors only, and in it we found the charges very moderate. In fact, always leaving churches out of count, there is little to be seen on any part of the island, the principle occupation being lace making. Still there is a pretty large pottery on it, but I suppose its produce is confined to the use of the two islands. There is a large fort just above the landing place, in which are barracks capable of holding a regiment, but it is nearly dismounted now; and though at one time a whole regiment was stationed there, I believe it is only garrisoned now by a very small detachment of the Royal Malta Fencible Artillery. As twilight approached we retraced our way to Mijario, where we got a boat and crossed to Marfa, where our Jehu was anxiously awaiting us, and by midnight we were once more set down in Valletta, each more highly satisfied with the day's enjoyment than another.

While in Gibraltar, I stated in a former chapter we grumbled much about having our field days on Saturdays, but here we had not that ground for complaint, as it has been but very seldom we have had them on that day. Still we have no lack of them, as no sooner does some distinguished visitor, such as a Crowned Head, a member of a Royal House, or some of those in exile, a foreign General, or Admiral, &c., show their nose on our shore than we must needs be turned out for their edification, though I am afraid they cannot leave much more enlightened as regarded our movements, as we have no ground at disposal of any dimensions where troops can be moved about and seen from any one point at the same time. Hence the usual marches past and a few changes of front, &c., are about all that we have room to do, at least when the whole garrison is turned out. One of these great displays was made on the occasion of the recent visit of the Prince of Wales on his return from India. The whole island turned out then, and what with bands playing, banners of all kinds floating in the breeze, and military demonstrations, there was a commotion such as is seldom to be witnessed in Malta, great as the island is for displays.

There was nothing of ceremony when the Duke and Duchess of Edinburgh sojourned here. They mingled with the inhabitants quite freely, and it may be said we scarcely knew that Royalty was living in our midst.

Our regiment, during our stay in Malta, where we still are, has been even more healthy than in Gibraltar. The principal disease prevalent here is a fever incidental to the climate, but which, if taken in time, is easily got rid of.

CHAPTER XXII

The Soldier's Pay

In bringing these rambling remarks to a close, it may be well that I should give the reader my frank opinion regarding military life.

As everyone knows there is a vast difference between both the recruit and the soldier of 1858 and those of 1877. When I first determined to serve Her Majesty in the first-mentioned year I had many difficulties to overcome, many privations to endure, and many extra articles to supply at my own expense. This has all been done away with now, as recent legislation has caused a searching enquiry into most of the complaints then made, and has put the soldier in a better position as regards pay and allowances; but although thus much good has accrued, the other side of the picture is somewhat dark, for I must frankly declare (no matter who may seek to deny the statement) the great out-cry in 1870-71 of re- modelling the army, has utterly failed in its object – nay, more, has almost ruined it altogether. A recruit at the time I joined was very often kept on a penny a-day for months after enlistment, till his kit, &c., supplied to him should be paid up. At best he could never draw more than 1Os a month, and he was indeed a saving and careful fellow who could draw full pay for a few months running. He required to be able to use the needle, and so patch up and keep in good order his necessaries, else he would find some small thing he wanted month after month. While here speaking of necessaries I may as well clear away a false idea that I know not a few outside the Army have got a hold of, and the recent speeches in Parliament – especially those supporting the Government – have been more likely to strengthen that idea than to dispel it. I refer to their belief that a private soldier has the rate of one shilling of pay daily. Now this I cannot deny as I am credited in my accounts every month with that sum, together with such amount of good conduct pay as my conduct may entitle me to receive; but I have long looked in vain for a War Minister to in-form his hearers what are the items that appear monthly on the debtor side of these accounts. Now the true state of affairs is this – A recruit on joining is served out with what is termed a free kit, viz.: – 1 tunic; 1 jacket; 2 pairs trousers; 2 pairs boots; 1 forage cap; 1 shako; 2 flannel (or 3 cotton) shirts; 3 pairs socks; 2 towels; 1 pair braces; blacking, polishing, cloth, brass, and shaving brushes; fork, knife, and spoon; sponge; razor and case; button-holder; a box of blacking; and great-coat, knapsack, and canteen with straps. Here is a complete rig out, as the sailors say; but then one knows these things are not manufactured from steel or cast-iron so that they could serve a man a life-time. Do you say, "Why, you are served out with clothing annually?" Well, what is it we are thus served out with annually? – a tunic, jacket) 2 pairs boots, and 1 pair trousers annually (2 pairs biennially), a shako every 4 and a great-coat every 5 years; but when any other of the foregoing are required then your shilling pays the piper. It may be that some months nothing of these are required, but in *every* one you have shown against you 3 1/2d daily for messing and washing; 2d or more for the benefit of the books and newspapers in the library you hear so much praised as belonging to every regiment for the use of the soldier; the same amount (and oftener higher) for the wear and tear of barrack-room furniture – mops, brooms, cans, &c. – to which must be added hair-cutting, marking, &c. This, I think, will show clearly I am not exceeding the mark when I say we drew lOs monthly when I joined first, but we can now draw the double of that, not 30s or 31s as many are led to believe. Any arithmetician can see that a regiment consisting of 600 or 700 men paying 2d each or more every month, and very often about a couple of shillings when leaving a particular barracks for barrack damages, do not sit rent free under the War Office authorities. The messing and washing mentioned above also require a little explanation, as we are always hearing of the soldier being "better fed, better clothed, and better housed than the working-man." The rations allowed are 1 lb. bread and 1 lb. beef to each man daily; and I defy any human being to live on that alone; so our threepence finds us in tea, coffee, sugar, potatoes, and vegetables, while the odd halfpenny goes for washing our clothing. Thus you see when everything is deducted our shilling dwindles away greatly; and what I have stated refers solely to regiments at home, for on this station, where we draw exactly the same pay, we have to supply ourselves with summer clothing in the shape of white coats and cap covers and these being in om for six months out of the twelve costs us on an average 5d or 6d a week for their washing (independent of the before-mentioned halfpenny), as we are expected always to turn out with them clean to parade. But regiments about to come to the Mediterranean will be glad to learn this is to be the last year of this regulation, serge coats and helmets being about to be served out by the War Office.

Year after year when the Army estimates are brought forward we hear the Secretary of State for War mourn over the number of desertions that have taken place during the year, and attributing the cause to the lower class of recruits as enlisting for the sake of the kit, and then deserting for the purpose of converting it into money. Against this I have not one word to say, as I know full well a great many of the desertions do arise from this; but has it never struck the Right Hon. gentleman that there may be cause for it on his own side? Instead of periodically sending hand- bills and circulars throughout the length and breadth of the land enticing young men to enlist by showing off the advantages to be gained by becoming a soldier, such as receiving a shilling a-day, being better fed, clothed, and housed, having the benefit of libraries and savings' banks, the opportunity of visiting foreign countries, &o., would it not be far better to show him how he will actually stand after he joins his regiment, such as I have shown above? for I can assure you it is not seldom I have heard an intelligent recruit, who showed every appearance of making a good soldier, say that he had been enlisted under an entire misunderstanding, and that he was justified in releasing himself as soon, in any manner, as he could find opportunity.

But I am digressing from my subject, which was the legislation of 1870 71. Of course, it will be seen I refer to Lord Cardwell's Act; and as it has now had a fair trial, I again, as emphatically as words can express, reiterate my statement that it has proved an utter failure. Where is the better class of recruits we were to get? Echo only answers. Where. This I can safely affirm, the recruits joining with me in 1858 were equal, if not superior, in physique and education to the recruits of 1876-77. By this Act men are enlisted into the army and their time expires before they have thoroughly mastered the rudiments even of what they came into it to learn. It is quite a common expression amongst them, "What do I care for the service; my time will soon be up, and I'll be back in civil life in a year or two;" and as regards their being better educated, an educated recruit is as great a rarity now as I have ever seen during my close on twenty years' service. However, the authorities seem to be determined that the recruits shall be better educated, as the compulsory clause has also crept into the army in the shape of their being bound to attend school a certain number of hours daily until in possession of a certificate. Now, what is the consequence of all this? Why, merely that they cannot be in school and do their duty at one and the same time. Hence they must needs be excused fatigues, &c. that would keep them away from school, and their more gifted comrades must do them for them. These uneducated recruits are not so far back but that they know it. Ask any of them, as the time for an examination for certificates comes round, if they are likely to pass for one, and they well tell you what a fool they would be to do so, and thus become available for parades and fatigues. All that is required to free them from a compulsory attendance is the *lowest* standard of reading, the *lowest* standard in writing, and the four simple rules in arithmetic; and yet I have known some of them commence attending immediately on their joining, and be still in attendance when their six years were completed, never having been able to master these simple studies. "Facts are chiel's that winna ding." Again, the Act, after it was properly in working order, was ultimately to do away with pensions altogether. I certainly wish some one would open the eyes of my dull apprehension on this point. I am serving twenty-one years at one shilling per diem, and after doing so am discharged with a pension of *eightpence* per diem, after my constitution has been undermined through service in foreign climes – aye, mayhap on many battlefields – so that I am unfit for a hard day's work, and must therefore accept a paltry pittance for light work for the few years before my worn-out frame returns to the dust from whence it came, and the eightpence to the exchequer. The recruit enlisting now-a-days draws one shilling and twopence daily for six years (for it must be borne in mind he draws the twopence of deferred pay which is not allowed a twenty-one years' man, though both perform the same duties); he returns to civil life and draws sixpence per day (the deferred twopence included) for another six years for nothing else but attending twenty-one drills in the year with some Militia or Volunteer Corps. He is in the hey-day of life and able, to perform a hard day's work – if he has had a trade before so much the better – for he was but a stripling cm joining, but he has now reached manhood's prime, or, as the saying is, a bone has been put in him and he has been taught not a little self- respect. How much, then, is saved? Again, if this Act is to continue, from whence are we to draw our non-commissioned officers? The late Duke of Wellington considered the sergeants the backbone of the British Army, but, unless they return to the long service, I ask again where these to come from are? Of course, at present I can see a soldier of one year's service taking his place amongst the corporals; but what is the result unless he be one who has been better brought up and has learned how to command *himself*? This early promotion over his comrades is apt to make him proud and haughty, and very often this brings his inferiors into crime in the shape of an unguarded reply to some offensive or too haughty expression. Insubordination towards a non-commissioned officer in the Army is very easy to commit, and is a most serious crime. Far be it from me to say one word against strict discipline, for where there are so many of different countries, religions, and temperaments mingled together, due respect for rank, &c., must be upheld; yet to my mind a non-commissioned officer in the British Army is often considered far too immaculate a being, and he often cloaks offences with his rank he would not dare do otherwise. Bat besides being apt to make them proud, are these new non-commissioned officers competent to discharge the responsible duties which daily devolve upon them? Have they had time to study the dispositions, feelings, and tempers of those under them, or learned how to command themselves, and govern those placed under their charge? After many years' experience of the Army I must say, that with a few exceptions they are not. Although I have been a private soldier the most of my time I always regretted seeing a good old sergeant leaving the Regiment. When I say good, I mean one who did his duty faithfully and fearlessly, for in the Army you will find eye-servants as well as in other spheres of life, but the soldier, be he sergeant or private, who performs his duties uprightly has nothing to fear. One order in the Army that I think would be better erased is that prohibiting non-commissioned officers using what they call too much familiarity with the private soldier. That a close intimacy between them may in some cases lead to bad consequences I do not deny, but to be made prisoner for being in their company (as I have often seen) is carrying the rule too far, as often this might happen between two brothers, or at least between old companions from childhood. The law is not relaxed even in these instances. There is no non-commissioned officer but knows that the intelligent private soldier is he who gives him least trouble in the performance of his duties, and, were this order in abeyance, he would only be too proud to accept one of them as a sharer of his joys or troubles, rather than those whom necessity compels him to make such. Yes; the Army has both its joys and sorrows; its hopes and fears; its pleasures and difficulties. Still, I must say I have nothing to regret in my past life as a soldier. I have done my duty to the best of my ability, and had I my life to begin over again, with no other prospect before me but working in a coal mine, I would most undoubtedly select the Army as a profession.

Certainly the British soldier has few domestic comforts - his is an active and stirring life - and the civilian who joins the Army in the hope of realising an easy and indolent life will find himself miserably disappointed. True, there are some would-be gentlemen in it, but they are greatly in the minority, and from that class (of whom better things might be expected) there generally emanate the sparks of any disaffection that exists. This Act has thoroughly destroyed the *esprit-de-corps* of some of our most distinguished regiments already. Old soldiers have ever been most jealous for the honour of their regiments; but in a few short years where will we find our old soldiers? "Why, in the Reserve," you say. Yes, if that means all corners of the world, for there is not one who will ever consider himself so much under control by it as he did when with the colours. Let all, then, who have the honour and prestige of the British Army at heart not rest until they have wiped this Act entirely from the Statute Book, or else that Army will very soon lose the character bestowed on it by Napoleon the Great of being the smartest in the world.

I expect soon to return to the scenes of youth, but only to find the companions of my early days all scattered and gone. Ah! the bright-faced children of my childhood; where are they? I shall gaze no more on the old familiar faces of those who roamed with me among the blooming heather of my dear fatherland. Their forms so full of life and beauty and their cheery voices are gone. The auld kirk-yard of Glenvale keeps the sacred dust of many of those who knew me in bye-gone days. The parental eye that beamed upon me with love and tenderness too deep for utterance is closed in the silent tomb. The affectionate heart that beat in such warm response to my every joy and sorrow is still, and mate is the voice which was once the sweetest music to my listening ear. But

"Still I've a Friend wha has watched over me.
An' guided my course in a strange countrie;
An, whan He tak's me whaur nae storms blow,
I'll meet a' the dear ones I lost long ago."

THE END

PART TWO

RANDOM RHYMES
BY
JOHN PINDAR
(PETER LESLIE)
LOCHGELLY, FIFE

EDITED
BY
Rev. A.M. HOUSTON, B.D.

MINISTER OF AUCHTERDERRAN

===============

CUPAR:
J & G. INNES, Publishers, *Fife News.*

————

MDCCCXCIII

PREFACE

John Pindar (Peter Leslie), the author of these "Random Rhymes,"
which are now given to the public in a more permanent form
than the columns of the Fife News and other weeklies, was
born at Glenvale, in "the Kingdom of Fife" about the year 1836.
His parents were poor. With a scanty education, he was sent
to the pits at the early age of nine. There he remained in dark,
dreary drudgery till his twenty-third year, when he enlisted in
a regiment of Fusiliers. Many of the poems were written during
his military experiences, so full of poetic incident and so plentiful
of romantic adventure.

Since this volume is published as a companion to his *Autobiography
of a Private Soldier*, it is unnecessary to say more here save to refer
the reader to that interesting story of his life. After many years
of loyal service for beloved Britain, Pindar retired. He lives hale
and hearty at Lochgelly a flourishing burgh in the parish of
Auchterderran, Fife. His scanty pension of one shilling a-day,
after deducting the rent of his classic garret, barely keeps soul
and body intact. Unfortunately, as the result of an accident he
is unable for labour of a manual kind, though he was some time
ago appointed hall-keeper to the Volunteer Hall, Lochgelly; but
his income from that source is very modest; so that purchasers of
this volume, who love the classic muse, will not only become his
patrons, but helpers of a worthy and now disabled son of Mars.

The poet has many friends, whose presence by times in the
garret sets his genial face ablaze. It is quite a treat to spend an
hour with him, to hear him con his favourite lays, and once
more recall to mind the memories of martial prowess. In the
hope that this genial feeling may be preserved, these poems are
now arranged in collected form, and the old Poet, expresses the
wish that he and his readers may be long spared to enjoy one
another's companionship in life.

THE EDITOR

MY AULD CRONIES

Air – "Nae luck aboot the house"

Draw in your seats, my canty frien's,
Aroun' my bright hearthstone,
An' I will sing a verse or twa
Aboot the days noo gane.
My loving frien's we've wander'd far,
An' felt life's chequered lot,
Since we played at the Nuck o' Hedge
An' built dams at the Ghut.

Chorus –

> *Oh, childhood's days were happy days,*
> *When we were young and free,*
> *An' pu'in flowers on Lauries braes*
> *Wi' hearts a' fu' o' glee.*

Those happy days, noo past an' gane,
We never can forget,
Our bright young hearts enjoyed then
A swing on Donald's yett.
I'm sure you mind the little school
Aince kept by Johnnie Glass –
We stealt his tawse to mend the haims
O' Nealie's cuddy ass.

In yon glorious, happy days,
Gude fun was never wantin' –
You mind we played at hide an' seek
In Harry Chisim's plantin'.
I'm sure ye mind the Roondel, too,
Where you, my cronies three,
Were won't to pu' the berries red
An' dauky on the tree.

I'm sure you mind the Singin' E'en'.
When for our cakes we went,
Wi' our new shoon an' daidlies clean,
Through a' the toons we kent.
Ae Singin' E'en', I mind it well,
When I was heavy laden
Wi' Singin' cakes – when doon I fell
In Sandy Cheaplin's midden.

Since then I've roved through distant climes,
Beyont the stormy seas;
But ne'er forgot the joyous times
When chasin' butterflees.
Excuse me noo, my dear auld frien's,
Although a tear may fa';
Ye ken we'll ne'er see days again
Like those noo far awa'.

JEANIE ROY

The sangs o' birds are heard again,
An' nature's face is fair,
The gowans blink upon the plain,
An' balmy is the air.
Love fills my soul – I canna tell
The pleasures I enjoy
When wandering through Pitcairn dell
Wi' bonny Jeanie Roy.

To shady nooks in that calm grove
At gloamin' I repair,
To tell my tale o' melting love
To my sweet lassie there.

Wealth's haughty look an' proud disdain
My peace can ne'er destroy
While to my bosom I can strain
My lovely Jeanie Roy.

Love rules the camp, the court, the grove –
Scott sang in accents fine;
An' I ha'e found a sweet, pure love
Can mak' my life sublime.
I sun mysel' in love's bright clime,
I've bliss without alloy;
For noo the bonnie lass is mine –
My charming Jeanie Roy.

THE COLLIER LAD

The wee bit collier laddie
Maun rise at early day,
And to the gloomy coal-pit
Wend his lonely way;
Far frae Nature's beauties,
Doon in his cavern dark,
He canna see the blooming flowers,
Nor hear the morning lark.

Though he works unknown to fame,
Doon in his dungeon grim;
The machinery o' the world
Is kept wagging on by him.
Commerce wud fail and languish,
The arts and science, too,
If it werena for the arduous work
The colliery laddies do.

He warms the king upon the throne,
The peasant in his cot;
And yet how dark and cheerless
Is his humble, chequered lot.
When the sun is shining clear,
Oh, do remember him!
Nature's sangs he canna hear
Where a' is dark an' dim.

OUR BROTHERS

P. Leslie, 71st H.L.I., India, 1860.

Our brothers roam in distant lands
Far ower the rollin' sea;
They're far awa' where palm trees wave
Ower India's sunny lea –
But though they roam where bonny flowers
Perfume the orient plain,
We hope wi' them to spen' bright hours
In oor dear hame again.

Our hearts were gloomy, sad, an' lane,
When they left hame langsyne,
But still we'll sing they're no' to blame,
Though sodgers in the line.
'Twas love for our kind-hearted Queen
Which made them cross the main;
Cheer up, they'll tread the dewy green
In oor dear land again.

When faint an' weary on the braes
Where tigers nightly roar,

They'll often think on happy days
Spent near the winding Orr.
To see their sweet parental hame
Nae doot their hearts are fain,
An' sit beside the auld hearthstone
In oor dear land again.

Keep up your heart, oh! mother dear,
An' dinna greet nae mair –
Hope for the best, come dry the tear,
It's needless to despair.
Just trust in Him wha brought life
The widow's son at Nain –
For he alone can bring to Fife
Oor brothers hame again.

MY AULD SWEETHEARTS

I mind when I was a young man
Some thirty years ago,
My heart was like a simmer day,
Without a shade of woe.
The gladsome days o' auld langsyne
Come never back again;
The present has owre muckle grief,
The past not much of pain.

But wi' the bonnie lassies dear,
I've spent delicious hours;
The world wud be dark an' drear
Without the blooming flowers.

I'll ne'er forget sweet Bella Gray,
An' lovely Mary Swan,
An' smiling Jane, wha cheered my heart
Ere sodger days began.

An' when I roamed through Erin's Isle,
My heart was ne'er forlorn;
For then I busk'd in the bright smile
O' little Bridget Horne.
In Erin's land I always had
Some soul-entrancin' thief
To steal my heart, like Mary Quin,
Or blue-eyed Nell O'Keeffe.

An' when afar in other lands –
In Malta's sunny clime,
I had my Teenie Gammie there
An' rosy Caroline.
Oh, some o' those dear lassies now
Are silent in the grave;
An' some, I ken, are, like mysel',
Still battling on life's wave.

Now a' the sweethearts I can get
(But this I shou'dna tell)
Are auld, an' frail, an' toothless –
Just something like mysel'.
I've often been invited in
Wi' some auld maid to dine;
But that is when I ha'e the tin,
Aboot the pension time.

I little thought in life's young days,
When wi' the lassies roamin',
That I wud miss their cheery smile
To bless life's cheerless gloamin'.

I feel auld age now coming fast,
An' early friends are gane;
While I maun shelter frae the blast
At a bachelor's hearthstane.

BELLA O' THE MANSE

There's mony laddies in the toon
Wha look asklent at me,
Because they canna get a blink
O' my sweet lassie's e'e.
But let them jibe, an' scoff, an' jeer,
The claim that I advance
Is that I ha'e a heart sincere
For Bella o' the Manse.

Her laughing face, an' comely mien,
An' bright expressive e'e,
Mak's this bonny lassie seem
A world o' love to me.
It's paradise for me on earth
To catch the winnin' glance
That flashes frae the sparkin' e'en
O' Bella o' the Manse.

Nae standing at the corners wi'
The frivolous laddies gay,
She kens that she's a servant lass,
An' mistress maun obey.
An' then, she disna waste her time
Wi' novel or romance;
I'll maybe yet can ca' her mine
Sweet Bella o' the Manse.

She disna rin in foolish ways,
Like lassies that I ken;
She kens a modest, virtuous life
Will aye attract guid men.
An' seldom is she ever seen
At concert, ball, or dance;
Within my soul she reigns a queen –
Sweet Bella o' the Manse.

To win her pure an' guileless heart
I'd roam this warld thro',
For then I's hae a sterling part
O' female nature true.
Awa', ye vacant-minded men,
Ye'll never hae a chance
To steal awa' my winsome hen –
Sweet Bella o' the Manse.

CLUNES GREEN BRAES

I've muse by Erin's tranquil rills,
An' climbed sweet England's flowery hills,
An' foreign lands I've wandered through,
Sin' last, dear maid, I gazed on you.
But during a' the years that's gane,
I've thought on thee in our Scotch hame –
Through troubled paths an' chequered ways,
I ne'er forgot Clune's smiling braes.

Mony Cashmerion maids I've seen,
Wi' comely forms an' sparkling e'een;
But light as fairies though they be,
They cudna win a smile frae me.

Let foreign dames be sweet an' braw,
There's nane like her that's far awa';
In fancy now my soul surveys
My bonny lass on Clune's green braes.

At lonely night I wander here
When stars are peeping bright an' clear,
And let my thoughts roam far away
To blissful scenes o' life's young day,
Where ance I roamed, dear Nell, wi' you,
And found thy heart both kind an' true –
But, oh! A few mair fleeting days
May bring me hame to Clune's green braes.

Can I forget the maid I prest
So gently to my beating breast?
Can I forget the roving eyes
That beamed on me 'neath Fifian skies?
An' lang may those bright eyes o' thine
In oor dear hame upon me shine;
Soon may I busk in their sweet rays,
When I come hame to Clune's green braes.

Ofttimes I wander here forlorn,
Pondering o'er life's early morn –
The joyous days when we were young,
Wi' truth an' love in ilka tongue.
My lovely Nell, you've been to me
A beacon on life's stormy sea;
Thy words, so sweet, my spirits raise,
Though far frae thee an' Clune's green braes.

THE KIRK O' AUCHTERDERRAN

Air – "The Auld Hoose"

The dear auld kirk, I lo'e it weel,
Where sainted dust repose;
It stands amang the leafy trees,
Near where the burnie flow.
Wavering memory brings to view
The days when, but a bairn,
I toddled wi' my father to
The Kirk o' Auchterderran.

Oh! Dear auld kirk, I've wander'd far
Since those unclouded days;
I've gathered in the ranks o' war
On India's sunny braes.
An' now, when auld, an' frail, an' gray,
I hear the psalms divine
Within the kirk o' life's young day –
The kirk o' auld langsyne.

Oh! Dear auld kirk, they've changed thee now,
An' made thee fair to see;
But the auld kirk o' other days
Will aye remain wi' me.
I'll ne'er forget our ain auld kirk,
Where oft I sat an' sung
The sweet old psalms in other times
When life and years were young.

Beneath the shadow o' your dome
My aged parents lie;
May I wi' them find my last home
Whene'er I come to die.
Why statesmen dare to hurt our kirk

Is what I've yet to learn;
May God protect an' prosper long
Our Kirk o' Auchterderran.

A RAMBLE ROUND LOCHLEVEN

Air – "Erin's Lovely Home"

'Twas on a lovely Sunday morn,
In the pleasant month o' May,
When Smith an' long Jock Pindar
Did tak' a walk so gay.
They left Lochgelly's flourishing toon,
Atween eleven an' twal',
An' travelled hard until they came
The length o' Scotland Well.

An' there they halted just a wee,
In Portmoak lone Kirkyard,
For they were anxious for to see
The graves o' Bruce an' Laird.
Young Bruce, he was a lovely bard,
Sang sweet in days of yore,
An' classified the sacred soil
Around Lochleven shore.

An' Doctor Laird wrought long an' sair
In Portmoak Parish Church;
An' solemn truths he would declare
To all within his reach.
When they had look'd around an' seen
Ilk place o' worth an' note,
Says Smith to long Jock Pindar –
"We'll go to Milnathort."

"For mony a body I ken here,
Wha'll baith be frank an' kind;
And bonnie lassies, blooming fair,
We'll get if you're inclined.
All poets love the lassies dear,
An' so does Pindar too;
So come awa' and never fear
You'll have no cause to rue."

"Agreed," says long Jock Pindar,
"That toon I wish to see,
Where lassies smile so bonny
Wi' love an' youthful glee."
They passed through auld Kinnesswood toon,
Upon their cheery way,
Where they saw maids like flowers in June,
That lovely Sabbath day.

Away they went wi' one consent
Right through Balgedie Toll,
And when they cam' to Powmill dam,
And heard the waters roll,
Says Smith to Poet Pindar –
"I am transported clean
Wi' admiration an' wonder,
So lovely is the scene.

"And yonder Burleigh Castle too,
Where many a lord hath been;
Lochleven clear, within our view,
Where Mary lived, our Queen.
The Standing Stanes of Orwell
We'll see as we pass by;
And the Auld Kirkyard of Orwell,
Where sainted dust does lie."

When they arrived in Milnathort,
At three in the afternoon,
They went and called on Mr Scott,
In the centre o' the toon.
There they fell in wi' Mr White,
An' had a friendly dram;
He gave his gig to them that night,
As they had far to gang.

He went and put into his gig
A young an' lively horse;
In a moment they were ower the brig,
An' fleein' through Kinross.
Suffice to state that Smith and Pate
Got safely hame that night,
And lang may they spend mony a day,
Wi' feelings o' delight.

Now my wee bit sang is o'er,
I've little more to say,
But they have roamed on foreign shore
Since that eventful day.
They've been where big streams wander,
O'er beds o' golden sand;
Yes, Captain Smith and Pindar
Have roamed a foreign land.

Though age and clime ha'e blanched their hair
Since those unclouded days,
They'll ne'er forget, 'midst a' their care,
Lochleven's flowery braes.
Though youthfu' days ha'e pass'd away,
With a' their glories shorn
They'll ne'er forget that smiling May,
O' their bright early morn.

They've had days dark and dreary
Since round the lake they ran,
Still they are blyth and cheery
When o'er a canty dram.
'Tis strange to think they've come from lands
Where might rivers roll,
To meet an drink a glass again
In auld Balgedie Toll.

Long Pindar's in Lochgelly toon,
And ofttimes muses o'er
The days when he did ramble roon'
Lochleven's classic shore;
While Captain Smith, his croney dear,
Lives in Balgedie Toll,
Where, like a king, he reigns supreme,
And tells his stories droll.

SMILING JUNE

Aince mair we greet thee, smiling June,
Wi' feelings o' delight;
Thou'rt clothed in robes o' flowery bloom,
Most beautiful an' bright.
The lark is in the cloudless sky,
And linties sing in tune,
To welcome, wi' their cheery strains,
The gentle days o' June.

The cowslip an' the heatherbell,
An' lovely fragrant rose,
Wi' a' their sweets, perfume the breeze
That o'er the landscape blows.

Oh, sweet to wander on the hills,
In the calm simmer noon,
Or pensive muse by rippling rills
In bonny days o' June.

The sweet flowers bloom on mead an' hill,
The lily, pure and fair,
Is waving in the morning sun,
An' balmy in the air.
O! wha wud choose the city's noise,
Its troubles, care, and gloom
An' lose the country's tranquil joys,
In the smiling month o' June.

MY FIRST REGIMENT

Calcutta, 1860

I made up my mind in the year Fifty-eight
Her Majesty's Service to join:
I was sworn to protect the Queen and the State
And all Her successors in line.
The 5th Fusiliers, distinguished old corps,
I joined in the Indian clime;
The gallant regiment that fought at Cawnpore
So brave in the year Fifty-nine.

Chorus –

>   *I've made a good change from the pick to the gun,*
>   *I never was better, my boys;*
>   *I've plenty of fun on the plains of Dum Dum,*
>   *To make me sing and rejoice.*

I have little cause to regret what I've done,
I never was better before;
I have got a shako as long as a lum,
With a bonny plume hanging o'er.
I've nearly a dozen of handsome white shirts,
Full-breasted, with buttons so braw;
Forbye ten new jackets, just come in from the wash,
As white as the new driven-snaw.

I've nine pair o' socks, which a needle ne'er saw,
And long-legged boots, seven pair;
And the shoemaker's ta'en my measurements awa',
To bring me some five or six mair.
I've five pair o' breeks, and six linen sheets,
Just from the mangle now come;
And at dinner-time I get pumpkin and leeks
And at night my tea mixed with rum.

And then I have plenty of nice damask towels,
With two pair of Dundee kid mittens;
And whene'er I please I can have roast fowls –
India is full of young chickens.
I have a fine comb, a new razor, and brush;
And if I want brandy or rum,
I get fifty rupees whenever I wish,
By writing to Bain at Dum Dum.

And I have the pleasure to see foreign places;
I'm sure I've seen more in a day,
Both men and women, with far blacker faces,
That e'er cam' from old "Jenny Gray."[1]
Let them call me at hame a long, foolish fellow,
For crossing the dark rolling sea;
Hurrah! My lads, there are few in Lochgelly
Who are happier this moment than me.

---

[1] A coalpit in Lochgelly where the author wrought in his early days.

THE YOUNG SODGERS SANG

'Twas when the flowers o' the simmer were bonnie,
An' burdies sang sweetly frae ilka green tree,
When I ta'en farewell o' my dear Caledonie,
An' gaed out to India a sodger to be.
I had wrought i' the pits sin' I was a wee callan'
An' keen, keen I was the big warld to see;
I've seen no my folly, an' tears are fast fa'in'
For those I ha'e left in my ain countrie.

I little kent then the hardships o' a sodger –
I had heard that his life was a' glorious and fine;
But often he's lain on the cauld grun' a lodger,
When marching at night in a foreign clime.
I often ha'e thought sin I put on a red coat,
A bonnie blue bannet, wi' plume hangin' o'er,
A waist-belt an' bayonet, although they look gaudy,
Are but a puir change for the claes I ance wore.

Oh, childhood's days o'er memory rushes –
The sweet, pleasant days nae mair to return –
When I roamed 'mang groves o' bonny broom bushes,
An' pu'd the gowans on the banks o' the burn,
'Twas then I was happy, blythsome, an' cheery –
In life's early morn nae sorrows kent I;
But noo my life is aye stern an' dreary,
Though beauteous an' bright in the Indian sky.
Beloved Caledonie, dear land o' my childhood,

Thou glorious land o' the brave an' the free,
Often I wander'd thy glens an' sweet wildwood,
An' sported wi' lassies upon the green lea;
But those days are gane, never mair to return,
While I, a puir wanderer, bound noo to roam
Far frae companions, which mak's me mourn
An' sigh for the joys o' my dear Scottish home.

BURNS' ANNIVERSARY, 1891

Sax score an' twal years now have gane
Since our sweet bard was born;
And here we've met to praise his name
On this his natal morn.
His fame is spread from pole to pole;
And every foreign clime
Has read the language of his soul
In strains the most sublime.

Awa' where mighty rivers glide,
Auld Scotia's sons to-day
Are looking hame wi' honest pride
To where he sang his lay.
His has been nae mushroom fame –
It's kent the world through;
The swarthy maids on India's plain
Can sing his songs so true.

Thousands o' Scottish hearts to-day,
Athwart the foamy brine,
Will cheer their hearts wi' "Scots Wha Hae"
And that sweet sang "Langsyne".
Though we are few, we yield to nane
In a' the country roun'
In admiration o' the bard
Wha sang by bonnie Doon.

Though mony bards we've had wha sang
O' mountain, vale, an' rill –
Like Nicol, Ramsay, Fergusson,
Aird, Hogg, an' Tannahill –
Aboon them a' in beauteous sang
Oor Robin tak's the stand;
For he's the National Poet o'
Oor glorious native land.

MARY, THE SWEET PRIDE O' LOCHGELLY

Sweet Mary, the pride o' Lochgelly toun,
She is such a winsome wee fairy;
Although you should search the hale country roun',
You'll no' find a lassie like Mary.
She dresses so neat, so modest and plain,
While ilka thing weel she can handle;
She disna indulge, like some that I ken,
In auld wives' clashes and scandal.

She works out-bye in a' kinds o' weather,
I wish I cou'd ca' her my dearie;
A lassie that's guid an' kind to her mither
Will keep her ain house blyth an' cheerie.
Last hairst, whin she shore on the fields o' Pitcairn,
She earned mair shilling than fifty;
There's no' a sweet lassie in a' Auchterderran
Mair sensible, bonny, an' thrifty.

Let nobles blaw o' their Norman descent,
Wi' their big name gilded in story;
I wad rather ha'e Mary, minus a cent,
Than a cor'net o' splendour an' glory.
I'll do all I can to mak' her my wife,
To love her's my pleasure an' duty;
The hills an' howms in the Kingdom o' Fife
Resound wi' the praise o' her beauty.

TO HENRY HUNTER, LOCHGELLY

Nae mair we'll see the golden days
When ower the hill we ran,
We ne'er thought then o' crooked ways,
That's aye the lot o' man.
In those sweet days, now past an' gane,
Our lives were a' sunshine –
Nae anxious cares in our bright hame
In yon dear days langsyne.

Ye mind, when wandering fu' o' glee,
By Leven's silver stream,
Juvenile days just seemed to be
A long sweet fairy dream.
We toddled then by stream an' glen,
Sweet meadow, vale, an' lea;
And ofttimes wished that we were men,
The strange world to see.

Those time are passed, those joyous days
Are flown awa' for ever;
An' we maun face the blasts that blaw
Across life's cheerless river.
We've seen the world an' felt its ills,
Its misery an' pain;
An' noo we lang for dance an' sang
O' childhood's days again.

Ye sweetly sing o' auld Lochore,
Reminding me o' days
We pu'd the berries, ripe an' red,
Upon the Harny braes.
Though in the land o' bright sunshine,
Oh! I remember still
Oor early haunts o' auld langsyne
Upon Benarty hill.

Perhaps once more on bank o' Orr
We'll roam at gloamin' grey;
Or hear the larks that sang so sweet
Wake up the summer day.
I'll maybe hear before it's lang
Thy cheery voice again;
So I'll conclude my simple sang
Amang the braes o' Spain.

IN MEMORY OF HANNAH THOMSON

Who died at Lochgelly, 14th September 1874, aged 8 years.

Fair young child, so sweet and canny,
We miss thy footsteps at the door;
Thou art gone, oh, dear wee Hannah,
To yonder bright and better shore.

Now our home is dark and dreary,
Since an angel voice is gone –
A voice once wont to make us cheery,
Singing round our bright hearthstone.

When the shades of night are falling,
We sit and dream, dear child, of thee:
Until we think we hear thee calling –
"Dear father, mother, come to me."

We see thy toys 'round us lying;
The creepie stool an' little chair
Now are vacant, an' we're sighing –
"Little Hannah sits not there."

But we'll submit wi' chasten'd sorrow –
Thou'rt gone a little while before;
We'll meet in the land of glory,
Where pain an' grief molest no more.

"Dear mother, hear that angel-voice,
Ringing sweetly in thine ear –
A voice that cries 'Rejoice! Rejoice!
Prepare to meet thy Hannah here."

THE WIDOW'S LAMENT FOR HER SON

Mysteriously killed on the railway, 1884.

My son, my son, what cruel fate
Hath thus untimely torn
Thee from my soul, while in the bloom
Of manhood's early morn.
No natural death was thin, my son,
And no kind friend was near
To save thy life while in the prime
Of manhood's bright career.

My son. My son, my loving son!
Beloved by one and all;
But death, who visits every one,
Gave thee a sudden call.
Now thou art gone, and left me here
To mourn thy early doom –
To wander forth and shed the tear
Of sorrow on thy tomb.

Loving memory long shall dwell
Around thy cherished name;
'Tis only here a short farewell
Until we meet again.
Thy mysterious death hath left
A vacant seat with me;
But though thou wilt not come again,
I soon will come to thee.

But when my earthly race is run,
And I am free from woe,
We'll meet again, my darling son,
Where tears have ceased to flow.
My thoughts of thee can ne'er depart
From this lone heart of mine;
I'll hear thy voice until my heart
Be cold and still as thine.

MAGGIE O' LOCHGELLY

I mind the days when I was young,
And Maggie's voice was mellow;
I'll ne'er forget the sangs she sung
Amang the whins so yellow.
Sin' then I've roamed 'neath sunny skies,
Beyond the foamy billow;
But foreign dames I cudna prize
Like Maggie o' Lochgelly.

I wunder if she minds the days
When to the school we ran,
And sailed our little paper-boats
On Sandie Reekie's dam.

And when refractory we wad be,
Our Schoolmiss, Peggy Broon,
Wad tak' the bauchel frae her foot
And pelt us on the croon.

When thinking o' those cloudless days,
So happy, calm, serene,
I only sigh and mourn now,
And tears start frae my een.
But though I'm wearin' doon the hill
Some comfort it wad gi'e
To ken that my dear Maggie still
Thought o' langsyne an' me.

SCOTT'S CENTENARY AT LOCHGELLY, 1871

Let auld Lochgelly cock her head,
An' sound her bugle horn –
In auld Fifeshire she's ta'en the lead
On our Scott's natal morn.
Her humble name through future time
Shall never be forgot;
For she has sung in strains sublime
The Centenary o' Scott.

Her wandering sons, a' scattered wide,
O'er mony a distant sea,
Will feel an honest Scottish pride
When they look hame to thee.
My native toon has honoured one –
The best that ever wrote;
I sang wi' glee, the night I read
Her praise o' Walter Scott.

Rejoice, thou flowery banks o' Clune,
An' droop thy head no more;
An' sing a sweet, melodious tune;
Thou lovely winding Orr.
The honest fame o' thy dear toon
Has spread to lands remote;
Henceforth her name is intertwined
Wi' that o' Walter Scott.

Oh dear Lochgelly, I am proud
A son of thine to be;
This body lies in death's cauld shroud
Ere I prove false to thee.
Let black disgrace – eternal shame
Be every Scotchman's lot
Who does not love the honoured name
O' our immortal Scott.

THE WANDERER'S RETURN

Lovely, smiling Autumn morn,
I see my village green;
Hear the burdies on the thorn,
Where beauty rules the scene.
I see young lassies, bright and fair,
A' skippin' o'er the lea,
And thoughtless callan's sportin' here –
But none remember me.

I stand an' view the ancient place –
The place where I was born –
While tears roll down my aged face,
Now withered an' careworn.

I see the cot where mother dwelt,
Near yonder hoary tree;
But strangers fill the early hame
That ance remembered me.

Is this my hame o' early days –
The hame I left langsyne?
Are these the glens an' flowery braes
I climbed in youthfu' prime?
Oh, do not laugh though bitter tears
Bedim my weary e'e,
To find the hame o' early years
A foreign land to me.

Ah, me how swift the years roll by –
The years so bright an' fine;
But now the sun o' youth's clear sky
Is set, nae mair to shine.
Sweet sunshine playeth on the stream,
An' flowers perfume the lea;
But, oh, the past – now like a dream –
Will come nae mair to me.

'Twas here I breathed love's tender tale,
Amang these waving trees,
An' chased alang the heathery vale
The bonnie butterflees.
Since then I've roamed in many lands,
Beyond the rolling sea;
An' now I view the hills again
Where none remember me.

I've seen the grand majestic domes
On India's' coral lea,
And wandered thro' her orange shades,
But happy couldna be.

Back to my ain bright Fatherland
My thoughts wad swiftly flee;
Na' now, forlorn, here I stand
Where none remember me.

EPISTLE TO WILLIAM BETHUNE

My kind auld frien', my dear Bethune,
You leave at last Lochgelly toon;
Ten fleeting years ha'e worn roon'
Since you an' I
Didst our social friendship croon
'Neath our ain sky.

But though you leave our auld Lochgelly,
You dinna cross the foamy billow;
You'll always be the same auld fellow
In Largo toon.
I'll see you when the summer's mellow,
An' birds in tune.

How very fast our bark sails doon
The stream o' time, towards the tomb;
Our fleeting days – oh, very soon,
They move quick by,
Then in the grave's Cimmerian gloom
Forgotten lie.

Dear Willie! In life's chequered scene,
The tear has often dimmed y,our een;
The little graves, now smooth and green,
An' still an' cold –

They tell o' sorrow that has been
In your household.

The dear wee bairns gane before
Are safe on yonder shining shore;
Although a parents heart feels sore
Their absence here;
They're home wi' God, an' never more
They'll shed a tear.

Lang may your other lammies be
Spared around their mother's knee –
Grief an' sorrow filled her e'e
For those now gane;
It was our Father's wise decree
To take them hame.

Nae doubt it fills the soul wi' pain,
An' mak's the tears to flow like rain,
When fell death has untimely ta'en
The sweet green flowers;
Have faith in God, you'll meet again
In Eden's bowers.

Since domiciled near Largo Bay,
You'll rove the hills in smiling May,
When Largo Law is bright and gay.
In summer-time,
You'll maybe come alang this way
For auld langsyne.

Now twenty years awa' have gane
Since auld Lochgelly was your hame;
For me, I'll aye be wond'rous fain
To see your face,
An' grasp you by the hand again

In fraternal peace.

Now, auld frien', may blessings shine
Around you, temporal and divine;
And though my uncouth rhyme
Is plainly dressed,
'Tis the genuine feelings o' the min'
That I've expressed.

May happiness, pure love, and peace
Around you flow, as years increase;
Do your affections always place
On things above;
And God will give you strength, an' grace,
An' peace, an' love.

THE LAST OF HIS REGIMENT

I'm the last of my Regiment,
Left standing alone –
My gallant companions
Are now dead and gone;
My young gallant heroes
So fearless and brave,
Are silent and cold now
In one bloody grave.

Why did I not perish
Along with my corps?-
But I'm here, broken-hearted,
Its loss to deplore.
No more from the scabbard
My bright sword will shine;

'Mong the wounded I'll die
On the banks of the Rhine.

Oh, sanguinary warfare,
When wily thou cease,
And the word enjoy
The blessings of peace.
My heart it is torn
With anguish and pain;
I am wretched, forlorn –
My heroes are slain.

RECOLLECTIONS OF CHILDHOOD

"Sweet childish days, that are as long
As twenty days are now." – Wordsworth.

Sweet smiling May, you bring to me
Bright dreams o' early days
When, free frae care an' fu' o' glee,
I spieled the heathery braes.
The birds that carol in the sky,
The flowers that deck the plain,
Call back the dreams days o' days gane by
That ne'er will come again.

Bright were the dreams o' life's young morn,
No tears bedimmed my e'e;
Robing chantin' on the thorn
No happier was than me.
An' now, when care sits on my brow,
Fond memory does retain
A glimpse o' happy days langsyne
That ne'er will come again.

The verdant meads, the bloomin' vales,
The sunshine bright an' fair,
The music o' the wimpling rills
Come back to me nae mair.
Now sombre feelings fill my soul,
When wearin' doon life's hill;
But yet the spells o' childhood's days
Around me linger still.

Oh, blissful days o' sweet sunshine!
O' fragrant flowers and braes!
Fond memory broods o'er bright langsyne,
Clear streams, and scented leas;
But brighter scenes aboon the sky,
When earthly days are gane –
With a' its beauty, earth on us
Is but a transient hame.

LOCHGELLY BRASS BAND

Bright, sunny days are coming now –
The birds begin to sing
Their welcome sangs that usher in
The balmy days o' spring;
An' through the lang bright summer nights,
Its music sweet and grand,
Will fill the air, and cheer the heart,
Frae our Lochgelly Band.

Oh, mony Bands I've heard and seen
In countries far awa';
But ane that plays upon the green
I think outshines them a';

They play the grand old melodies
O' our dear Fatherland;
I dance wi' glee, whene're I see
Our famed Lochgelly Band.

An' mind, the lads wha play so weel
In a sweet Scottish tune,
Dig coal below, or rin a wheel
Amang bad air an' gloom;
An' yet, I dinna think in Fife
There's ane that plays so mellow,
Frae Anster-West to Torry toon
Like our's in auld Lochgelly.

When through the bonnie streets they steer,
The lads an' lassies cry –
Here come the Band we love to hear,
They cheer the heart and eye.
Clad in their robes o' bonny blue,
They play both sweet and grand –
The little bairns on the streets,
They cheer Lochgelly Band.

Music, "heavenly maid", was sung[2]
In ancient Greece langsyne;
And we, the men o' modern days,
Still love the strains sublime.
Then, dear Lochgelly, tak' pride
In our bright cheery Band –
Lang may they play, lang may they bide
A credit to the land.

---

[2] "When music, heavenly maid, was young." - Collins

EPISTLE TO HENRY COOK

Secretary, Fifeshire Miners' Association.

Dear Harry, -

Whether I write a poem or sang,
I fear I'll mak' it rather lang;
But if you're no' so very thrang,
Perhaps you'll read it;
And if you see a word that's wrang,
Just never heed it.

Weel, first and foremost, I intend
The bye-gone ages to defend;
I trust a patient ear you'll lend
To my bit tale,
And criticisms you can send
With the next mail.

I'm conservative in feeling,
My politics there's no concealing;
But, while to you I am revealing
My thought in rhyme,
Memory is backward wheeling
To an earlier time.

But my remarks I won't confine
To any country, age, or clime;
Perhaps before I end this rhyme
You'll pause and wonder
At the poetic flight sublime
O' Lang Jock Pindar.

'Tis now some dozen years, or more,
Since I left dear auld Scotland's shore
To roam where mighty river roar,

And mountains high,
In wild, majestic grandeur, tower
Up to the sky.

I've wander'd lang 'mang Eastern scenes,
Where bright, eternal summer gleams;
By fairy dells, romantic streams,
I sat langsyne,
Engaging the refulgent beams
O' sweet sunshine.

The mind of men can ne'er conceive
The beautiful, the primitive
Simplicity of maids like Eve –
On Cashmere's plain
The lovely things, oh, soon wad have
Your heart in twain.

When the earlier race of men
Lived in mountain, cave, and den,
The human race were happy then;,
But now, you know,
That mighty instrument, the pen,
Levels all below.

In this age of learning, now
Every man cocks up his pow,
Exclaiming I, as well as thou,
Can show my knowledge –
The auld world did merrily row
Without her college.

Go, mingle in the city's din,
Or in the country wayside inn,
You'll find the tinker, wi' his tin,
Hold up his cheek,

Declaring he reads Homer fine
In classic Greek.

It grieves my soul, and fills my eye,
To think that ancient chivalry
Fled with the golden days gone bye –
Leaving in its place
Sanctimonious hypocrisy,
With scowling face.

Liberty and equality,
Brotherly love, fraternity,
On every hand is now the cry,
Both loud and keen –
Banish our old nobility,
Dethrone the Queen.

The Radical Press sounds her horn,
Because the Marquis of Lorn
Takes a princess to adorn
His ducal hame –
The laddie's worth a thousand foreign
Proud German game.

The papers every day proclaim
Such awful deeds that I refrain
Even to mention such by name,
Or my muse here
Would blush and hing head wi' shame,
And drap a tear.

In this great age of vice and crime,
Divorce Courts wi' adultery shine;
'Twas better to have lived langsyne
Wi' Goth and Vandal;

I dinna like the present time
O' clash and scandal.

Where is that golden age to which
Mankind are striving hard to reach?
I doubt we're far yet frae the beach
O' perfect bliss,
Notwithstanding all we preach,
In worlds like this.

There's no compassion between
The present days and days that's been
Antediluvian times, I ween,
Were better far
Than the days that we have seen
O' cruel war.

Kings upon their thrones are quakin'
Nations o' the earth are shakin' –
While the God o' war is takin'
Supreme delight
In the broth o' hell , and makin'
Mankind to fight.

Think o' the tears that widows shed,
In mourning for their gallant dead;
Oh, civilisation, hide thy head,
And boast no more –
Thou'rt makin' battle-plains run red
With human gore[3]

Mourn with me, all Nature mourn
For widow's hearts wi' anguish torn;
The infant that's yet unborn

---

[3] The war with France and Germany

Shall curse the day
That saw his father's manly form
Stretched in the clay.

Come, mourn, ye stars and rolling seas;
Mourn, sweet flowers and waving trees;
And mourn too, oh, whispering breeze
With wailing moan;
Creation, mourn for wars like these,
Wi' heavy groan.

When shall that glorious morn appear
When cannon, pistol, sword, an' spear
Are numbered wi' the things that were?
And brotherly love
Shine o'er the world, bright and clear
Like stars above?

Oh, for some calm, sequestered spot,
Some silent, uninhabited grot;
Away where lotus islands float
In summer seas –
There I would spend my days, remote,
With peace and ease.

There I would hold communion wi'
The mermaids o' the mighty sea;
The wailings o' humanity
And bitter strife
Would never more abide wi' me,
To sour my life.

This world is all a fleeting show –
So sang Tom Moore, some years ago;
The poor have many wants below

The bright blue sky;
Human distress mak's tears to flow
Down from my eye.

Still, in the land, beneath the palm
I still can chant at evening calm
A lovely verse from some sweet psalm;
And aye I find
That Gilead's soul-consoling balm
Can cheer the mind.

The miner, weary and care-worn,
Sad in spirits and forlorn,
Must wend his way at early morn
To toil and slave
Where no beauteous flowers adorn
His gloomy cave.

Without the miner where would be
Our county's great prosperity? –
He makes the iron ships to flee
Across the ocean,
And keeps the world's machinery
In active motion.

Far from the worlds mighty din,
Down in his cavern dark and grim,
He canna hear the lark's sweet hymn
Wi' joyous sound;
The light of nature shines but dim
Beneath the ground.

I've read you little poem with pleasure,
To me it is a perfect treasure;
And the rhyme is in a measure
That's my delight;

I shall be glad when you have leisure
Again to write.

Take my advice and ne'er refuse
To court your hamely Scottish muse
The poetic talent ne'er abuse,
But gi'e her string –
She is eloquent when ye choose
To let her sing.

Although I'm in a rhyming mood,
For want of space I must conclude
A rhyme that's far from being god;
But you'll dispense
With what is vulgar, low, and rude,
And tak' the sense.

May stream o' bliss around you glide,
Domestic peace at your fireside;
An' sorrow, want, and care keep wide
O' your hearthstane;
And wife and bairns be the pride
O' your dear hame.

TO A MOSQUITO

Calcutta, 1860.

Y' wee impudent, wicked thing,
How weel ye like, on sportive wing,
Around my head to bum an' sing,
An' mak' me claw
Whene'er you put your venomous sting
Into my jaw.

If for a moment you but see
Me try to shut my droosie e'e,
'Tis then you strike your loftiest key,
An' doon you'll light
Upon my body, my blood to pree
Wi' a your might.

Wee wicked thing, upon my word,
To bite me so is rather hard,
I canna mount Chowringo Guard
Without you there;
Ha'e mercy on a sodger bard,
His blood to spare.

Far worse you use me than the bogs,
Your fellow-chums, the stinkin' rogues
Wha ower me crawl like parritch cogs,
Wi' swelled-up doup;
An' then at night the big bullfrogs
Around me loup.

To tell the truth, I hate you all,
Bogs and bullfrogs, great and small;
Wi' a the varmin that do crawl
Upon me here;

But faith, my billies, I maun tholl
Your bites to bear.

'Twill be a happy day for me,
When from your presence I can flee
Across the saut an' briny sea,
And Scotia view –
A land that's hitherto been free
Frae thing like you.

LITTLE BOBBY (THE POETS DOG)

"The first to welcome, foremost to defend" – Byron.

Thou art a dog, my Bobby dear,
Possessing kindly ways;
A noble friend, true and sincere,
Deserving all my praise.
Thou'rt free from man's degrading sins –
There lurks no human guile
Within thy soul, while kindness beams
In thy confiding smile.

But do not prove thyself, dear Bob,
A craven-hearted coward;
I hope thou'lt bite the heels no more
Of canteen Davie Ewart.
I trust thou'lt prove a soldier brave,
Where're thou meet'st thy foes;
Face them bravely, Bob, and leave
Thy teeth marks on their nose.

Aye bite them hard upon the nose,
Thou white-wooled little Bobby;
Give to thy enemies a dose
Of Maltese hydrophobia.
If e'er thou fight with older dogs,
And see mischief a-brewing,
Just run to me for shelter, or
To Private Winkie Ewing.

But while thou toddl'st thro' the rooms
Of Company letter "I",
Thou'lt get a welcome smile from all –
A cosy place to lie.
And when thou die'st, beneath the wave
Of the mighty rolling sea
May thou, dear Bobby, find a grave
Where fools can't bread on thee.

THE DYING SOLDIER'S FAREWELL TO HIS MOTHER

The stars are peeping from the sky,
The deadly battle's o'er;
While dead and dying round me lie
In pools of reeking gore.
But mother, dear, I soon shall be
One of the noble slain –
A sweet, affectionate smile from thee
I'll ne'er behold again.

Dear mother, I can never see
Again our banners flying;
The battlefield my grave must be –

Oh, mother, I am dying.
I've fought for home and fatherland,
Where thousands round me fell;
Oh, for a touch of thy dear hand –
But mother, oh, farewell!

My mother, dear, you'll ne'er again
Embrace your soldier son;
His warfare's o'er, his sword's laid down,
His earthly fight is done.
Oh, soon I'll be from sorrow free,
Where sinless angels dwell;
It's growing dark, I cannot see –
Sweet mother, dear, farewell!

DROOKIT STOUR

Air – "The Drunkard's Ragged Wean."

Every intelligent Scotchman knows that drookit stour is only a
Combination of dust and water, or, if you like, gutters or clabber
But it looks more kindly and Scotch-like to designate dust and
water. *Drookit stour.*

Gibraltar. May 1879.

It's a waefu' sicht to see a man lost to sense and shame,
A man wha ance cud boast, ye ken, o' a respected name;
I've seen his hand stretched forth to help the needy an'
   the poor,
But noo he's lyin' unco low amang the drookit stour.

An honoured elder o' the kirk – a bailie o' the toon –
A merchant whase honest fame was spread the country
   roon',

A maist respected man was he, but noo he canna
  procure
A better lodgin' than to lie amang the drookit stour.

Prosperity's brilliant sun upon his path did shine,
Until he ta'en unto his heart the cursed demon wine;
He little thought that by-an'-by this demon wud illure
Frae actions guid, and bring him doon amang
the drookit stour.

King Alcohol soon masters a' wha come within
  his sway,
The wealthy an' the poor alike become his greedy prey;
Doctors, lawyers, minister too, he often does secure,
An' brings them doon upon their croon amang
  the drookit stour.

Just see yon gallant sodger lad, wi' medals on his breast,
Against the foes o' Britain he has dared and done
  his best;
But here's a foe he cannot fight – a demon grim
  an' dour,
Alas, my sodger lad is doon amang the drookit stour.

I speak frae sad experience; the demon drink has been
An' enemy to me throughout the many years I've seen;
This vicious foe wud crack my croon, an' nose wud
  ofttimes clour,
An' soil my bonny scarlet coat amang the drookit stour.

SMILING JULY

All hail! Lovely month,
Wi' rosy perfume,
Following so brightly
Thy sweet sister June.
Like the midsummer's bride,
Thy clear sunny sky
Cheers the hearts o' thy lovers,
Sweet smiling July.

Thy calm, beauteous face
We love now to see,
We'll embrace thee wi' feelings
O' pure ecstasy;
Thy beauty can banish
All tears from the eye,
While viewin' thy glory,
Sweet smiling July.

How sweet to repose 'mong
Thy dewy flowers,
That luxuriantly blossom
In yon fairy bowers.
In the calm hours o' night
We cheerily can hie
Away to the meadows,
Sweet smiling July.

May each lonely heart
Feel thy happy sunshine;
Oh! Warm and affections
Wi' raptures sublime.
May cauld, gloomy cares
At our bosoms ne'er lie,
While thou'rt so near us,
Sweet smiling July.

EPISTLE TO J. BAXTER, LOCHGELLY

Although at present I must cling
To an isle where bells forever ring,
Perhaps before another spring
In Caledonia,
Wi' you I'll dance the Highland Fling,
Dear brother Johnnie.

To see auld Scotland's heathery hills,
Her smiling plains, an' windin' rills –
The very thought my bosom fill
Wi' hope so bright;
For, oh! I love auld Scotland still,
Wi' pure delight.

Where is the land beneath the sun
That's fought and bled as she has done? –
See the vict'ries she has won
O'er superstition;
I'm glad to think that I have sprung
From such a nation.

Wha wadna love the glorious land
Whence ha'e sprung that heroic band
Wha bravely fought, wi' heart an' hand,
In freedoms cause? –
Twas them wha gave to us our grand
Religious laws.

But time wud fail me now to tell
O' Wishart, Hamilton, and Cargill,
Sandy Pedan, Walter Mill,
An' many more,
Wha rung aloud the gospel bell
In days o' yore.

Our poets, too – we've few or nane
To match wi' Burns, Bruce, or Grahame;
Where is the bright auld Scottish hame
But's heard their strain?
Where they're read or not, disgrace an' shame
Their fireside stain.

Though sodgerin' in this bonny clime,
I often have a heart and time
To sing a sang o' auld langsyne;
Though far awa',
It wafts me back o'er ocean's brine,
Heart, soul, an' a'.

But I maun quit my uncouth sang,
My flights are neither high nor lang;
I feel my muse gang aff the fang,
My hearty Jock;
I'll light my pipe – it ne'er comes wrang
To tak' a smoke.

ISABEL

'Twas in the vernal season
O' the sweet breathing spring,
When trees put on their robes o' green,
An' birds begin to sing,
The bonny flowers were blinking sweet
In Lowery's fragrant dell,
When I first saw my smiling lass –
The rosy Isabel.

The orient blush o' simmer's morn,
The roses' sweet perfume,
The fragrance on the breezes borne,
The maiden smiles o' June
Are no' so sweet to me as she
On whom my thought aye dwell;
Both day and night my thoughts are wi'
The rosy Isabel.

When the gentle morn is breaking
Oot owre the waving trees,
An' a thousand sweet birds singing
Upon the simmer breeze,
Oh! Then the music o' her voice
Comes owre me like a spell,
While in each flower I recognise
The smile o' Isabel.

Her rosy lips are fu' o' smiles,
Her een wi' love are beamin';
Her bosom pure, like sparklin' dew
Upon the meadows gleamin';
An', oh! She spoke so soft an' sweet,
Her words like music fell
Upon my ears the night I gave
My heart to Isabel.

THE DRUCKEN MINER

There you go, kick up a shindy,
Hame again, an' roarin' fou,
Spent your whole pay in the Mindy,
And the rent noo wearin' due.

Oh, you are a bonny fellow –
Nane wi' you can blaw an' brag,
You're the best man in the "Nelly",
Aye puts oot the biggest darg.

No' a wife in a' Lochgelly
Kens my sorrow, grief, an' care;
Oh, you drucken man, it's really
Mair than I am fit to bear.

Last fortnicht auld Jamie Dandie
Gave his wife twa pounds an' mair;
But you ca'd me a dirty randy,
And tore my bonny yellow hair.

Selfish, dirty, drucken body,
You've nae thoucht for wife or wean;
You maun get your beef an' toddy –
I maun pick a penny bane.

If you had a spunk o' feelin'
You would try to mend your ways;
Oor disgrace is past concealin' –
*Sans*⁴ credit, meat, an' claes.

Look at honest Charlie Ramsay,
He has bonny bairns four;

---

⁴ Without

And a cleaner wife than Nancy
Ne'er was in Lochgelly Store.

Your honest wife and little bairn
Gi'e you little thoucht or care;
Jock, ye dinna want to learn
How to keep things nice an' square.

When the public-houses close,
You maun rin wi' Tammy Dawer,
Doon an' visit Kate McDose –
A famous shebeen in the Moor.

There you'll drink till early morn,
Till you've spent your last bawbee;
Oh, I wish I'd ne'er been born,
To suffer a' this misery.

I'm ashamed to meet a grocer
On the streets o' oor braw toon,
For we're indebted to them a',
Frae Sandy Air to Billy Broon.

Wi' the Parliamentary squad,
You can spout an' Irish story;
But canna tell if Preston Bruce
Belongs to Radical or Tory.

Do you wonder though I'm sulky,
When you ken I hae a pair
O' new shoon wi' Charlie Wulkie,
Ready made this month an' mair?

An' I daurna see the drapper
Since you got that suit o' claes;
No' a farthing ha'e ye paid him
For these last twa hunder days.

Be ashamed to think your shadow
Never darkens a kirk-door;
But to rin for drink you're ready
Ony day ten miles an' more.

Drink has been oor ruination
Since the day I was your wife;
Misery and degradation,
Hunger, cauld, domestic strife.

Drink has made your carcass lazy;
Last pay, only seven days,
Wouldna keep the cat in gravy
Far less buy us meat an' claes.

Deeper aye in debt we're sinkin',
No' a penny in the store,
Caused through your infernal drinkin',
Lazy, loafing Johnnie More.

Man, I mind when we were married,
I was then your bonny Bell;
Sair has been the heart I've carried
Since you swore to love me well.

Now, I'll leave you a' thigither,
Slavin' days wi' me are done;
Rin awa' an' tell your mither
That she has a worthy son.

When you swear to leave off drinkin',
Swear forever to abstain;
Not till then, my Jock, I'm thinkin',
Can we fill one house again.

LINES ON THE RECEPTION OF MY MOTHERS PORTRAIT

I see thy dear sweet face, mother,
Through my fast flowing tears;
The lineaments I trace, mother,
Of the happy byegone years.
Since then I've wandered very far,
And mingled in the ranks of war;
But thou hast been my guiding star
In every land, dear mother.

Oh! I have found since then, mother,
How wayward I have been;
And I may ne'er again, mother,
At thy dear side be seen.
Thou'rt sinking in the vale of years,
While I, with many hopes and fears,
Must lonely roam in other spheres,
Far from home and thee, mother.

The world's bitter blast, mother,
Has fanned my cheek since thou
Didst strain me to thy warm breast,
And kiss my fair young brow.
But here thy features mild I see,
With cheery smile and kindly e'e,
That once so sweetly beamed on me
In our bright home, mother.

Throughout my wild career, mother,
I've found no friend like thee;
Thou've shed the unseen tear, mother,
At lonely night for me.
I know full well that I've distress'd
The kindest parent and the best,

And broken both her peace and rest,
Since I left home, mother.

Though in foreign clime, mother
I hear thy voice so fine
Singing the strains sublime, mother,
That cheered my heart langsyne.
But these bright days have passed away,
My hair at last has turned grey;
But love for thee can ne'er decay –
My love, oh! Blessed mother.

I know thy genuine worth, mother,
Among the scenes of strife;
My heart's been drawn forth, mother,
To her who gave me life.
But fleeting time shall soon be o'er,
When we at last on yon bright shore
Shall meet again to part no more –
No more to part, dear mother.

THE AULD KIRK

The Auld Kirk, the Auld Kirk,
You'll aye be dear to me;
I lo'e you weel, although, I am
A member o' the Free.
I'll ne'er forget the dear Auld Kirk
O' Chalmers, Welsh, an' Broon;
Oor ain Kirk – lang may it flourish
In ilka Scottish toon.

The Auld Kirk, the Auld Kirk,
What memories you bring
O' fighting days on Scotland's braes,
Against a tyrant king.
Cameron, Renwick, an' Cargill –
These names - enough for me,
To mak' me lo'e the Auld Kirk still,
Now flourishing pure and free.

The Auld Kirk, the Auld Kirk,
You're changed sin' Forty-three –
You can elect your shepherd noo
As well's U.P's an' Free.
My mither sleeps beneath your dome,
An' my auld faither too;
I hope, in spite o' auld Gladstone,
We'll keep oor Auld Kirk true.   .
The Auld Kirk, the Auld Kirk –

The Auld Kirk, the Auld Kirk,
The Englishmen that noo
Represent our Scottish Shires,
They dinna care for you.
Episcopalians every one,
They dinna care a straw
Although oor Kirk was banished clean
Frae Caledonia.

The Auld Kirk, the Auld Kirk,
Lang, lang may Scotland see
Fraternal love to your young bairn
Born in Forty-three.
While I breathe, an' move, an' live,
You'll aye be dear to me –
Like my forefaithers, I wad give
My life for sake o' thee.

I FONDLY CHERISH

Still I fondly cherish
Loving thoughts o' thee;
Thou can never perish
From my memory.
Sad and lone we parted,
Cursed by cruel fate;
Now I'm broken-hearted,
Poor, and desolate.

Here upon my quiet post,
In the silent night,
I see thee on yonder coast,
Lovely, pure, and bright.
Our lives were happy then,
Smooth as summer streams;
But, Jeanie, we'll ne'er again
Enjoy Elysian dreams.

I see life's bright morning,
When thou were to me
A sweet flower adorning
Scotland's bonny lea.
With thee I can ne'er share
Sunny hours again;
My life is fraught with care,
Misery, and pain.

Feelings fresh and early,
Spirits bright and gay,
Now are cold and surly –
Youth has passed away.
In folly's giddy ring,
Round about I've whirled,

Till I am a poor thing,
Weary o' the world.

Here I lonely wander
O'er the rolling sea;
Day and night I ponder,
Dearest Jean, on thee.
Though in pain I languish,
My prayer is that thou
Ne'er may feel the anguish
That burns in me now.

SIR PEEL TEEL

Lang Sir Peel Teel, jist skin an' bane,
Wisna pleased to bide at hame;
But for a sodger he has gane –
Daft gowk is he;
But only has himself to blame
That's owre the sea.

To mak' a sang we whiles did fee 'm;
An' often we've been happy wi' 'm;
An' mony a canty dram wad gi'e 'm
When on the spree;
'Twad cheer oor hearts again to see 'm
That's owre the sea.

He was a merry, social chiel,
To sing a sang, or dance a reel;
An' for a glass wad face the deil,
When in his glee –

To speak the truth, we lo'ed him weel
That's owre the sea.

Weel did he love his Caledon –
Land o' Burns an' Willy Thom,
Wha ha'e immortalised in song
Hill, vale, an' lea;
But noo he's crossed the ocean's foam,
An' owre the sea.

His legs were lang, an' thin his brans,
That bore him up in short harangues;
While in his toon for makin' sangs
Ne'er matched was he;
But now he wanders foreign lan's,
Far owre the sea.

A minister you wudna name,
But Sir Peel Teel was sure to ken;
An' bards, frae Homer doon to Grahame,
Their birth kent he;
We hope to see him ance again
That's owre the sea.

We loved to sit an' hear him tell
How he would hie to some lone dell,
An' calmy read for hours himsel',
In summer nichts,
O' glorious men wha fought an' fell
For Scotland's richts.

He whiles lay in Colchester camp
On an iron bed, wi' blankets damp,
Which sometimes gave his legs the cramp,
An' sair was he;

But stern duty made him tramp
Far owre the sea.

He had his faults, like money mair,
An' loved the lassies, sweet and fair;
They often made his kind heart sair,
An' filled his e'e;
For little cash he had to spare
That's owre the sea.

TO A WEE BIRD

Oh, burdie, were I jist like thee –
Had little care, but up an' flee –
I'd strike upon some plaintive key,
The air of charm –
Like other birds that's full o' glee
An' void o' harm.

I'd chirp awa' through hill n' glen,
Far frae the haunts o' wicked men;
I'd never let the world ken
My calm retreat;
I'd live serenely in my den,
Resigned to fate.

AULD BETTY HUNTER

Auld Betty Hunter, I ne'er can forget her,
Wha lives in her cot at the tap o' the toon;
For tellin' droll stories I ne'er heard a better,
I could listen to her frae September to June.

In the lang winter nichts, we assemble thegither
Around her fireside, for she always mak's room;
An' we lo'e her so weel that we aye ca' her "mither" –
Oh, seldom is Betty's fireside ever toom.

Her fund is exhaustless o' Scotch wit an' humour,
And to her ghost stories there ne'er is an end;
Her memory's so strong, she can sing ilka song
That our national poet, Robbie Burns, e'er penned.

But the mighty deeds o' brave Willie Wallace
Are a theme she likes weel to lecture upon;
She kens a' the troubles that ever befell us,
Sin' the day that King Fergus ascended the throne.

Prince Charlie's memory she cherishes dearly,
She tells a' the hardships he ever gaed through;
Though she had trodden Prestonpans and Culloden,
A better description she cudna gi'e you.

She love Caledonia – she is Scotch to the Bane –
An' her feet ha'e ne'er left her ain parent earth;
When speaking o' nations, she ne'er can find ane
To compare wi' the glorious land o' her birth.

The shades o' gloamin' are fa'in around her,
Mony lang years in the world she has been;
But she wears doon the lone hill to the tomb,
May her last end be happy, calm, an' serene.

A NEW YEAR'S EPISTLE TO SERGEANT MAJOR CAMPBELL

A Guid New Year, my Auld Pay-all,
I wish you frae my very soul;
An' while on this terrestrial ball
May you be happy,
An' always ha'e within your call
A wee bit drappy.

In yon dear land where we were born,
How mony friends on this new morn
Will drink your health frae jug an' horn
In social glee;
Whilst we are wandering lands that's foreign
Beyond the sea.

Around the cheery, bright fireside,
Our aged parents will preside,
Far frae their sons, a' scattered wide
On life's rough main,
Imploring Heaven's power to guide
Us hame again.

There's music in the magic name
O' that sweet, kindly Scotch word "Hame";
May black disgrace an' burning shame
Rest on the villain
Whase love for hame's no' in a flame
O' purest feelin'.

The sodger in a distant clime,
The sailor on the foamy brine,
The wanderer 'mang scenes sublime
Does often mourn

To see again, in summer time,
His native burn.

Dear Jamie, lad, both you an' I
Ha'e roamed 'neath mony a brilliant sky;
An' tears perhaps ha'e dimmed the eye
When we thought on
Our glorious land o' liberty –
Sweet Caledon.

Bright land o' Burns an' Tannahill,
Green meadow, mountain, vale, an' rill,
The music o' thy rivers fill
My soul wi' love;
Our native land, we'll mind it till
We cease to move.

You ken it's lang since I did raise
My humble voice in Scotland's praise;
Amang her glens and brumlie braes
Perhaps we'll sit
Enjoying our declining days
In calm peace, yet.

May you enjoy a bright New Year,
Blest wi' happiness, health, an' beer –
A social glass at times does cheer
The heart o' man;
Tak' my advice, an' ne'er be sweer
To pree the dram.

Although I roam in this bright clime,
I aye can find both room and time
To ha'e a glass for auld langsyne –
The days gane by;

A friend wha mak's my life sublime
I value high.

Oh, mony New Years may you see,
Is the earnest wish o' bards like me;
May peace and great prosperity
Rest on your head,
An' bairns bless your memory
When you are dead.

May a' the blessings I can name
Adorn your sweet, conjugal hame;
An' love's sweet, pure, unselfish flame
Your path illume,
Until you gang where peace doth reign,
Beyond the tomb.

A LOST LIFE

> *"But thoughtless follies laid him low,*
> *And stained his name" – Burns.*

A.L. had gone round the gigantic circle of the sciences, had dipped
deep into the mysteries of creation; but vicious companion-Ship had
converted what might have been a glorious man into a Confirmed
misanthropist.

What have I done, what have I done,
Beneath the circuit of the sun –
I've only in vile courses run
Since I was born;
I ne'er did try black sin to shun
In any form.

I love what all good men detest –
The filthy song, the obscene jest,
I've rolled myself in pleasures nest
Till now I find
Every thought within my breast
To sin inclined.

My life hath sported in the beam
That play'th o'er life's pleasant stream;
The unbridled valves have let the steam
Of passions warm
Rush me where no quiet rest gleam
In life's dark storm.

But what is life? A pleasant dream –
A real enjoyment – a gleam
Of sweet sunshine, till in the stream
Of Lethe we lie;
Till then I'll bask in life's bright beam
And cares defy.

I've no desire, no inclination
To try a moral reformation,
Although I'm fit to fill a station
Of worth and trust;
I love a life of degradation,
For drink I must.

What care I for learning fine,
Or all the sciences sublime –
In learned languages I shine
And show my knowledge;
I'd shame the Greek and Latin science
In school or college.

I might have been a great physician,
Or lawyer in a proud position;
But, being void of strong decision
To choose a trade –
I now must bear good men's derision,
And beg my bread.

I can feel great inspiration
From the drink's intoxication;
Then I can give a grand oration –
Most eloquent;
I could grace the highest station
In Parliament.

When strong drink had my passions fired,
Sots like myself thought me inspired,
My drunken songs were so admired
By staring asses;
My wanton muse, she ne'er grew tired
'Mong drink and lasses.

Voltaire's sceptre I could sway,
And tune the lyre like Thomas Gray,
And wander through the Milky Way
Up to the moon;
And beat the clergy every day,
Like sceptic Hume.

But here I am, a pest on earth,
A man that's void of moral worth;
I laugh and sing in scenes of mirth,
And curse the great
Thick-headed sons of noble birth
Who rule the State.

Among the virtuous sons of men,
My breath would poison such as them;
But here I hold my trembling pen,
And laugh at sin;
I love the vulgar, selfish den
Of vice and gin.

I cannot mend my life, nor flee
From all the scenes of sin I see;
Few are the men I know that's free
From human errors;
But I'm so bad, that hell to me
Has lost its terrors.

I've spent my glorious manhood's prime
Where sin in all its forms shine;
The laws, both moral and divine,
Have lost their hold
Upon this vicious heart of mine,
Now black and cold.

Depart from me, ye saints, depart!
And leave me with my wicked heart;
Till death comes, with its fatal dart,
To end this life –
I shall frequent the busy mart
Of sin and strife.

Now, gentle reader, do not be
A slave to passions vile;
Oh, keep the heart aye pure and free
From sin, deceit, and guile.

ROBERT BURNS

Right weel ha'e ye sung o' our dear native land,
O' her glens, sunny braes, sweet and bonny;
Byron and Scott, they will both be forgot,
Ere thy name's lost in green Caledony.
Round a' the world thy fame is now gane –
Thy sangs, melodious and cheery.

Banish awa' both sorrow and pain –
Under their spell, wha is dreary?
Ramsay, and Ferguson sang very weel;
Nicol, Hogg, Tannahill, sweet and fairly;
Sweetly too, sang Gilfillan, Macneal –

Nane o' them cud sing "Rigs o' Barley".
Amang a' the bards o' Scotland I ken
There's nane like Robin, sae clever;
I've often been cheered wi' his canty strain
On the banks o' a bright Orient river.
Nae bards ha'e we in this modern time
Able to sing a sang like "Langsyne" –
Lang shall it flourish in our misty clime.

Proud is auld Scotland o' her darling son,
Oh! His name she forever shall cherish;
Enshrined it shall be in the hearts o' the free
Till the mountains o' Scotland perish.

FIVE ROBINS

The chirpings o' my Robins sweet
Aye cheer the hearts o' men –
There's Robin B, and Robin T,
Robin F, and Robin G,
An' Perthshire Robin N.

Five Robins ance in Scotland here
Did sing melodious, sweet, and clear;
But tho' they've flown, we still revere
Their glorious names;
For, oh! They sang wi' hearts sincere
O' dells an' plains.

They sang by river, bank, and shaw,
O' bonny lasses, fair an' braw;
But tho' they've gane frae us awa',
Their sangs are here –
"Louden's Braw Woods," "My Nannie O'" –
Our souls to cheer.

The swarthy clans beyond the sea
Ha'e heard an' sung o' Bessie Lee;
My Robins's sangs can never be
Forgot until
Scotch thistles cease to cock their e'e
On plain an' hill.

"Oh, why I left my hame?" Oh me!
I've sung that sang when o'er the sea,
Until tears trickled frae my e'e,
When nights were calm –
Awa' on India's fragrent lea,
'Mang groves o'palm.

Burns, Nicol, an' Ferguson –
Their fame has through creation run;
Auld Scotland's glorious days are done
When she's unwillin'
To tak' a pride in Tannahill
An' Rab Gilfillan.

Where'er a Scotsman's feet have trod,
At hame or on a foreign sod –
My Robins' sangs have their abode
In his heart warm,
To cheer him on life's dusty road
O' wind an' storm.

Where Ganges roll o'er scented plains,
Where Hindoos guard their sacred fanes,
There you will hear my Robins' strains
By Hindoo maids
Sung sweet at night, when silence reigns
In orange shades.

An' now, when I am old an' gray,
An' youthfu' days a' passed away,
These Robins round me chant their lays
As sweet an' fine
As when my heart was young an' gay,
In days langsyne.

THE BAILIE'S FAREWEEL TO THE SCHOOLBOARD

The School Board's elected, an' I am not there,
Still I won't fill my mind wi' thoughts o' despair;
But mony a sweet Miss will let the tear fa'
For the kind-hearted Bailie wha smiled on them a'.

My thanks I return quite hearty an' free
To ilka a dear Miss wha flung glances at me;
May sorrow an' care at their hallan ne'er ca' –
Is the wish o' the Bailie wha smiles on them a'.

May happiness, peace, an' prosperity glide
Around ilka neuk o' their cheery fireside;
An' bairns aye gang to the school neat an' braw –
Is the wish o' the Bailie wha smiles on them a'.

May our bairnies grow up in knowledge an' truth,
An' virtue adorn their walk in their youth;
An' may they ne'er follow such men as Bradlaugh –
Is the wish o' the Bailie wha smiles on you a'.

May brotherly love, instead o' discord,
Adorn the men o' the present School Board;
An' lang may each member his ain horn blaw –
Is the wish o' the Bailie wha smiles on you a'.

TO DR NELSON

Devoted to your calling you have always been,
Oh! few like yourself in the Burgh we have seen;
Constant in attendance on patients everywhere,
They all receive, at you hand, kindness, skill, and care;
Onward as swift time doth march, I love you better still;
Right well you serve our village with energy and skill.

Now forty years have passed away since you came to Lochgelly –
Energetic still and strong, with brain that's never shallow,
Loving-hearted gentleman! Here I declare I never
Saw your equal in the town – you're aye so frank and clever.
Of all the doctors in the town, I'm sure that we shall find
None like you – more brave and true, considerate and kind.

OUR TOON

Inscribed to Bailie Dick, Lochgelly.

Dear Bailie Dick, dear Bailie Dick,
The good auld days are gane
Since you used to wedge the mell an' pick
In the auld "Little Dane",
An' I, your laddie,
Drove "Wee Star"
In bonny days langsyne –
Lang ere I joined the ranks o' war
In India's sunny clime.

Auld village school, auld village school,
The tears drap frae my e'e
When I recall to mind the lads
Wha sported there wi' me;

For some repose in other lands
Beneath a foreign lea,
While others, like mysel', are still
On life's stormy sea.

Clear winding Orr, clear winding Orr –
My bright, my early hame –
Upon thy smiling banks I sang
In happy days now gane;
An' when afar, in Orient climes,
In fancy I wud hear
The murmer o' thy tranquil rill,
Like music in my ear.

Dear banks o' Clune, dear banks o' Clune,
Thou'rt sweet, fresh, an' fair;
An' in the leafy month o' June
I still can wander there.
For weel I ken the young laird
O' Glencraig's bonny ha'
Will let me spiel the broomy braes
When gloamin' shadows fa'.

My dear auld toon, my dear auld toon,
You'll aye be dear to me,
Until I sleep inside the tomb –
My heart is still wi' thee.
Can I forget life's bright young days,
When owre these hill I ran,
An' pu'd the berries, hips, an' slaes,
Near Davie Aitkens dam?

My bonny toon, my bonny toon,
Frae thee I'll roam nae mair;
I'll bide where thy sweet lassies bloom,
Like roses, pure an' fair.

Although grand cities I ha'e seen
Athwart the foamy brine,
Their grandeur couldna please my e'en,
Nor cheer this heart o' mine.

IN MEMORIAM – ROBERT BAIN

Rest, warrior! Thy battles now are o'er
On Crimean plains and India's coral shore –
Boldly thou fought up Alma's rugged height,
Engaging all the power of Russia's savage might;
Regiments, French and British, assembled there
To cut the claws of the Russian bear.
Battles fierce were ofttimes waged before –
At Waterloo, Vittoria, and Cawpore;
I know no battle fought without a plan –
None, at least, like bloody Inkermann.

ACROSTIC

Traveller o'er life's stormy sea,
How well I love to welcome thee;
Enrapturing tales to me you bring

From that dear land where linties sing.
I love to read thy pages through,
Firm old friend, so kind and true –
Every week with something new.

Nature's wonders, so grand and fine,
Entrance my soul with thoughts sublime;
What an earnest friend you've been to me
Since thy bright face I first did see.

NEW YEAR'S EPISTLE TO SERGEANT DONALD FERGUSON, KINROSS

"Should auld acquaintance be forgot,
And never brought to min'?
Should auld acquaintance be forgot,
And days o' auld langsyne?"

Dear Donald, -

Mony lang years ha'e o'er us gane
Since you an' I left Scotia's hame
Our country's honour to maintain
Beyond the sea;
An' were we young, we'd fight again
On India's lea.

Lingering memory brings to view
The varied scenes we wander'd thro';

But time wud fail to tell to you
What we ha'e seen
Since first we served, like sodgers true,
Our gracious Queen.

Where is the place we hinna seen?
Where is the place we hinna been? –
An' back again on Scotland's green –
Sweet flowery plain;
Oh, mony strange sight met our e'en
Far owre the main.

We've seen the Himalaya hills, sublime,
Awa' in Punjaub's balmy clime;
An ofttimes drank the Spanish wine
To mak' us hearty –
Dear Donald, we enjoyed it fine
A social party.

We've seen Benares, Lucknow, Cawnpore,
An' heard the deadly cannon's roar
Among the hills aboon Lahore,
In days gane by –
We dinna want baith reek an' gore
'Neath yonder sky.

We sodgered in the Grecian Isles,
Where grandeur reigns an' beauty smiles,
An' where sweet maids, wi' winning wiles,
Wud mak' us cheery –
I've seen me then gang twenty miles
For ae sweet dearie.

We'll ne'er forget the days langsyne –
Bright, sunny days, when in our prime;
An', though I say't, few in the line

Could us surpass
For fighting, or in courting fine
A bonny lass.

You were a young bit callan when
You went through India's hard campaign;
The sights you saw amang the slain
I canna tell
Like you, wha on the sanguinary plain
Fought long an' well.

The mutiny was scarcely o'er,
When our distinguished Highland corps
Another bloody campaign bore,
Wi' heavy loss –
But here you are, still to the fore,
In auld Kinross.

Seventy-first! Famed Highland corps!
Although we hear thy name no more,
We'll ne'er forget the garb we wore
In years noo past –
The auld name we will aye adore
While life doth last.

I'm wearin' now towards three-score,
A crabbit, surly bachelor,
Hirplin' daily round my door,
Wi' stick in han' –
Wi' nae domestic bliss in store
For me, puir man.

Where is the loving, kindly dame
Wha, for my sake, wud change her name,
To light my ingle, grace my hame,
An' cheer life's gloamin' ? –

I'd like to see her at my hearthstane
A loving woman.

Though some few years ha'e o'er me gone
Since I beheld your dear son John;
Jist let him ken that I think on
The guid auld times,
Ere he was up to manhood grown,
In Southern climes.

Now, auld dear frien', oh! lang may you
An' your wee wifie toddle through
The scenes o' life, and never view
Disheartening care;
Your frien's be honest, kind, an' true –
Is Pinders prayer.

Frae my Scotch heart I wish you here
A bright an' happy, guid New Year,
Wi' mony frien's and hearty cheer
At your hearthstane,
An' matrimonial bliss shine clear
In your Scotch hame.

Now, Donald, lad, you'll think it time
For me to close my uncouth rhyme –
Although it's far frae the sublime,
At that don't wonder;
But I'm your frien' while I can sign
My name, JOHN PINDAR.

THE NIGHT I LEFT CARTMORE

The night was calm, no clouds were seen
Athwart the jewelled sky;
The starry hosts, bright and serene,
Were peeping sweet on high;
The smiling moon, with silvery beams,
Was spreading glory o'er
The flowery banks and winding streams
The night I left Cartmore.

Since that dear night I've wandered far,
And mony places seen;
I've mingled in the ranks o' war,
And battled hot and keen.
But when I stood on fields o' strife,
And heard the cannon's roar,
'Twas then I thought on my dear Fife
And scenes around Cartmore.

Although I've seen Hindostan's hills,
Majestic and sublime,
Their savage grandeur ne'er could please
This lonely heart o' mine;
For, still my thoughts would fly away
To peaceful scenes of yore –
I'll ne'er forget life's early day
And friends in old Cartmore.

EPITAPHS

Here lies the banes o' gluttonous Will,
Whom death has overpowered;
He'll never rest until he has
His grave chums all devoured.

———

Here rests the dust of one who had
A heart to think and feel,
Though in this world he bore a name
As hard as any steel.

EPIGRAMS

Greasy Jock greasy Jock, put your head in a pock,
And conceal your lee-telling mouth;
No word that you say, in a whole blessed day,
Contains the essence of truth.

———

Gab and Guts, Gab and Guts, they tell me your wuts
Have procured you an' elegant wife;
Y' ne'er should ha'e been higher than mucking a byre
On some muirland farm in Fife.

Andrew, my lad, may your heart ne'er be sad,
As you roam through this world o' ours;
You've a canty sweet dame at a cheery hearthstane,
And bairns – God bless the sweet flowers.

———————

Dear Johnnie, dear Johnnie, our early days bonny –
You'll mind them, the bright days o' yore;
You've laddies sin' syne, now grown to me,
While I'm still an auld bachelor.

———————

Geordie Glen, Geordie Glen, among learned men
You like to craw and to caper;
But ae thing I'll tell you, you're a puir silly naething,
Whase language is jist smoke an' vapour.

———————

Robert Knight, Robert Knight, forty years ha' ta'en flight
Since you came to the toon o' Lochgelly;
And, though you ha'e been eighty years on life's scene,
You are still a hearty auld fellow.

———————

Robert Mill, Robert Mill, you've a resolute will;
You're a man I respect and esteem;
Though far I have trod o'er a Southern sod,
Your equal I seldom have seen.

ON HEARING THE REV. T. DEWAR

Mr Dewar, Mr Dewar, your sermon is pure –
Yea, eloquent, learned, sublime;
But mankind are jolly, wicked, unholy –
They treat with contempt what's divine.

———

To sail o'er the billow, and visit Lochgelly,
Would to me be delightful and pleasant;
May nae sorrow befa' till I meet wi' ye a' –
So fareweel, dear mother, at present.

———

If men would only try
To be kind to one another,
We would have a sunny sky,
And always smiling weather.

MY NATIVE LAND

O, glorious land, renowned in song
My soul shall cling to thee,
Where'er my weary footsteps roam
In lands beyond the sea,
Sweet voices o' my early days
Come back to me in dreams;
An' memory brings before my gaze
Green meads and gushing streams.

At night, while on my silent post,
In dreams my soul will stray
To tranquil scenes on Fife's dear coast –
The scenes o' life's young day.
I backwards through the mist o' time
Oft cast a tearfu' e'e;
And, pensive, muse on auld langsyne
And friends so dear to me.

O' beauteous land, so fair an' grand,
Thy sons, so brave and free,
Are looking back, through memory's track,
Bright island-home, to thee.
But, though sweet Scotia's bonny shore
We never mair may see,
The land that out Scotch hearts adore
Our guiding star shall be.

Though fragrant breezes roun' me play,
An' maidens sweetly sing,
Nae peace nor happiness can they
To my lone bosom bring.
Should I return to Scotland's braes,
I'll never wander more
Through other lands, but end my days
Besides my native Orr.

OUR JAMIE COME HAME

Dear Kate, put on your cloak, an' rin
Awa' to Cuparha',
An' tell Tam, Graham that Jamie's hame
Frae the gallant Forty-Twa.
I ken he'll be right glad to see
My son, so brave an' braw;
For he was aince a sodger too,
In countries far awa'.

Chorus –

> *Gae, sound the news through Cuparha'*
> *Mak' vocal hill an' plain;*
> *And tell the kindly neebours a'*
> *That Jamie's hame again.*

My puir auld heart feels young again,
Wi' joy the tears doon fa';
For my puir laddie noo has been
Owre twenty years awa'.
My sodger lad made Russians reel
Owre Alma's rugged broo;
He's served his Queen an' country weel –
God bless my laddie noo.

I feel a Spartan mither's pride
At the honours he hath won;
Five medals dingle on his breast –
I'm prood o' such a son.
An' best of a', there's ane o' them
The Cross o' Queen Victoria –
The highest honour man can gain
On battlefields so gory.

His aged father wud hae been
A happy man today
Had God but spared him to ha'e seen
His brave son, Jamie Gray.
The night he died, he prayed to God
For blessings on our child –
Our Jamie was in India then,
Engaged in battles wild.

My darling son, your warfare's o'er
On fields o' bluidy strife;
Nae mair you'll tread a hostile shore,
Nor leave your bonny Fife.
And, if you should think o' a wife,
Dear Jamie, there is ane
Wud cheer your pilgrimage through life –
An' that's young Maggie Graham.

JEANIE MUNRO

Air – "The Laird o' Cockpen"

Wha hisna heard o' young Jeanie Munro?
Wha hisna heard o' young Jeanie Munro? –
I pray you, beware o' this maiden, so fair,
For bright are the eyes o' young Jeanie Munro.

When the Colonel cam' on parade,
Full mony a blunder an' stammer he made;
For the evening before, as to the mess he did go,
He met the bright eyes o' young Jeanie Munro.

The big Major, too, has been smitten indeed;
He has turned a Papist to be o' her creed;
Instead o' the church, now to mass he does go –
An' a' for the sake o' young Jeanie Munro.

The Lieutenant and Captain for her fought a duel,
An' the Quartermaster drowned himsel' in a pool;
While the heart-stricken Adjutant walks to an' fro
Alang the Parade, crying "Jeanie Munro."

The Paymaster, too, has been caught in her snare,
And he crawls about, wringing his hands in despair;
His books are a' wrang, an' he swears he will throw
Himsel' owre the brig for young Jeanie Munro.

Yon fiery-haired Ensign – oh! woeful to tell,
Yest'reen, wi' his gun, put an end to himsel'.
Because she told him to let his beard grow
Before he could cheek up to Jeanie Munro.

Last night at tattoo, the Pay-Sergeant an' a'
Cam' into his room wi' a face white as snaw,
Lay down on his bed, gave a kick, and cried, - "Oh!
I'm dying this night for young Jeanie Munro."

The Drum-Major, Bugler, the Piper, Pioneer,
Sergeant-Major, an' privates are smitten, I fear;
An' through a' the Regiment, wherever you go,
You'll find someone crying – "Oh! Jeanie Munro."

But what do you think o' the Apothecary,
Wha fattened on nothing but rice an' hot curry? –
He won Jeanie's heart in a fortnight or so,
An' ended the flirting o' Jeanie Munro.

BOB MILL, THE CARRIER LAD

Folk say that the best men to the Commons are sent,
To rule the affairs o' the nation;
But the carrier lad is always content
To drive your goods frae the Station.
Come dry day, come wet day, it's a' ane to me,
I've a heart an' a hand that is willing
To help a friend 'cross life's troubled sea
While I'm able to earn a shilling.

Amid summer's heat, or wintery winds howlin',
I drive to the Station aye cheery;
An' wha can say they e'er heard me growlin',
Wi' visage grim, sulky, an' dreary?
My kind-hearted chum in lang Cowdenbeath
Is kent as a jolly good fellow;
I'll gi'e him a glass to sweeten his teeth
Next time he comes east to Lochgelly.

When gowans bloom sweet on green Birnie Brae
An' hills wi' their vocal notes ringing,
My voice you can hear at the dawn of the day
Whistling, humming, or singing.
As lang's I get plenty o' meal to my *Mill*
I'll envy nae lord in creation;
But I trust to merit respect an' goodwill
While driving your goods frae the Station.

MY MITHER'S AULD HEARTHSTANE

My native hame, my native land,
Oh! tak' me there ance mair:
I lang to leave this sunny strand,
Though beauteous, bright, an' fair.
Gi'e orange groves an' brilliant skies
To those wha love the same;
Enough I've seen to mak' me prize
My mither's auld hearthstane.

My native hame – oh, blissful spot!
I wish that I could share
The love and pure affection
O' dear frien's dwelling there.
How fragrant is the memory yet
O' golden days lang gane,
When lads and bonnie lassies met
At mither's auld hearthstane.

Lang years ha'e flown o'er my head
Since youth's unclouded morn;
But hope still whispers in my soul –
Oh, dinna be forlorn;
For, there is praying for thee now,
In thy sweet Scottish hame,
A parent, kind, wha kissed thy brow
Beside the auld hearthstane.

Through wandering years o' martial strife
Among the Southern isles,
I've ne'er forgot my native Fife,
Where steadfast friendship smiles.
Though bright, romantic lands I've seen,
Believe me, there is nane
Contains a brighter spot on earth
Than mither's auld hearthstane.

THE LASS O' PITKENIE

Ha'e you seen my wee lassie, wha lives in yon toon,
As blithe, sweet, an' merry's a lav'rock in June?
Be it sunshiny weather, be't frosty or rainy
You'll aye get a smile frae the lass o' Pitkenie.

The pure flowers o' simmer, in sweet regal bloom,
May spread o'er Pitkenie their richest perfume;
But the sweetest flower there is my lovely Teenie –
My ain bonny lass on the braes o' Pitkenie.

On the braes o' Pitkenie sweet roses are blushing,
An' Orr's rippling river is glowing an' flushing;
But I carena a strae though its beauties are many,
Unless they are shared wi' the lass o' Pitkenie.

I might wander again to some sunny clime,
Perhaps find a grave 'neath the shade o' the vine;
But till life's latest day I will think on my Teenie,
The bonny sweet rose on the braes o' Pitkenie.

MY LITTLE TOONY

Air – "Piper o' Dundee"

Oh! tak' me back to our toon,
To our toon. To our toon,
O! tak' me back to our toon,
My bonny Lochgelly.
And I will never wander mair
Through other lands, though rich an' fair,
Nae land on earth can e'er compare
Wi' ane far owre the billow.

I love my little toony, my toony, my toony,
I love my little toony, my bonny Lochgelly.

Though flowers bloom here in simmer pride,
An' streams through orange forests glide,
Oh! tak' me where my brithers bide,
In bonny Lochgelly.
I'll ne'er forget my early days,
When I pu'd berries, hips, an' slaes,
Lang ere I roam'd the palmy braes
Where Ganges roll so yellow.

To Scotia's Isle my soul shall cling,
Where thistles wave an' linties sing;
Wi' sangs I'll mak' the couples ring
When I come owre the billow.
I'll crack wi' you o' days land gane,
When we were young an' a' at hame,
I'll canty sit at your hearthstane,
In bonny Lochgelly.

THE ROSE O' DUNNIKIER

The lassies o' Kirkcaldy toon
Are bonny, sweet, an' gay;
Their cheeks are like the rose's bloom
In smiling, flowery May.
But their sweet smiles can ne'er illume
A soul wi' love sincere
For my pretty Maggie Home –
The rose o' Dunnikier.

Her rosy moo', her e'e sae blue,
An' teeth like shining pearls,
Mak' Maggie worth a score or two
O' pale-faced city girls.
When flowery fields we wander through,
Her voice, sae sweet an' clear,
Mak's vocal ilka plain an' dell
Around auld Dunnikier.

Oh, smiling maid! Pure love like thine
Is mair than gold to me;
The happy day I ca' thee mine,
I'll dance and sing wi' glee.
I wudna change my lot in life
Wi' Rosslyn's noble peer,
An' leave my bonny lass in Fife –
The rose o' Dunnikier.

JOHNNIE YACH, THE YOUNG RECRUIT

Awake! Awake! Young sleepy head,
The pipes are playing roond yer bed;
Awake! Arise, an' gang on parade,
Or you'll be late in the morning

Chorus –

> Heu, Johnnie Yach, are ye wauken yet,
> And are yer traps a' shinin' yet? –
> If you are late, you're sure to get
> The guardroom in the morning.

The bugle soonds upon the square,
The Sergeant-Major's already there;

Wi' dirty shoon and unkemm'd hair;
Dinna gang on parade in the morning.

Brave young sodger, I love you weel,
I ha'e a heart to think and feel;
But a young sodger late for drill
Is a sorry sicht in the morning.

And, oh, beware o' Spanish gin,
Sold in these dens o' filth an' sin;
Be sober, an' strive hard to win
Sincere respect in the morning.

Strong drink's the cause o' a' the crime
Created in the British line;
Abstain frae such, an' you will shine
A healthy lad in the morning.

Sodgers like you, ance young an' brave,
Now fill the drunkard's gloomy grave;
Because to night they were a slave
At night an' early morning.

Now, here's six things to bear in mind –
Be *truthful, honest, brave,* an' *kind,*
Vigilant, sober, an' you'll find
Yersel' a sergeant some morning.

MY PITHEAD LASSIE

Oh, ha'e you seen my chatty queen?
Wha sings so sweet an' mellow, O!
There's no a queen like bonny Jean
In toon o' auld Lochgelly, O! –
In toon o' auld Lochgelly, O!
In toon o' auld Lochgelly, O! –
She is the flower amang them a'
Wha works upon the "Nellie," O!

I'll hae this lassie, sweet an' fair,
Though she has ne'er a guinea, O!
High-born dames can ne'er compare
Wi' my young handsome queenie, O!
Wi' my young handsome queenie, O!
Wi' my young handsome queenie, O!
There's no a flower on bank or bower
So fragrant as my Jeanie, O!

Hame frae her work she comes at e'en
Wi' spirits light an' cheery, O!
An' mak's her mammy's housie clean,
My bonny, weel-faured dearie, O!
My bonny, weel-faured dearie, O!
My bonny, weel-faured dearie, O! –
Lang Cowdenbeath and Little Raith
Hisna a lass so cheery, O!

My modest, couthie little Jean
Is gaun to leave the "Nellie", O!
An' at my side she'll soon be seen
A braw wife in Lochgelly, O!
My Jeanie o' Lochgelly, O!
My queenie o' Lochgelly, O! –
The laddies roun' about the toon
Ca' me a lucky fellow, O!

AULD LAUNCHERHEAD

Auld Launcherhead, auld Launcherhead,
It's fifty years an' mair
Since on thy brumley braes I roved,
When summer skies were fair.
Nae wonder that the tear should fa'
Doon frae my misty e'e,
When waverin' memory does reca'
Those bye-gane days to me.

I see the village worthies still,
Wha roved in days o' yore
Alang the broo o' Clune's green hill
To view the winding Orr;
An' I can hear auld Billy's voice,
Wha rang the evening bell –
He's sleeping near the tranquil scenes
In life he loved so well.

Dear Launcherhead, thy sunny braes,
I see them, bright an' fair;
Amang the scenes o' other days
I breathe the fragrant air.
The little birds sing on the tree,
The grass is waving green;
But, oh ! how sad the change to me,
Where nae kent face is seen.

Auld Launcherhead, thy murmuring breeze
Is fraught wi' grief an' pain,
When I think on the joyous days
That ne'er will come again.
The gloomy shades o' gloamin' fa'
Upon my native hame;

Life's early friends are now awa'
And left me here alane.

Auld Charlie's gane, wha used to play
The auld Scotch fiddle weel;
I mind, when little laddies, we
Wud toddle at his heel.
His wee clay hoose, in ruins now,
Is roofless, cauld, an' bare;
The silent bat an' hoolet mak'
Their gloomy dwellin' there.

An' now, when grey hairs croon my brow,
I love to muse an' sing
O' early friens a' vanished now
Frae where I spent life's spring.
Auld Launcherhead, auld Launcherhead,
Few summer suns can shine
Ere I repose amang the dead –
Dear friend o' auld langsyne.

BURNS' BIRTHDAY, 1879

Ye men o' bonny Scotland's Isle,
Wha roam by Tweed an' Clyde,
Maun ken that we admire the bard
Wha sang by Afton's side.
If y' but heard our voices now
In this braw foreign clime,
You'd cock your ears, erect you brow,
To hear us sing "Langsyne".

Chorus —

> *For auld langsyne, my frien's,*
> *For auld langsyne;*
> *We'll sing the sangs o' Scotland yet,*
> *Though in a foreign clime.*

I've stood by Ganges' yellow tide
Upon a Januar' morn,
Far frae the bonny land I love –
The land where Rab was born.
An' 'mang a hundred Scotchmen there
I've raised this voice o' mine,
Until re-echoed through the air
That glorious sang, "Langsyne."

Whare'er a Scotchman's feet may roam,
His heart aye fondly turns
Back to his bonny, tranquil home,
His country, and his Burns.
His memory will wander back
To where sweet voices, fine,
Are singing roon' a Scotch hearthstane,
That sang o' sangs – "Langsyne".

Go, roam the world thro' an' thro',
Traverse a' foreign plains,
An' there you'll find some Scotchman true,
Singin' his canty strains.
Last New Year's morn my glad ears heard
That dear sang sung sublime;
Oh! heart-felt sang o' our dear bard –
The Scotchman's sang, "Langsyne."

THE SEVENTY-AN'-ONE

From the Grenadier Guards to the Hundred-and-Nine,
Distinguished regiments that form the line –
I challenge ye a' to show me, if you can,
A braver corps than the Seventy-an'- One.

Chorus –

> *Then hurrah! hurrah! for our country an' Queen,*
> *We're ready to fight when a foe's to be seen;*
> *Our gallant corps, boys, stand second to none –*
> *Let's shout high the deeds o' the Seventy-an'-One.*

Go, search its auld records, they prominently tell
How the Glasgow heroes both fought and fell;
The Crimean plains an' wide Hindostan
Resound wi' the deeds o' the Seventy-an'-One.

On mony a sanguinary field in Spain
The Seventy-an'-One did bright laurels gain;
On the slopes o' Vittiria, the gallant Cadogan
Fell gloriously leading the Seventy-an'-One

But time wud fail me, dear boys, to tell
The deeds o' the corps we a' love so well;
Wha carried the day at Seringapatam? –
History exclaims, 'Twas the Seventy-an'-One.

In the year eighteen hundred an' sixty-three
The Seventy-One were where the gallants should be;
In storming the Craig Picket, wha led the van? –
'Twas Colonel Hope wi' his Seventy-an-None.

Now let us, brave comrades, fill high the glass,
In memory o' those wha fell in the Pass;
Although they are sleeping in Hutti-mor-dan,
Their memory is green in the Seventy-an'-One.

A CANTY GLASS

When I am oppressed wi' care an' grief,
An' feel life's lot so dreary,
A canty glass gi'es me relief,
An' mak's me blithe an' cheery.

Chorus –
    Then fill your glasses, drink to the lasses,
    The dear sweet flowers o' creation;
    We a' ken weel a bonny wee lass
    Is the pride o' our dear nation.

Abstainers in these modern days
May think they're free an' happy;
I never felt life's pleasant ways
Except when o'er the drippy.

    Then fill your glasses, &c.

Awa'. Ye very unsocial crew,
Your principles I scorn;
We Scotchmen find a friend aye true
In auld John Barleycorn.

    Then fill your glasses, &c.

Though thus we sing, we don't abuse
The drink which mak's us frisky;
But he's a fool wha wud refuse
A glass o' real Scotch whisky.

    Then fill your glass, &c

Then tak' your dram where'er you pass,
 Whether on land or ocean;

To the soul-enlivenin' glass
Aye cling wi' fond devotion.

Then fill your glass, &c.

THE MELODIES O' HAME

I've wandered thro' this world noo
Some thirty years an' mair,
An' heard the sangs o' foreign lan's
Float on the balmy air;
But, oh, hoo cauld an' spiritless,
Unmeanin', poor, an' tame –
Hey dinna touch the true Scotch heart
Like melodies o' hame.

Chorus –

> *The melodies o' hame,*
> *The melodies o' hame,*
> *There's nae sangs like our ain sangs,*
> *The melodies o' hame.*

I've been enraptured wi' the sangs
O' Erin's lovely plains,
As I should be when litenin' to
Her maist delightfu' strains;
But though they're sweet and tender,
Even them I canna name
Amang our bonny heart-felt sangs,
The melodies o' hame.

Oh, sweet Scotch sangs, ye bring to me
A glimpse o' early days,

A vision o' the sunny past –
My smiling native braes,
Whare I roamed in by-gone years
Wi' the lassie o' Torbain,
An' made the vales re-echo wi'
The melodies o' hame.

'Mang gorgeous scenes I've stood
In the calm an' silent night,
When a' the world was sleeping,
An' wee stars peeping bright.
In fancy then I'd wander
Back to the auld hearthstane,
And hear my mither sing aince mair
The melodies o' hame.

Awa' whare mighty Ganges
Does roll its yellow tide;
Awa' where western rivers
Through majestic forests glide –
There you'll find Auld Scotia's sons
Spreadin' their country's fame,
By singing our undying sangs,
The melodies o' hame.

NORA KILLEEN

A winsome sweet fairy is Nora Killeen,
A lass light an' airy is Nora Killeen,
Nae rose o' the simmer so sweet as the kimmer –
Sae, gallants, beware o' young Nora Killeen.

That snuffy auld body, the Laird o' Pinmore,
Whase years maun now number auchty-an'-four,
Said he felt a' the vigour o' sweet seventeen
When he gazed on the charms o' Nora Killeen.

Last Sabbath the priest had his nerves a' unstrung,
He gave out his text as a psalm to be sung –
When mounting the pulpit his auld eyes had seen
The enrapturing beauty o' Nora Killeen.

The doctor, the lawyer, the banker, the joiner,
The bailie, the draper, the baker, and miner,
Inside a lunatic asylum have been,
A' caused through the beauty o' Nora Killeen.

But ten o' her lovers have gone to the sea,
While some mair are sleeping beneath the green lea;
Still thro' the hale village saut tears frae the een
Are copiously flowing for Nora Killeen.

But Nora has married big Fagan O'Neal,
A dealer in tatties, pork, ham, and oatmeal;
Now ahint his auld counter, wi' apron sae clean,
Stands the heart-ensnarin' young Nora Killeen.

TEENIE BAIN

Let Cowdenbeath blaw o' her lasses sae braw,
Wi' their red cheeks like roses in June;
They a' maun gi'e place to the sweet modest grace
O' my Teennie in Lochgelly toon.
She sings like a lark round my cheery hearthstane,
He heart is confindin' an' warm;
She lichtens my care, an' my sorrows she shares,
In the vale o' sunshine an' storm.

This canty, this bonny, sweet wifie o' mine
Is a radiant sun in my hame;
The blink o' her e'e gi'es me pleasure sublime –
Oh, there's nae wife like sweet Teenie Bain.
Now I whistle an' sing, because I ha'e won
A bright lassie wha mak's me her care;
There's nae toon in Fife that can show such a wife
As my Teenie, sae thrifty an' fair.

When frae my wark in the gloamin' I come
To my housie, sae tidy an' nice;
What a heaven o' bliss to get a sweet kiss
In the fauld o' our ain paradise.
Her bright, sunny smile drives awa' care an' gloom –
Nae wonder I'm fond o' my queenie;
I've nae cause to wish for the peace o' the tomb
While blest wi' the smiles o' my Teenie.

THE BANKS O' CLUNE

I've mused upon Benarty's hill
When nature's sweets were singin',
And toddled oft by Inchga' Mill
When bonny flowers were springin';
An' I ha'e roved thro' Colin's crags,
Her glens an' lovely rills,
An' mony a pleasant day I've spent
Upon the Torry hills.

Aboon them a' I lo'e the Clune –
That spot's aye dear to me;
For there I spent life's sunny day
In wandering o'er thy lea.
Doon by the bonny Butter Well
I sat in days o' yore
When the shadows o' gloamin' fell
Upon dear winding Orr.

I see Clune Babby's ivy cot
Upon the rosy broo;
But she is dead an' a' forgot –
The auld cot's lonely noo.
Clune Babby's gane to that far land
Frae whence she'll ne'er return
Again to roam upon the braes,
Or muse alang the burn.

The Clune, the Clune, I lo'e the Clune –
Bright spot, I lo'e thee well;
Oh, when my weary days are dune,
Lay me in yon calm dell –
Lay me in yonder flowery glen,
Beneath the hazel tree,
Far frae the haunts o' wicked men
And drunken revelry.

MARY, THE FLOWER O' FERMOY

The Tipperary mountains are shrouded in gloom,
An' wintery winds rave down the glens o' Fermoy;
While mournfully I lie, in my cauld barrack-room,
Lamenting the loss o' my heart's pride an' joy.
Gae, range through the world o' beauty an' grandeur –
Seek sweet – foreign lasses where silver streams rin;
Your dark orient maids, wi' their riches an' splendour,
Want the artless beauty o' young Mary Quin.

The lark, he can sing in the blue sky sae cheery –
The lambkins can gambol an' sport on the lea;
But sorrow maun reign in my bosom sae dreary,
Since the flower o' Fermoy has flown frae me.
The beauty o' simmer can yield me nae pleasure;
Nane kens o' the anguish that's now dwellin' in
My lonely heart, sin' I've lost my treasure –
The flower o' Fermoy, my young Mary Quin.

Her beauteous form is gracefu' an' slender,
And bright is the glance o' her love-laughing e'e;
But, oh, her kind words, sae melodious an' tender,
Are gi'en to another, mair favoured than me.
But though I should mingle in scenes o'' commotion,
An' win a high name in the battle's wild din –
Enshrined in my soul be the purest devotion
For the flower o' Fermoy, my young Mary Quin.

THE LASS O' CUPARHA'

I've seen the sweet maidens o' Erin an' Spain,
Forbye other lassies far owre the dark main;
But though they are a' baith winsome an' braw,
They're no like the lassie o' auld Cuparha'.

I've sat where the Ganges does murmer alang
The banks where re-echo the Hindoo maid's song;
Even there, my lone thoughts wud wander awa'
To the bonny sweet lassie o' auld Cuparha'.

Your ladies, wha spring frae the great names o' earth
May look wi' contempt on a plebeian's birth;
But the fairest damsel the Peerage e'er saw
Cudna' shine wi' the lassie o' auld Cuparha'.

Your high-born beauties are seldom sincere –
Their love lies in titles, wi' thousands a-year;
But coronets an' wealth wudna' change her ava
Wha blooms in her beauty in auld Cuparha'.

Her heart is my ain, she is constant an' true,
Sae, gallant young callants, I carena for you;
Owre conquests o' beauty you brag an' you blaw,
You'll ne'er win the lassie o auld Cuparha'.

She is honest an 'kind, sweet, modest, an' fair,
The flower o' the village – I'll tell you nae mair;
But soon I'll return frae lands far awa',
An' claim the dear lassie o' auld Cuparha'.

MAGGIE KIPPEN

Let those wha like to sing in the praise
O' foreign dames so braw;
The subject o' my simple lays
Does far outshine they a'.
Across life's wild an' stormy sea
My barque wi' her I'd lippen;
There's nane on earth so dear to me
As my sweet Maggie Kippen.

She'e kindly, couthie, bright, an' fair,
Which ony ane can see
Wha likes to watch he modest air
An' bonny laughin' e'e.
Let thoughtless laddies laugh an' stare
When owre the green we're skippin';
You winna find anither pair
Like me an' Maggie Kippen.

I like to sing the lassies' praise,
As Burns did langsyne
Although like him I canna raise
A sang so sweet an' fine;
But I ken weel, had Robbie seen
Her through Lochgelly trippin',
He'd match her wi' his bonny Jean –
My ain dear Maggie Kippen.

THE FLOWER O' BALGEDIE

Although I ha'e wander'd in lands fair an' bonny,
An' seen comely maidens beyond the dark main;
Yet 'mang foreign flowers I never saw ony
To match wi' my lassie, young Elsie McLean.

She is as sweet as the morn when wee birds are singing,
An' pure as the dew-draps that lie on the plain;
You'll no' find a sweet flower in garden bower springing
That can be compared wi' young Elsie McLean.

Had I just been twenty, an' aye in my glory,
I then might have hoped her affections to gain;
But though I am auld, grey, wizened, and hoary,
A sang I maun sing to young Elsie McLean.

There canna be ane in the hale o' creation
That wud try her pure reputation to stain;
May she aye be kept frae the contamination
O' villains wha wud injure young Elsie McLean.

May heaven smile on thee, my sweet dark-eyed maiden –
Thy heart be a stranger to sorrow an' pain;
Nae black clouds o' life mak' thy heart heavy-laden,
Thou flower o' Balgedie, young Elsie McLean.

Oh, may the sweet sunshine o' love an' o' gladness
Illume thy young heart o'er life's gloomy main,
Wi' nae trials nor cares to fill thee with sadness,
Thou flower o' Balgedie, young Elsie McLean.

FAREWELL TO LOCHGELLY

Air – "Roy's Wife."

Fare thee well, my dear Lochgelly,
Fare thee well, my dear Lochgelly,
I maun leave thy bonny braes
And cross the raging foamy billow.

When far awa' in India's clime,
Where the orange groves bloom yellow,
I'll think o' bonny days langsyne,
And loving friends in dear Lochgelly.

When far upon a foreign shore,
Wi' my spirits lone an' dreary,
My thought will fly to scenes of yore,
When often I was blithe and cheery.

Fare thee well, my friends so dear,
May your days be bright and mony;
Fare thee well, my heart is sweer
To leave the lasses, sweet an' bonny.

May health and plenty bless this place
Where ance I roved a thoughtless fellow;
The tears are trickling doon my face –
Oh, fare thee well, my dear Lochgelly.

My love I leave to all behind;
'Tis hard to tear my soul asunder
Frae mony friends wha proved so kind
To the rantin' poet, Pindar.

MY AIN DEAR WIFE

Do you mind the happy days langsyne,
When you, a country maid,
First vowed an' promised to be mine
In Pirnie's hazel shade?
Now mony fleeting years we've seen
Since first I did admire
Your guileless heart an' witching een,
My cheery wife, Dunsire.

Though forty years ha'e passed since you
Became my loving wife,
You've been to me affectionate, true,
The pleasure o' my life.
For, to secure the worlds wealth,
We never did aspire;
Content, while God hath gi'en us health,
My modest wife, Dunsire.

Throughout our lengthened pilgrimage,
The tear has filled our e'e;
But a'e our trust's in Him wha rules
The earth, the sky, an' sea.
We've aye a dud our backs to cleed –
A pantry, house, and fire;
There's little mair in life we need,
My coothie wife, Dunsire.

We've twa braw sons at our hearthstane,
An' ane far owre the sea;
While twa bit lasses bless our hame,
On Fifeshire's pleasant lea.
Twa wee pet lambs frae us are gane
To join the angel choir;

We'll meet them in the fold aboon,
My bosom wife, Dunsire,

Although upon life's troubled sea
We sair an' hard ha'e fought;
We aye ha'e been contented wi'
Our present humble lot.
Soon frae this lowly vale o' life
We'll rise to worlds higher,
Oh, never mair we'll part when there,
My bosom wife, Dunsire.

TEENIE WAUKINSHAW

Brag o' your fact'ry lasses braw,
Wi' smiles so sweet an' fine;
But nane o' them can match ava
This bonny lass o' mine.
My dear lass is young an' bonny,
An' fair without a flaw;
Here aboot you'll no find ony
Like Teenie Waukinshaw.

Her pure sweet heart is free frae guile,
The fragrance o' her breath
Does mak' the bonny flowers smile
Alang the verdant heath.
Your noble-born dames wud frown
On such a lass as she;
She's mair to me than the British crown –
The pithead lass for me.

When frae her wark she comes at nicht,
Wi' bright smiles in her e'e,
She mak's her mammy's labour licht
By working frank an' free.
The wet pit claes afore the fire,
She lays them in a raw;
Nae wonder that I do admire
My Teenie Waukinshaw.

I dinna think I'd gang far wrang
To mak' the lassie mine;
The lass that works and sings a sang
Will mak' her hoosie shine.
If she wud only say the word,
I'd dance, an' sing, an' craw,
An' draw aince mair my guide auld sword
For Teenie Waukinshaw.

A KISS

Inexpressibly pure and sweet
Is a delicious kiss,
A very heaven of love on earth,
A paradise of bliss.
To press a maiden to thy breast
And kiss her lips divine,
'Tis only then that man is blest
With happiness sublime.

MY AULD COMPANIONS

Peter Leslie (Late 71st H.L.I.), 60 Main Street, Lochgelly, Fife.

A Guid New Year, my comrades dear,
And happy be you ane an' a';
This night we are assembled here
To crack o'er days now far awa –
The bright and happy days of yore,
When we were young and in our prime,
And members o' that gallant corps,
The bravest in the British line.

Fond memories bring before my gaze
Familiar scenes o' auld langsyne,
When marching up the orient braes
Awa' in India's sunny clime.
Wi' you this night I'm glad to join,
An' shake hands wi' you ane an' a';
May happiness around you shine
When frae you I am far awa'.

God bless you a' an' keep you weel,
Companions o' my martial days;
Nae words can tell you what I feel,
Though I should write a thousand lays.
But while I've health an' strength to raise
In simple song this voice o' mine,
Our Regiment's deeds I'll ever praise –
Our happy hame in days langsyne.

An' you, dear sir,[5] we love to see,
An' hear your weel-kent voice again;
You led us up Umbeyla's hill
To honour, victory, an' fame.

---

[5] General Hope, C.B.

But though our sun's in life's decline,
An' gloamin' shades around us fa'
We'll aye remember auld langsyne,
An' happy days now far awa'.

PRIVATE THOMSON'S CHRISTMAS RESOLUTION

Malta. 1874.

I, PRIVATE SANDY THOMSON, swear
That I'll abstain till next New Year
From drinking whisky, gin, or beer,
Brandy, rum, or wine.
Should I this resolution break,
And my fair promise gang to wreck,
Let Marwood hing me by the neck
In twenty yards o' twine!

IN MEMORIAM – HENRY HUNTER

Who died at Lochgelly, 18th september, 1876, aged 40 years.

"And art thou gone, and gone forever." – Burns.

Malta, 1876.

My loving friend, and thou art gone
Into the sunless land;
While I am far from thee at home,
Upon a Southern strand.
Though many years have passed away
Since I beheld thy face,
It seem to me but yesterday
When we wander'd thro' the place.

Friend of my youth, I'm far away,
Beyond the rolling wave;
But my sad thought have gone to-day
Home to thy lonely grave.
Thou've found a grave 'mong kindred dust –
Affection's tear was shed,
When thy mourning friends stood round
Thy last low narrow bed.

Companion of life's pleasant hours –
Bright friend of other days –
No more we'll pull the summer flowers
Upon Benarty's braes;
No more we'll rove o'er heathery hills,
When falls the evening dew;
No more by Scotia's winding rills
I'll roam, dear friend, with you.

My loving friend, thy memory
Shall bright to me appear;

Thou'lt live in friendship's hallowed thought –
Affection's balmy tear.
Thy early death hath filled my mind
With melancholy's gloom;
But oh, dear friend, I hope to find,
Like thee, a Scottish tomb.

Sleep on. Dear friend, and take thy rest
In a quiet Scottish grave;
While I must ride, with grief oppressed,
O'er life's tempestuous wave.
My bosom friend, we'll meet again
Beyond the rolling spheres
No more to part – Farewell, till then,
Dear friend of early years.

TO A BEREAVED MOTHER

Young mother, dry thy tears and weep no more,
Thy child's not dead, but gone before;
The little child thou loved so well,
In sinless Paradise doth dwell.

He glanced at earth, then passed away
To blissful realms of endless day;
Look up from earth to heaven, where
Thy little one sits bright and fair.

MY AULD KNAPSACK

Guid frien' you've been to me, auld pack,
Nae mair you'll dingle on my back;
But let us hae a parting crack,
For my heart's fou
Wi' grief an' sorrow noo to tak'
Farewell o' you.

'Tis noo eleven years an' mair –
Lang years to me o' joy an' care –
Sin' you an' I together were
Acquainted first;
An' though you've made my lang back sair,
I never cursed.

You've kept my auld kit weel thegither
In sunny an' in stormy weather,
An' a' the letters frae my brither
That I ha'e gotten;
Forbye the Bible frae my mither –
A sweet love token.

I've had you stowed so full o' shoes,
Stockings, tow'ls, an' tartan trews,
Besides a year o' "Peoples News,"
Which made you heavy;
You've made the sweat rin owre my broos
Like draps o' gravy.

When wandering India's sunny clime,
'Mong grandeur stern and sublime,
At night my head wud oft recline
Upon your tap,
Where I've enjoyed a sweet, bit fine,
Refreshing nap.

Yon day you fell in Ganges river
I thought to tine you a' thegither,
When auld Forsyth, smart an' clever,
Rescued you clean
As you were sailing like a feather
Adoon the stream.

'Twas only ance that I can mind
That you, auld pack, was left behind,
When in a gloomy stored you pined
For saxty days,
While I was fighting Pagans blind
On Punjab's braes.

Four times we've crossed the Southern main,
And traversed mony a fragrant plain,
An' noo we've come abroad again'
Alas! To part:
To leave you on the soil o' Spain
Will break my heart.

If your successor chance to be,
Just like yoursel', a frien' to me,
Perhaps we'll whiles in social glee
Enjoy a crack;
But I'll remember till I dee
My auld knapsack.

LOCHGELLY NO MORE

Fareweel to Lochgelly, where happy I've been;
Fareweel, My dear mither, o' you I will dream;
For now I maun gang to a far distant shore,
And maybe return to Lochgelly no more.

Oh, mither, dear mither, if I had but known,
I'd been kinder to you in the days that are gone;
An' have had less sorrow for what I ha'e done,
For you, dearest mither, I've been a bad son.

Fareweel, my auld father, I oft did you wrong,
But love in my bosom for you it is strong;
I hope we shall meet on a happier shore,
Although I return to Lochgelly no more.

Fareweel, my dear brothers, and sisters so gay,
My love with you all, for I must away
To India's drear plains, where cannons do roar,
And I'll maybe return to Lochgelly no more.

Dear Harry and Johnnie, I hope you'll engage
To comfort our parents in their old age;
Oh, be kind to them both, and do what you can
For Davie, for Angie – oh! mind little Ann.

Fareweel, my dear country, my own lovely land –
Fareweel to thy mountains and valets so grand,
Fareweel to thy rivers and shell-spangled shore –
I'll maybe return to Lochgelly no more.

Fareweel to thy green plains and bonny cool shades,
That often have sheltered our lovely Scotch maids;
Fareweel to the thistle, which I do adore –
I'll maybe return to Lochgelly no more.

LOCHGELLY AGAIN – 1879

Oh, mony lang years o'er my Scotch pow have gane
Since I left you a' in our dear Scottish hame,
To wander to India, beyond the wild main;
But now I've returned to Lochgelly again.

Again I can gaze on my bright native hills,
And list to the flow of her murmuring rills,
And wander ance mair by bank, dell, and plain,
Since now I've returned to Lochgelly again.

The days o' childhood are now gane for ever,
Our barque's sailing fast down life's stormy river;
My heart at this moment is free from all pain,
Since now I've returned to Lochgelly again.

It is not the flow o' the glass passing round
That cheers me in seeing my dear native ground;
'Tis the sunshiny faces that mak' my heart fain,
Since now I've returned to Lochgelly again.

Sit near me, my dear friends, and let us a' sing
A sang o' langsyne till the cupples do ring;
Freedom and pleasure this ae night maun reign,
Since now I've returned to Lochgelly again.

PART THREE

UNPUBLISHED POEMS BY JOHN PINDAR

PINDAR POEMS FROM *THE COWDENBEATH AND LOCHGELLY TIMES & ADVERTISER*, 1895–1897

===============

COMPILED
BY
JAMES CAMPBELL

===============

MMXVI

PREFACE

The following rhymes were written by John Pindar, (Peter Leslie,) and were found while I was researching the *Cowdenbeath & Lochgelly Times & Advertiser* covering the period January 1895 to December 1897.

Prior to this time Pindar had produced quite a number of poems which appeared regularly in the columns of the "Fife News." At one time he also produced a book called *The Autobiography of a Private Soldier* which was printed by the "Fife News" in Cupar, in which he gives an account of his life from birth (1836) to the time he came out of the army in 1877.

There was also a small book of his poems produced by the Rev. A.M. Houston, B.D. minister of Auchterderran, named "Random Rhymes", containing some 159 pages of John Pindar's work.

However, I believe that most, if not all, of the works contained in this small book are works by Pindar that, up until the time that they appeared in the "Times" of 1895 -1897, had never appeared in print or been published.

James Campbell
Crosshill, Fife, 2016

PINDAR'S NEW YEAR ADDRESS TO THE BRAW LASSES AND LADS O' BONNY LOCHGELLY, NEW YEAR DAY, 1895

Air - "Wha'll be King but Charlie."

A guid New Year I wish ye a',
Nae fireside dull an' dreary;
But blessings at your hallen ca'
To keep you blithe an' cheery.

Chorus -

> *Then laddies a' an lassies braw,*
> *You can be blithe an' frisky,*
> *Without the aid o' drink ava;*
> *Nae pleasure in the whisky.*

The year that's gane, left mony a hame,
Wi' grief an' melancholy,
May we a' thrive in ninety five -
Ilk lass an' laddie jolly.
Then laddies a', &c.

May care an' want be strangers to
Ilk lass an' sprightly fellow.
An' friendship reign sincere an' true,
Through a' oor bonny Lochgelly.
Then laddies a', &c.

Dear burgh toon, nae son o' thine
In sorrow be repining,
But social love and joys sublime
At his bright fireside shining.
Then laddies a', &c.

Domestic peace can never be.
Among your burning glasses;

Awa wi' bacchanlian glee
My ain dear bonny lasses.
Then laddies a', &c.

False pleasures ever lurk within
Your so-called social drappy,
Without its aid we a' can be
Healthy, strong, an' happy.
Then laddies a', &c.

May he wha rules the stars aboon,
Send blessings sweet an' mony,
An' keep awa our bairnies a'
Frae the curse o' Caledonie.
Then laddies a', &c.

Lang may our lads an' lasses sing,
Wi' voices sweet an' mellow,
That soberness is sure to bring
Prosperity to Lochgelly.
Then laddies a', &c.

MY AULD PICK SHAFT

And must we part my dear auld friend?
A friend on whom I did depend,
But now your toil is at an end,
My auld pick shaft.

Afore piece-time I've seen us hole
Some three square yards o' guid splint coal;
I then was young and could control
My auld pick shaft.

You wisna made o' firey birch,
But guid Scotch ash that would far reach,
When I, my arms out would stretch,
My auld pick shaft.

Ae morning I had just my clothes off,
When wi' grief I saw your nose off,
You wis the last I got frae Joseph,
My auld pick shaft.

That nicht I didna tak you hame,
Some slashin' brusher chiel I ken,
Broke you ower some muckle stane,
My auld pick shaft.

Had I but catched that brusher chiel
Wha broke my shaft an' Tam White's steel,
I'd made him like a rotten squeal,
My auld pick shaft.

We've gi'en mony a hearty stroke
When we were buckled in the yoke,
Lang afore the brusher broke
My auld pick shaft.

But tho' nae mair we can prevail
Against the coal, we baith maun fail;
But now you'll dae for plantin' kail,
My auld pick shaft.

TO JENNY ON HER MARRIAGE DAY

Lochgelly, 1895.

I'm happy dear lassie to ken you are married
And settled in life wi' an honest young man;
To mak his days blithsome, happy, and cheery,
I ken you will do the best that you can.

A braw cantie hoose, an' a cheery hearth-stane
Are sure to delight a fond husband's e's;
A cosy bit hoosie will keep him at hame -
Gloomy hames maks husbands gang whiles on the spree.

Pull baith the gither, an' care, want an' sorrow,
Shall flee frae the hame devoted to love;
Hae mutual esteem an' respect for ilk other,
While hand in hand through the world you rove.

An' here I beseech you my sister Jenny
Strive hard to keep debt frae your door far away;
Be honest in life, an' you'll never want a penny
To keep off the wolf on a dark rainy day.

An auld bachelor may ken very little
Aboot the sweetness o' pure matrimony;
But to mak peace, should tempers be brittle,
Moisten them weel wi' love's sweet honey.

Should the ills o' life mak you lonely and dreary,
Cling to our Father wi' love and devotion;
His complacent smile will mak your days cheery,
While sailing o'er life's dark gloomy ocean.

THREE ACROSTICS

Ferguson, Hemens and Clare

F our and twenty years dear bard,
E ncompassed all thy years below,
R ight well thou wrote and gave to us
G lowing songs to cheer our woe
U nder the gloomy cares of life
S orrow was thine, and ceaseless strife.
O 'er thy lowly dying be
N one was there a tear to shed.

H eaven born singer, delightful bard,
E nshrined in our affections and regard,
M any cares were thine and domestic strife,
E mbittered thy short and unhappy life,
N ever was the captain worthy to be
S incerely loved by a good wife like thee.

C ompanion of the rural muse;
L asting fame sweet bard is thine,
A mongst our British bard thou shine;
R eason fled at last and left thee
E ngulfed in gloom and lunacy.

THE BONNY LASS O' GRAINGER STREET

When the sun cheers the warld wi' his smiling ray,
An' lambkins frisk bonny on mead, glen an' brae,
Oh, then what a pleasure wi' Jenny to meet -
Wy ain bonny lassie o' auld Grainger Street.

I ne'er saw a lassie sae fair, sweet an' braw,
When I'm twenty ane I will tak her awa,
She's modest an' handsome, she's pure an' discreet -
My ain bonny lassie o' auld Grainger Street.

At nicht I slip doon to her auld faither's door,
As silent's the cat on a saft carpet floor,
A tiral on the pane, then my joys are complete -
Wi' my bonny lassie o' auld Grainger Street.

My lassie can sing the dear sangs o' langsyne,
Tam Glen, Robin Gray, an' a Crony o' Mine,
But I'll be her Crony, jist you never leet,
I'll steal the sweet rose oot o' auld Grainger Street.

On the green Shiram brae when gloamin's are fine,
I meet wi' this sweet little lassie o' mine;
Oh, then what kisses delicious an' sweet
I get frae my lassie o' auld Grainger Street.

My ain chosen Jenny is lovely an' fair,
There's nane in the village wi' her can compare;
An' while my young heart in motion will beat,
I'll ne'er forsake Jenny o' auld Grainger Street.

OOR POET'S NATAL DAY

Recited at the Largo Burn's club by Mr William Bethune.

Peter Leslie, Late 71st H.L.I., 26th January, 1895.

We'er a' met again on our bard's natal day,
To honour the name that will never decay;
When this happy day to Scotchmen returns,
Their souls are on fire wi' the sangs o' our Burns.

O' sweet Scottish bards we've a hunder or twa,
Wha hae sung o' our lads an' lasses sae braw;
But still frae their sangs the heart fondly turns –
To the matchless strains o' our ain Rabbie Burns.

Ferguson, Ramsay, Tanahill, an' Macneil,
Hogg, Nicoll, Gillfillan, hae sung weel,
But a' our Scotch poets now in their urns -
The king o' them a' is our ain Rabbie Burns.

Gala Water, Young Jessy an' Eppie Adair,
Tam Glen, Corn Rigs, an' the sweet Banks o' Ayr,
Duncan Gray, Logan Braes, we a' sing in turns;
Oh, where is the bard like our ain Rabbie Burns?

Awa owre the sea in some far foreign clime,
What thousands this nicht will be singin' Lang Syne;
An' joy may rest on some Scotch heart that mourns
It's absence frae the land o' our Rabbie Burns.

Let eternal disgrace, infamy, an' shame,
Envelope the darkness for ever the name.
O' the cankerous churl wha scoffs at, or spurns
The land that gave birth to our ain Rabbie Burns.

Let your rhymers jeer, ca' me vulgar an' vain,
That a' I can give is cauld kail again;
But kail cauld or het when next birthday returns,
May I be among the admirers o' Burns.

EPISTLE TO A DEAR FRIEND

J.W.S.

May you hae friens' sincere an' mony,
Baith honest men and lasses bonny,
But I'll say this, my trusty crony,
   where'er you be,
Sincere an' true you'll no find ony
   Surpassin' me.

Kind hearted, canty, social frien',
Bright happy days we baith hae seen
Since first we trod the dewy green
   Around Cartmore;
Since those bright days we baith hae been
   On foreign shore.

But our ain land's the land o' flowers,
O' sylvian shades an' rural bowers,
We've often spent delicious hours
   On our dear braes;
You an' yer wifie, canty baith,
Inhalin' the pure simmer's breath
   'Mang flowers sae fine,
Wavin' ower the sweet verdant heath
   In simmer time.

A fortnicht noo I've haen to bide,
A prisoner at my air fireside;
I chanced to let my tea-pat slide,
An' broke the handle,
An' burnt my fit; noo I confide
In Dr Dendle.

My fit wis burnt into the bane,
Whalk caused me muckle grief an' pain;
But Pindar is himself again,
An' far frae dreary;
But joggin' at his simple strain
To keep him cheery.

I sometimes think that I've done wrang
In wastin' time wi' fruitless sang;
But noo I'm far ower auld to gang
'Mang lasses fair;
I've noo to spend my cheerless lang
Nichts in despair.

But though auld bachelor I be,
The bonny bairns I love to see;
Their prattlin' fill my heart wi' glee -
Be't lass or laddie;
But I hae nane to cry to me
Ta, Ta, or daddy.

But in this warld weel I ken
O' sour an' selfish married men,
Wha mak' their hooses but an' ben -
Domestic hells;
Gie me instead the silent glen
Where quietness dwells.

Matrimonial sweets to me
Can never here my portion be;
But still I love the blinkin' e'e
O' lasses yet;
The lowe o' love's young day, you see
I'll ne'er forget.

Blessings temporal, an' divine,
Aroond your ingle brightly shine,
Pure happiness an' peace sublime
On life's rough wave,
Until you reach the perfect clime
Beyond the grave.

SUMMER COMES AGAIN

"Thus we salute thee with our early song.
And welcome thee, and wish the long." - Milton

John Pindar, Lochgelly, 1st May, 1895.

Oh! bonny are the woodlands noo
Sin' winter's gane awa',
Our hills noo show a verdant broo
Instead o' driftin' snaw;
Cauld wintry winds hae ceased to blaw
An' gowans deck the plain -
Bright nature cheers the heart o' a',
Sin' summer comes again.

Sweet warblin' birds are trillin' forth
Their sangs o' love an' glee,
An' flowery garlands wavin' bright
Upon the sunny lea;
We noo can rove the the heathery dells
Wi' bosoms free o' pain -
Within the soul pure pleasure dwells,
Sin' summers comes again.

Supreme the joys o' summer days
To muse by vale an' hill,
An' listen to the music o'
Some sweet murmurin' rill;
The cuckoo in its calm retreat,
The lark's melodious strain,
Mak's the heart wi' pleasure beat
Sin' summer comes again.

Delightful scene o' peace an' bliss
To hear the kirk bells ring
On Sabbath morn, while round our path
The flowers o' nature spring;

Upon this smilin' world here
We canna aye remain,
But let's rejoice in sunshine clear
Sin' summer comes again.

Our sweet Lochside, our rural scenes,
Our plains, our vales, our shades,
Are lively wi' braw smilin' queens -
Our ain Lochgelly maids;
Noo youth an' age can roam the fields
Where summer beauties reign,
An' taste the joys that nature yields
Sin' summer comes again.

LINES KINDLY ADDRESSED TO MRS ELSPETH ERSKINE, ON HER EIGHTY-SECOND BIRTHDAY, 27th May, 1895

Lang twa an' auchty simmers noo
Hae come an' vanished frae your view,
Since you wis mammie's little doo,
In days langsyne;
An' here you are still strugglin' through
The vale o' time.

You're a grannie o' grannies here,
Whose bairns' bairns roond you steer;
At eventide may licht shine clear
Upon your path;
A' that's livin' is drawin' near
The gates o' death.

Great changes here your eyes hae seen
Since your bright years were sweet sixteen;
Your best an' dearest bosom frien'
Has gane away,
An' left you here on life's rough scene,
Noo auchty-twa.

Benarty Hill, the river Orr,
Our green Lochside, an' sweet Cartmore,
Those tranquil scenes in days of yore,
You roved among;
Nae thocht nor care at out hearts core,
When years are young.

Methuselah's years o' earthly time
Were nine hunder an' saxty-nine;
But after a' these years; your mine,
Grim death he cried,
The holy Bible book divine
Jist says he died.

When a' his length o' years were gane,
They wud appear as short as ane,
Though in the world noo there's nane
That lives sae lang;
But to the grave our lang last hame
We a' maun gang.

The tears o' sorrow never stain
Your aged cheek while you remain
A wanderer, where grief an' pain
Attend our race;
But there's a hame where pleasures reign,
An' perfect peace.

You've had your share o' worldly strife
Since you became a mither, wife,
You've found misfortune unca strife
On life's dark wave;
Though deein' here we enter life
Beyont the grave.

My dear auld frien' in life's decline,
Your settin' sun in beauty shine,
To rise again in yon bright clime,
Sae bright an' fair;
The trials o' life, the cares o' time,
Ne'er enter there.

THE HAME OWRE THE SEA

Air - "Land o' the Leal"

Just a wee bit sang, Ann,
No sae very lang, Ann,
Aboot yer ainsel,
In the hame owre the sea.
When the night are still, Ann,
I often sigh my fill, Ann,
To see your young face,
In the land owre the sea.

You wis a prattling thing, Ann,
An' whiles to me wud sing, Ann,
A canty wee sang,
In the hame owre the sea.
I hope I'm no to blame, Ann,
In leavin' you at hame, Ann

We'll a' meet again
In the hame owre the sea.

Oh! soon I'll see your face, Ann,
Beamin' wi' love an' grace, Ann,
In our native place -
Our sweet hame owre the sea.
The sicht wud please my e'e, Ann,
Yer wee roond face to see, Ann,
Toddlin' owre the green,
In the hame owre the sea.

Langsyne I kissed yer brow, Ann,
An' kaimed yer sunny pow, Ann,
Methinks I see thee now
In the hame owre the sea.
I think on days noo gane, Ann,
When roond the bright hearthstane, Ann,
You dangled on my knee,
In the land owre the sea.

Oh! May you sail through life, Ann,
Free frae the world's strife, Ann,
An' be a sweet wife
In the land owre the sea.
Ay keep yer spirits high, Ann,
I'll soon see Scotia's sky, Ann,
An' to your presence fly
In the hame owre the sea.

THE DOONFA' O' COOPERHA

Lochgelly, June, 1895.

Venerable place; and is this a'
That now remains o' Cooperha' -
A ruin bare, a desolate wa'
Is what I see.
Nae wonder though a tear should fa'
Doon frae my e'e.

Silent now is every room,
The smiles o' beauty nae mair illume,
The dear auld Raw's now fu' o' gloom,
An' dark an' drear,
The hoolets owre the riggin' soon,
Will nightly stear.

The families were scarcely gane,
When hordes o' savage vandals came,
Wha smashed the window's glass an' frame,
Wi' hellish glee.
In a' the Raw a bright hale pane,
You canna see.

Had this happened in days o' yore,
When knowledge passed the workman's door,
An' ignorance in streams galore,
Flowed through the land,
We might expected little more,
Frae savage band.

Bit savage instincts still do rage,
In this mighty progressive age;
The wretches wild wha did engage
To wreck the Raw,

Maun a' hae come wi' mash an' wedge
In ilka paw.

Auld Cooperha' in days langsyne,
Nursed healthy lads an' lassies fine;
When'er the sun begins to shine,
He strikes her wa',
They've lived till nearly ninety-nine
In Cooperha'.

I canna tell auld Cooperha',
Why you hae been condemned ava,
A healthier place I never saw
Wi' my twa een;
For pure an' cool the breezes blaw
Across your green.

Had the governin' powers instead,
Condemned that auld hole Launcherhead;
But she is left I'm much afraid,
To sing an' craw,
When you are numbered wi' the dead -
Bright Cooperha'.

In years gane by, bright families here
Assembled in their social cheer;
But dear auld Cooperha', I fear,
Nae mair we'll see
Bonnie lasses an' bairnies dear
Aroond your knee.

What changes has the world seen,
Since Eve came forth in Eden green;
Where now you stand, the sea hath been,
An' forests high,

Where birds wud sing sweet an' serene
To earth an' sky.Auld Cooperha'; theme o' my sang,

Auld Cooperha'; theme o' my sang,
Frae your grey wa's I'm wae to gang,
Here you hae stood for centuries lang,
But my heart's sair
To see you numbered now amang
The things that were.

THE RENOVATION OF THE OLD COAL ROAD

Respectfully dedicated to the Commissioners, Lochgelly, june, 1895.

GENTLEMEN:-

Alloo me to congratulate you
On the pleasant road you've made,
Wi' hard whinstane a' nicely laid,
Baith up an' doon;
O may your guid names never fade
Frae oor braw toon.

In tranquil hours o' gloamin' grey,
Baith auld an' young can roam that way,
Admirin' nature bright an' gay,
In simmer time;
You've made oor toon, I'm proud to say,
In beauty shine.

Ye chosen nine, lang may you be
Link't by the chain o' harmonie;
Believe me, sirs, I'm glad to see

That strife ne'er dwells
Aroond your board, but a' agree
Amang yoursel's.

Had I a grand poetic soul.
Your praises high I wud extol,
But in a wee garret hole
I coorie doon;
But while bluid through my veins does roll,
I'll love oor toon.

Wha wudna love oor burgh fair?
Where oor wee anes are taught wi' care -
For learning's neither scarce nor rare,
But shinin' clear;
An' preachers too, wha can compare
Wi' those we've here?

We've doctors famous for their skill
There's few in Fife their shoon cud fill,
When I am sick, a drap or pill
I get frae them;
They do their best when I am ill,
To ease my pain.

We've female teachers nice an' fine,
Where a' the female graces shine;
May a' their pleasures be sublime
While wanderin' here;
May they get husbands in their prime
By next leap year.

Noo drumlie dubs nae mair are seen
Alang this road sae neat an' clean;
We noo can walk abroad at e'en

Wi' feet dry shod;
Since the Auld Gig Coal Road
Has been made nice an' snod.

Some fifty years hae passed an' gane
Since I wroucht in the Little Dane;
Although a sma' bit laddie then,
I'll ne'er forget
O' fa'in' owre a muckle stane
At Donald's Yett.

But I am proud to ken that you
Hae made a road the Queen might view;
Noo cycle lads can spin richt through
To Stationhead,
Alang the road sae trim an' new,
That you hae made.

Mony a lad an' lassie noo,
When gently pass the e'enin' dew,
Alang that road like lovers true,
Will sing an' kiss;
When the sleepin' world canna view
Their raptured bliss.

I often tried in my young days,
An ungrammatic song to raise
In my dear little toony's praise;
An' still I sing
O' flowers upon the Birnie Braes
In vernal spring.

Dear burgh toon, lang may you be
Frae anxious thochts an' sorrow free,
An ilka man an' wife agree

At their fireside,
An' streams o' blessings frae on high
Aroond them glide.

Noo gentlemen, your humble bard,
Whose sangs before you've ofttimes heard,
Will do his best withoot reward,
Your praise to soon',
Until he fills in some graveyard,
A lonely tomb.

THE PITHEAD LASSIES

Three little fairies a' blythsome an' bonny,
It's heartsome to hear them singing wi' glee;
Through a' our burgh you winna find ony
Sae fair an' sweet as my ain lassies three;
Owre at the Newton, works Jeannie an' Mary,
Twa sweeter lassies your never did see;
While Nannie is jist a love-breathin' fairy,
Wi' twa rosey lips a pleasure to pree.

Dear little Nannie, sae modest an' canny,
Owre my affections she'll ever hold sway;
The heart-killin' fairy, sweet, bright, an' airy,
Is workin' jist now on auld Jenny Gray;
Oh! soon may I see Jean, Mary, an' Nannie
In hames o' their ain, cosie an' cheerie
Although I lo'e them, ye ken that I manna
E'er think o' ane o' them for my dearie.

The beauty an' charms o' love-sparklin' e'en
Brings back ither days to this heart o' mine;

In life's sunny morn on the Tollyhill green,
I roamed wi' Teenie my love o' langsyne;
Female affection, sae pure, sweet, an' tender,
Is the dowry o' Mary, Nannie, an' Jean,
Pure love far outshines the great regal splendour,
Surroundin' the throne o' rajah or queen.

THE BONNIE LASS O' COLQUHALLY

When the sun hides his head owre the hill o' the Clune,
An' the bright beamin' staries are a' peepin' doon,
Like angels o' mercy on our braw burgh toon,
I hie to the lass o' Colquhally.

Although humble the station she does occupy,
Lookin' after the household an' workin' oot bye;
The sweet little lassie is the pride o' my eye -
My bonnie young lass o' Colquhally.

Her transparent bosom is a stranger to guile,
She is free o' deception, o' cunnin', an' wile,
While her een are aye beamin' wi' loves rosey smile;
O' fair is the lass o' Colquhally.

Sweet lovely flower in a' the graces excellin',
My soul wi' the purest affection is swellin',
In a month or twa mair I'll hae a nice dwellin'
Wi' the bonny lass o' Colquhally.

Wi' sic a braw lassie for my sweet wifie here,
A carena a button for the prince or the peer;
A' the love o' my nature is pure an' sincere,
For the bonnie lass o' Colquhally.

THE DRUNKEN WIFE

Oh sic a wife, plague o' my life,
O what am I to do,
For wi' her raggin', fechtin' strife,
My heart is broken noo.
I do the very best I can
To keep her trig an' braw,
But still she tak's the cursed dram,
An' deaves me wi' her jaw.

Yestreen when frae the pit I cam',
Wi' claes wet to the skin,
The fire wis oot, nae dinner made,
My housie cauld within;
Wee Charlie, greetin' in his bed,
Said mammy wis awa'
To pawn my sark in Cowdenbeath
Alang wi' Jean McCraw.

The neebours ken that I hae been
To her a husband kind,
An' though I say't, a better ane
In Fife ye winna find.
When'er I speak, she's sure to bring
The dishcloot owre my jaw,
Then like a fiend she'll roar an' sing
Prince Charlie's noo awa'.

Ae day I made my auld hoose clean,
An' washed my Charlie's claes,
Wishin' in my heart I ne'er had seen
The cause o' a' my waes;
When hark! a kick cam' to my door,
A shout, an' wild hurrah,

It wis my wife come home again
Wi' her dear frien' McCraw.

She's left me noo in sic a state
That I'll ne'er win aboon,
Just yesterday she selt claes aff
My laddie's coat an' shoon;
Twa blankets, an' my lang lum hat,
This week hae run awa',
The washin' tub, the parritch pat,
Twa picks, the mash an' a'.

The little bairnies on the street
Molest me when they can,
They shout an' cheer, an' cry "Look! here
Comes drunken Katie's man".
The morn I shall cross the Firth,
An' join the Forty-Twa,
An' leave her wi' her drunken mirth
An' bosom frien' McCraw.

THE HILLS O' THE CLUNE

Air - "Bundle and Go."

Far, far hae I wandered since life's early morn,
I've seen great countries beyond the wide sea,
An' danced wi' sweet lassies in lands strange an' foreign;
But back to Scotia my thought wud aye flee.
Their bright sunny skies, an' flowers bloomin' bonny,
Their sweet orange groves, an' vales o' perfume
Made me think mair o' green Caledonia -
The plains o' Lochore, an' hills o' the Clune.

Though the towerin' Himalayas kiss the bright sky,
Nae charms for me like the Clune's flowery hill,
Where oft I reposed in bright days now gone by,
An' heard the murmur o' Fitty's calm rill.
The Ganges an' Jumma may sing to the Hindoo;
To me they sang but a mournful tune,
Amang a' their beauties I sighed for a sang
Frae my ain dear stream near the hills o' the Clune.

Memory dwells in the land o' our childhood,
Although in faraway lands we may roam;
The burns, the hills, the glens, an' the wildwood
Are near to the heart when far frae oor home.
Amang orient beauty I oftimes wud dream,
That I was layin' my weary head doon
On the verdant banks o' my bright flowin' stream,
That sweetly sings through the vale o' the Clune.

CRAVING A SON FOR HIS MOTHER'S DEBT

Your mother owed me John Bent,
Some eighteenpence or more,
The night before she died and went
To yon celestial shore.

I know it well my dear Macnair,
But I am much afraid,
You'll have to wait till we go there,
And see the money paid.

AUCHTERDERRAN

A lovely place is my old village home,
With its old grey kirk and ivy-crowned dome,
Green in my memory where'er I may roam,
The sweet village I left long ago.

When bound by the speed of bright orient scenes,
Memory would whisper remember the streams,
And flowery banks where the old bard still dreams
Of blissful days in the dear long ago.

In all my wandering I ne'er have forgot
The village school where we wrestled and fought,
Dear to my soul is the sweet little spot
I left long ago, long, long ago.

The trees waving there are still full of song,
And the wee burn flows tunefully along,
The grassy dells I wandered among,
In the sweet long ago, long, long ago.

The friends I left near that old village home,
Now sleep in their mools' neath the old kirk home,
Never again shall I hear the sweet tone
Of dear voices I heard long ago.

THE LASSIE O' THE MOOR

I ken a dear lassie baith charmin' an' gay,
Her breath has the sweetness o' pure flowers in May,
The love that she's kindled in this breast o' mine,
Can only expire wi' my last day o' time.

She's sweet as the rose on Benarty's green hill,
An' pure is her heart like Leven's clear rill;
Oh! hasten the time when I'll take her awa',
My ain lovely Phemmie, meek, modest, an' braw.

A font o' pure joy an' sweet pleasure to me,
Is the love-dartin' glance o' her laughin' e'e;
Though big my heart be it only has room
To enshrine the image o' sweet Phemmie Broon.

A palace o' grandeur may look bright an' fair,
But love an' affection is whiles absent there;
Independent I'll be, contentit, though poor,
Wi' my bonny lassie wha bides in the Moor.

The love for my lassie is pure an' sincere,
She's a' that I live for in life's valley here;
The world's wealth to me can never secure
Calm peace withoot Phemmie, the lass o' the Moor.

My days shall be sunny an' absent frae care,
When Phemmie an' me are a young wedded pair;
I'll then be a stranger to sorrow an' gloom,
When I press to my heart my ain Phemmie Broon.

SUSAN O' DUNNIKIER

The sun set ahint the hill,
The twinklin' stars were peepin' doon,
A' nature quiet an' labour still,
An' silent lang Kirkcaldy toon.
That calm sweet nicht I'll ne'er forget -
The moon abune wis bright an' clear,
When up the fragrant glen I met
My lovely Sue o' Dunnikier.

But when the simmer days were gone,
An' dreary winter had set in,
My peerless Susan's soul had flown
Frae this warld o' pain an' sin,
An' left me lanely in life's vale,
To sigh an' shed the unseen tear;
Oh, cruel death why didst thou steal
My bonny Sue o' Dunnikier.

Noo my lassie's sainted form
Lies silent in the lanesome grave,
Nae mair wi' me at early morn
She'll listen to Forth's dashin' wave;
She's gane where tears can never flow,
In yonder mansions fair an' clear,
An' left me mournin' here below,
For my dear Sue o' Dunnikier.

Ye lovely flowers sae pure an' fair,
That bloom sae sweet owre vale an' lea,
Oh, hing your head in sad despair,
An' mourn an' sympathise wi' me.
Mourn wi' me ye winds o' heaven,
Mourn oh forests dark an' drear.
Sorrow noo my heart has riven
Sin' I've lost Sue o' Dunnikier.

Oh, cheerin' hope, to meet again,
Although she's vanished frae my view,
The few days that I may remain
On earth will pass like mornin' dew.
While through the earthly scene I roam,
Her memory will linger here,
Whether on land or ocean's foam,
I'll mind the lass o' Dunnikier.

CORA

My charming young Cora,
Cares, trials, and sorrow,
Be strangers to you in this valley o' woe,
May sunshine and gladness
Dispel gloom and sadness,
And you will be happy whenever you go.

I ken you are canny,
And kind to your mammy,
We a' should be kind to our mither so dear,
An unkind word spoken
Has oftentimes broken
The peace o' the mither an' made her heart drear.

We'll ne'er find anither
To equal our mither,
So worthy o' our love, respect, and esteem,
A friend constant and true,
Be kind to her noo,
She's wearin' awa' frae life's troubled scene.

Lang may you be cheery,
A heart dull and dreary
Is no for a lassie o' beauteous sixteen,
The sad tears o' sorrow
Ne'er fa' frae my Cora,
Her days in the world be pure and serene.

HAPPY NOO, JEANIE

Oh, we are happy noo, Jeanie,
We are happy noo;
Sin' I hae gien ower drinkin',
An' gettin' myself fu'.
I'm wae to think dear Jeanie,
I did my means consume
On cursed drink, but noo fareweel
To misery an' gloom.

I hae te'an the pledge, Jeanie,
Resolved to drink nae mair
O' whisky bad that drove me mad,
Wi' grief an' dark despair.
Our bairns noo are blithe, Jeanie,
Nae sorrow noo they ken,
Just listen to their laughin' glee
As they run but an' ben.

Their little hearts are glad, Jeanie,
To see sic changes noo;
Nae mair they run wi' fricht to see
Their faither roarin' fu'.
While I breathe an' move, Jeanie,
I never shall again
Fill your young confidin' heart
Wi' sorrow, grief an' pain.

A MITHER'S ADVICE

Dear Aggie be canna, tak' care o' yoursel',
Keep far frae the lad wha wud fecht an' rebel
Against a' that's guid, for he never can be
A laddie to please your auld father an' me.

Dear mither, dear mither, ye ken very weel,
That Tammy's a sober, a real thrifty chiel';
He's no like my father, wha whiles likit you
On Pay Saturdays when he got roarin' fu'.

That's the reason, my lassie, I want you to ken,
That ye ne'er can be happy 'mong tipplin' men;
Nae poverty, sorrow, wud be seen ava,
If the drinkin' customs were banished awa'.

Dear mither, my Tammy is sober an' kind,
To indulge in strong drink the lad's no inclined,
But at our ain fireside it canna be wrang,
To enjoy a glass owre an auld Scottish sang.

My lassie, when first your dear father an' me,
In the bonds o' wedlock did try to agree,

Vicious companionship led him astray,
But whisky nae mair hauds him under its sway.

Dear mither, young Tammy, he telt me yestreen,
Where strong drink is ragin' he'll never be seen,
Sae gi'e me your blessin' an' happy I'll be,
For Tammy's the laddie I mean to gang wi'.

Dear Aggie, ye ken that I hae dune my best
To lead you in paths that Our Father hath blest;
In your hard trials here seek counsel frae God,
His bright smile can lighten life's dark gloomy road.

LINES KINDLY ADDRESSED TO MR ALEXANDER HUGH

Its lang since we did discover,
A genuine poet like you,
Your madrigals pleases the lover,
They are kindly, brilliant, and true.

We scan the newspapers in vain,
For something to read and admire,
Sweet, pure, and delightful your strain,
So pregnant with beauty and fire.

If a fault you have it is this;
For a bard your songs are but few,
What I say don't take it amiss,
You're the pride of our rhyming crew.

You are still exalting in youth,
Arise from your lethargic chair,

And sing of love, beauty, and truth,
And charm the hearts of the fair.

Already you're known to fame,
This laurel encircles your brow,
You'll live to secure a great name,
Co-existent with Byron and Rowe.

Although with your ledgers and bills,
Your time is devoted each day;
Forget not Parnassian rills -
Remember the Muses I pray.

The bright beams of fancy and wit,
Blend sweetly in every line;
Arouse ye great bard, let us get
Some more of the grand and sublime.

Your tuneful accents, strike the mind
Of a humble admirer like me;
But count me a friend, and you'll find
Me generous, loving, and free.

Forgive me this song in your praise,
Ere I hide my head in the tomb;
But one thing I know, your sweet lays
In beauty immortal shall bloom.

THE OLD COT IN PLANTATION STREET

Respectfully dedicated to Robert McQuillen, late 93rd
highlanders.

In Plantation Street whaur oor famed Page wis born,
Stands an auld cot in ruins noo grim an' age worn;
The dingy auld wa's are noo conquered by age,
Whaur dwelt Jenny Baxter an' auld Mary Page.

To me that auld cot is still grand in decay,
Memory dwells there than can ne'er pass away;
Though auld noo an' grey, an' chequered my lot,
While feelin' exists I'll mind that auld cot.

Oh, weel do I min' the bright days o' langsyne,
When my brither an' me wi' aunty wud dine,
In the auld cottage there noo roofless an' bare,
Wi' her Launcherhead bairns her bannock wud share.

Frae that lowly cot sprung a brave sodger son,
Wha stood on the field where great battles were won -
A hero, a man, in the Crimean clime,
Noo nearly the last o' Sir Colin's Red Line.

In dear Lochgelly there's strange faces noo,
Micht question if my simple story is true;
Ay, true as the Gospel, which mony can tell,
Wha's kent the auld village as lang as mysel'.

In simmer's sunshine, an' in winter's wild wind,
Near that auld grey cot a strange pleasure I find;
Rumination at times mak's the silent tear fa',
As I linger at nicht near the dark gloomy wa'.

Auld venerable cot, noo lonely an' still,
Like those that's awa' I maun wear doon the hill,

But while the Lord spares me on life's troubled stage,
I'll mind aunt Jenny an' auld Mary Page.

LINES TO MR CHARLES WILKIE

C ontentment reign in your domicile,
H eaven's sweet blessings upon you smile,
A ffection's bright smile, pure and sincere,
R eign round your hearth in the world here;
L aud and bless you Maker always,
E ncompass your home with songs of praise,
S orrow and pain may you never know,

W hile wand'ring through this valley of woe;
I llume your mind with works of men
L ike Chalmers, Guthrie, and Bishop Ken,
K eep your mind serene, and you shall be
I nwardly happy on life's rough sea,
E nvy I know has no home with thee.

THE LASS O' COWDENBEATH

'Twas when the flowers were bloomin' fair,
An' tassels waved frae ilka tree,
When first I met young Mary Clare
Wi' love an' beauty in her e'e.
My bonnie lass, sweet an' sincere,
I've sworn to protect till death,
There's no anither lassie here
To match the lass o' Cowdenbeath.

Since first I heard her silvery voice,
Happiness to my soul has flown,
She's made a lonely heart rejoice,
She's promised now to be my own.
Her loving heart will be a throne
On which I'll reign in bliss supreme,
The smiles will lighten up my home,
That sparkle frae her bonny een.

For world's gear I dinna care,
Just gie me health to work an' toil;
Content wi' that, I'll seek nae mair,
But just my Mary's cheery smile.
When wi' age we hirple doon
To sleep the silent clods beneath,
The fragrance o' our lives will bloom
Like flowers upon the Hill o' Beath.

IN MEMORIAM

CECILIA BURGESS.

"Her memory long shall live alone
In our hearts as mournful light,
That broods above the fallen sun,
And dwells in heaven half the night."

TENNYSON.

Peter Leslie. Lochgelly, 14th March, 1896.

And thou art gone, oh! Cecilia dear,
Where sorrow reigns no more.
Gone to the mansions bright and clear,
On yonder peaceful shore.
Though young in years the spoilers came
And plunged our home in gloom,
The music of thy silvery voice
Is silent in the tomb.

God's chast'ning hand was laid on thee
With sufferings sore oppressed,
But He hath taken thee away
To be with Him at rest.
We saw thy years expanding bright,
Like flowers in smiling May,
But God hath called thee, and to-night
We wipe the tears away.

Thy pure and blameless life hath closed
In spring of life's young morn,
Thy voice is hushed, and we are left
Now lonely and forlorn.
No more beneath these azure skies
We'll hear the voice again,
That filled our home with music sweet,
From thy delightful strain.

But here our tears shall flow apace
For our young daughter gone,
Nature must pour its sorrow forth
For our departed one.
The tears we shed upon thy grave
Shall with affections swell,
Oh, Lord! enable us to say,
Thou hast done all things well.

Thy memory enshrined shall be
Within our sad hearts here,
Until we hear thy angel voice
In heaven sweet and clear.
Oh! what a blessed, cheering hope
To us poor mortals given,
That sundered hearts shall meet again
To part no more in heaven.

OUR WEE PET LAMB

Our wee pet lamb frae us is ta'en,
An' we're left lonely noo.
We miss her smile an' prattlin' glee,
An' fair sweet sunny broo.
The second lamb o' our wee fauld,
Death has untimely torn,
Noo in the silent grave lies cauld
Her pure angelic form.

Nae mair we'll strain her to the breast,
Or round her cradle creep,
Be still, O soul! our lamb's at rest,
In Jesus blessed sleep.

Sorrow's nicht will soon be o'er,
This earth is no our hame,
Lord, gie us grace to reach the shore,
Whaur our wee Mary's gane.

THE PLEASURES O' CHILDHOOD

Lonely I roam on a far foreign soil,
Far frae the joys o' my sweet native Isle,
Where happy I wandered in life's young day,
But pleasures o' youth hae a' fled away.

I've dear recollections o' the green braes,
Where grew the sweet gowans, hazels, and maize,
An' roved through the dell at calm gloamin' day,
But joys o' childhood hae a' fled away.

In those bright days I had nae thought nor care,
The warld afore me was bloomin' an' fair,
Free as the lark in the bright simmer day -
How youth's golden age has a' fled away.

In those lovely times - sweet days o' langsyne,
What harmless joys an' pleasures were mine;
As blithe as the lambs in the sweet sunny May,
Was my young heart in the days far away.

I'm wearin' fast to the land o' the leal,
Where bliss is substantial, an' joy is real;
There, I shall never feel nature's decay
In the glorious realms o' endless day.

A MEMORY

"Far oft thou art but ever nigh;
I have thee still, and I rejoice;
I prosper, circled with thy voice;
I shall not lose thee tho' I die" - TENNYSON.

The bright sun was spreading his sweet beams below;
The glad earth was laughin' an' lovely to see,
An' the auld Contel burn was murmurin' low,
A cheery pure sang owre the gowan-decked lea,
The dewdrops were kissin' sweet flowers on the scene,
That waggit their heads in luxurious bloom;
A' nature was jubilant like my winsome queen,
When we met that day on the banks o' the Clune.

I've sailed owre the sea an' traversed lands foreign,
But her memory in my bosom maun dwell,
I canna forget the dream o' life's morn
When we roved owre the braes near Clune Bably's Well;
Sad was our parting 'neath the green hazel trees,
Still the sun of hope would our bosoms illume,
That I would return frae wild stormy seas
To wander aince mair owre the banks o' the Clune.

Again when I trod the scenes o' my childhood,
The bleak winds did rattle an' rave;
But Teenie, my lassie, the peerless an' good,
Was hid frae my een in the mould o' the grave,
Oh, never again shall her sweet laughin' face
Be seen on the hills 'mang the long yellow broom;
Sad now is the look o' the aince cheery place,
Since Teenie nae mair wanders owre the sweet Clune.

Perhaps her pure spirit will oft wander near
The place where we met in days of yore;
The music o' her voice will sound in my ear

When wanderin' alane on the banks o' the Orr,
Frae yon happy land where Teenie is roamin',
Wha kens but her spirit will often come doon,
An' meet wi' her lover in the hours o' the gloamin'
Among fairy flowers on the braes o' the Clune.

GOING FOR A SOLDIER

I left my bonny country toon
In the sweet month of smiling June,
When nature's face was a' in bloom,
Oh fair to see,
And bonnie waved the yellow broom
Ower bank an' lea.

But smilin' nature cudna cheer
My heart, I felt so lone an' drear,
As frae the village I did stear
That lovely morn,
And birds were singing sweet an' clear
On dewy thorn.

Though hills an' vales were vocal round
Wi' a' sweet harmonious sound,
Nae pleasure in their voice I found,
My heart was fou
Wi' thocht an' grief as I gaed doon
The Avenue.

I taen my way by Auchtertool,
An' passed its bonny silver pool,
An' passed the glen where once a duel
Was deadly fought

Wi' Sandy Bosewell an' Duncarn,
Boot feeding stot.

On Baubee Farm I stood a wee,
And backward caist a straining e'e,
Thinking that I still might see
My dear wee toon,
But I just saw the level lea
In flowery bloom.

My native friends, I've thocht sin syne,
Had I returned at the time,
There wudna been a British Line
Ere seen my face,
I was surely born to join
The fighting race.

What made me leave I canna tell,
My friends at home a' loved me well,
But their advice heedless fell
Upon my ear,
It maun ha'e been yon whisky gill
That brought me here.

I'm sure you mind Kinnesswood toon,
When ower the stair you flang me doon;
An' on the stanes did crack my croon,
An' nose wi' clure,
Which made me six weeks keep my room
A' through thy po'er.

Strong drink creates an appetite,
Destroys talents though pure an' bright,
An' ruins the soul which is the light
O' immortal man,

To guide him in his heavenward flight
To the better lan'

I've known men to occupy
Positions eminent an' high,
When you stapt in an' made them lie,
Wi' want an' woe,
Oh, cursed drink come tell me why
Men love you so.

Men, yes, an' lovely women too,
Hae often been disgraced by you,
Heaven what a sight, a woman fou
Wha hisna seen,
The dignity o' her fair sweet broo
So low an' mean.

My kind auld mither spak to me
Wi' persuasive voice an' kindly e'e,
That I my folly soon might see,
An shun your ways,
Indeed she'd often prophesy
You'd end my days.

Ye maidens o' my native land
Oh, never gie your Scottish hand,
To him wha wudna tak' his stand
Baith firm an' sure,
An' join the happy temperance band
Wi' principles sure.

EPISTLE TO TREASURER A. HUGH

Lochgelly, 3rd June, 1896.

My dear young bard, pride o' Lochgelly,
Wha writes in strains sublime an' mellow,
Your poetry, dear friend, I tell ye,
Has always been,
To me like Burns, Hogg, an' Shelley,
Where bright thoughts gleam.

Perhaps you may baith rage an' storm
At me to write in such a form,
I'm frae the shire where you were born -
A grand Fife toon;
Where blyth you roamed in life's young morn,
A canty loon.

You may think my presumption strong,
Unpoetical, an' very wrong,
To send you neither poem or song,
But vulgar rhyme,
Which you might think is rather long
For you to sing.

But surely you'll no angry be
At this bit rhyme sent on to thee;
I ken your heart is kind an' free,
An' wont rehearse
The imperfections you shall see
In my crude verse.

I can't lay claim to such a mind
Like Burns, our bard inspired, refined,
My Scottish Muse is unca blind
In her crook'd way;

But you'll forgi'e her if she's kind
In what she says.

Our sweet poets ha'e sung their fill,
Ramsay, Burns, an' Tannahill,
They've classified each stream an' rill
In Caledonie,
An' sung the praise on bank an' hill,
O' lassies bonnie.

Lang years hae passed since your young een
First gazed on Fifeshire's forests green;
When often you ha'e happy been,
When wanderin' wi'
Some bonnie, handsome, smiling Jean,
Wi' love-lit e'e.

The happiest days o' our short life,
We've spent amang the hills o' Fife;
Ye ken there's bonnie lassies rife,
Fair, sweet, an' gaudy,
Wud rax the stays to be the wife
O' a Scotch laddie.

Although I've rovedin a hostile soil,
Far frae my bonnie native Isle;
I ha'e returned a short wee while,
Wi' you to sit,
Right cheery owre a female smile
In dear Fife yet.

But now, dear bard, I think its time
For me to close my uncouth rhyme;
Although my thoughts are no sublime,
You needna wonder;
But I'm your friend while I can sign
My Name John Pindar.

THE AGE OF MY BRAVE REGIMENT

Air - "Wearing o' the Green."

One hundred years have passed away,
Since our brave fighting corps
Was formed up first in bright array,
Upon our Highland shore.
And what is more, our gallant corps
Ne'er saw a cloudy day;
For where the fields of fame were fought,
It nobly held the sway.

Chorus -

> *Then hurrah, hurrah, for the Seventy-First,*
> *Its gallant deeds do shine*
> *As bright as those of any corps*
> *That form the British Line.*

The marshal glory and renown,
We have a noble share;
Whenever military deeds were done,
The seventy-first was there -
Cape of Good Hope and Hidostan,
Rilea, and Fountes de Honor;
Those sanguinary fields our fathers fought
in brilliant days of yore.

Vimiera, and Corunna too
Pyrenees, and famed Victoria,
And on the plains of Waterloo
They reaped eternal glory.
At Orthes, Nive, and Almaraz
They linked their bayonets there,
And reeling sent the Frenchmen back
With shouts of grim despair.

And we, the men of modern times,
Can proudly speak and tell
How in the sultry orient climes
Our regiment fought and fell.
Some regiments glory in the name
Which on the colours shine
But few there are, oh! gallant corps,
Can be compared with thine.

Remember, brave young soldiers,
Our noble Seventy-One
Have fought and bled on many fields
Beneath the foreign sun;
And should the bugle sound to-morrow,
Rouse us to fight again,
Remember the dear won glory
We ever must maintain.

The spirits of our forefathers
On yon celestial shore
Would frown upon a craven heart
In their distinguished corps.
To us they have bequeathed a name
Of glory and renown,
Achieved on fields of storied fame
For country, queen, and crown.

Our regiment great and glorious.
The gallant Seventy-One,
Has ever stood victorious
Where noble deeds were done.
Then let each soldier fill his cup,
And give three ringing cheers,
Our corps at first was formed up
This day one hundred years.

MY WEE STUMPIE WEAN

My wee bonnie bairn, my sweet butterba',
There's music an' gladness in your cheery craw;
Losh me, but your tearin' the cat by the nose,
An' skelt a' the milk for young Charlie's drap brose.

Noo you've gotten the shears, an' you'll very soon
Mak' lang silken ribbons o' mammy's black goon;
Was there a laddie in the world like that,
My sweet - lod he's fa'in owre the big parritch pat.

My sweet golden angel what's wrang wi' ye noo,
You've hurt on the auld pat you're fair sunny broo;
But noo dinna greet my ain darlin' lammie,
An' you'll get a braw horse the morn frae mammy.

I canna be watchin' you Jamie like this,
But gi' your dear mammy a nice like kiss,
I canna sit a' day wi' you on my knee,
So rin awa' oot till I mask daddy's tea.

In a very short time my Jamie cam' in,
The blood tricklin' doon frae his sweet rosy chin;
Imitatin' big laddies at kickin' fitba'
He skinned his wee chin on a new paintit wa'.

I washed his roond facie an' put him to bed,
Wi' a mither's prayer an' a clap on the head;
Though sair is the fecht wi' a wee stumpie wean,
When he sleeps at my breast my sorrows are gane.

THE YOUNG SOLDIER'S RETURN

After two severe campaigns in Egypt and Chitral.

We've a' met again roond the cheery hearthstane,
To ha'e a bit crack on the days that are gane;
How are you, dear father, an' how are you a',
Sin' I left Lochgelly to roam far awa'?

When I left my village in days o' langsyne
To meet a stern foe in Egypt's hot clime,
My bonnie wee sisters sae fair, young an' braw
Were the pride o' my heart when I gaed awa'.

I met sister Bella wi' bright laughin' e'e,
An' Henny, sae kindly an' bonnie to me,
I'm glad now to see them a' happy an' braw
Sin' I returned frae the lands far awa'.

It's heaven on earth when kind friends fondly meet
By a cheery fireside to mingle sae sweet,
In the lang winter nights when the dreary winds blaw,
An' ha'e a bit crack on the days that's awa'.

I see the bright scenes o' my life's early day,
The green Tolly Hills an' the sweet Birnie Brae,
Smiling summer deck'd them in gowans sae braw
In yon bonnie days afore I gaed awa'.

In Chitral my thoughts on memory's wing
Wud whiles wander hame to this bright cheery ring;
In fancy this sweet social circle I saw
While meeting a grim foe in lands far awa'.

Let sorrow an' trouble this ae night depart,
While the sunshine o' bliss beams bright on each heart;
Dull care at our hallen this night needna ca',
While we ha'e a bit crack on the days that's awa'.

THE LASSES O' LOCHGELLY

T hou bonny lasses o' oor auld Lochgelly,
H ear me for a wee, an old sodger fellow;
E ntranced I am wi' thy voices sae mellow.

L ang may you be strangers to sorrow an' pain,
A nd a pleasant husband may ilk lassie gain,
S incerely I wish frae this auld heart o' mine,
S uccess to you a' wi' sweet pleasure sublime;
E ndevour to lead a pure, bright, holy life,
S in is ever present wi' anger an' strife.

O nward an' upward let your motto be,

L earn to do well, an' shun bad company;
O bserve what I say, keep your conduct serene,
C ut evil companions, low, vulgar, an' mean,
H ave nothing to do with a young man ava
G iven to swearin', banish such far awa',
E nduring sweet creatures I'll noo say nae mair,
L ang may you tread paths o' the virtuous an' fair;
L oving husbands I hope ilk lassie will find,
Y outh's still on your side, keep an innocent mind.

THE LASS O' CONTEL RAW

Sweet lovely maid o' Contel Raw,
I maun gang noo far awa',
Frae oor bright plains an' rural ha',
An' cross the rolling ocean.
Duty calls me to Africa's plain,
Where terror an' grim murder reign;
Our gallant countrymen are slain
Across the rolling ocean.

In grief let love be still our balm,
To mak' our hearts tranquil an' calm,
Though I maun wander where the palm
Waveth over the ocean.
In a' the changes I may see
On Africa's bright, but bloody lea,
My heart shall be the same to thee,
Far ower the rolling ocean.

Sweet Scottish maiden ere we part,
Oh! let me clap thee to my heart,
Dearer, sweeter to me thou art,
Than a' the wealth o' the ocean.
Fareweel, my pretty Fifeshire queen,
Calm your bright but tearfu' een,
I'll soon return in Contel green,
Back ower the rolling ocean.

EPISTLE TO COLOUR-SERGEANT W. ANDERSON

He was a warrior stern and keen,
And had in many a battle been. - SCOTT

John Pindar, late 71st H.L.I.

A soldier every inch thou art,
And borne a most distinguished part,
You've bravely fought wi' gallant heart
On field o' fame,
And now in civil life you start
Wi' an honoured name.

In all the places that you've seen,
Throughout the name you've been,
A soldier to our gracious queen,
What soldier durst
Charge you wi' an action mean
In the seventy-first.

Many long years have flown away,
Since through the scenes o' life's young day,
You roamed your native fields in May
'Mong flowers so green,
Since then in many a hostile fray
You've battled keen.

Romantic lands you've soldiered through,
From Kyber Pass to bright Corfu;
And cimmerian Crimea too,
Your eyes have seen;
But time would fail to tell to you
Where you have been.

Wherever rang the British arms;
Where'er was sounded war's alarms -

That was the music had the charms
For men like you;
Thou art what Shakespeare proudly terms
A soldier true.

When nations on the earth are shakin',
And kings upon their thrones are quakin',
In such commotion lets be takin'
Supreme delight,
Our trade is brisk when kings are makin'
Their soldiers fight.

Should all the world in peace agree,
And mankind live in harmony,
Our profession of chivalry
Is gone for ever,
A popular trade since Sandy[1] crossed
The Indus river.

How grand to be a son of Mars,
And fight in great immortal wars,
And though you get some cuts and scars
That's soldiers fame;
Yea! should you fall 'mong crimson cars,
You glory gain.

But should war's sound be heard no more;
And silent aye the cannons roar,
And peace reign all the world o'er
You need not sigh
Since what you've done on foreign shore,
In days gone by.

Upon your breast five medals gleam,
Which must command respect, esteem,

---
[1] Alexander the Great.

Where'er your martial form is seen
Thou son of Mars;
The world will see that you have been
In brilliant wars.

Now, after all your scenes of strife,
Glitter and pomp of martial life;
In your new home may blessings rife
Be yours, until
Death takes you and your loving wife
To Zion's hill.

May streams of bliss around you glide,
Domestic peace at your fireside,
And sorrow, want, and care keep wide
Of your hearthstone;
And wife and children be the pride
Of your Scottish home.

ISABEL

Flower of the village, I'll never
Forget a lassie like thee,
Thy mind is brilliant and clever,
And sweet love beams frae your e'e.

I hear thy sweet delicious voice
Thrill forth a cheery lay,
Which makes my very soul rejoice,
And drives dull care away.

Thy form's engraven on my mind,
Nothing shall ere efface

From out of the chambers of my soul
The brightness of thy face.

From scoundrels and villains vile
Thy path be ever free,
A wicked man who would beguile
An angel such as thee.

From virtue's path, my Isabel,
I know you'll never stray,
But keep your life pure and serene
Like flowers in smiling May.

When this world dissolves away,
And nature's mountains riven,
Oh! may thy bloom in endless day
A fragrant flower in heaven.

SCOTCH POETS

Caledonia has given birth
To Burns, Scott, and Grahame,
And the lovely poet, Michael Bruce,
Who sang near Leven's stream;
Nicol, Macneal, Moir, Motherwell,
Ramsay, Ferguson, Tannahill,
Have all sung sweet and well,
And classified through Scotland wide,
Each mountain, stream, and dell -
Their songs are sung the world through
Wherever Scotchmen dwell.

EVENING

The silver moon is beaming
O'er the evening's birth,
The twinkling stars are peeping
O'er the smiling earth.
Nature's hushed in calm repose
And bright the brilliant sky,
And every gentle gale that blows
Wafts tales of days gone by.

THE SODGER LADDIE

Tak' my advice, my young laddie,
An' marry the lassie sae braw,
Frae here doon to lang Kirkcadie
You'll no find her equal ava.
Although you ha'e wander'd in lands
Beyont the saut sea far awa',
You are hame where bright beauty stands
In a lass, the best you e'er saw.

Egypt's plains may be glorious
To a sodger lad in his prime,
Or even in India victorious,
Where you fought 'mang granduer sublime.
I've kent you a lang time, but noo
Your frien's in the doonward decline,
The hair is noo grey on my broo,
Still I lo'e the days o' langsyne.

Let medals adorn the breast,
O' sodgers like us in a fight,
Believe me, I'd rather be pressed
By a braw Scotch lassie at night.
In my auld domicile, weel ye ken,
I muse ower the days that are gane,
I've nae kindly wife o' my ain
To brighten my cheerless hearthstane.

THE FLOWER O' CRAIGDERRAN

One smiling June morn I happen'd to wander
Amang the green fields o' bonny Pitcairn,
When I met my dear lassie sae charmin' an' sweet,
A fragrant rose frae the braes o' Craigderran.

My heart was transported when Jean I first courted,
But fate has now parted my lassie an' me,
But the wealth o' the world, although it were mine,
I'd part wi' it now for a blink o' her e'e.

In calm hours o' gloamin' we oftimes would wander
On Balgregie Braes, were waves the green fern,
Admirin' the beauty o' nature's pure granduer,
What joys were mine wi' the flower o' Craigderran.

Far, far ha'e I wander'd since that lovely morn,
Amang scenes o' danger, o' dashin', an' darin',
Still abune excitement my heart was forlorn
When I thought o' Jeanie, the flower o' Craigderran.

Dreary the world since I parted wi' Jeanie,
O' seein' her again I'm nearly despairin',
Lang years maun gang by ere I can share
The smiles o' my lass on the braes o' Craigderran.

SOCIALISM

If Socialism wud banish sin
Frae this bright land o' ours,
The lion wi' the lamb wud rin
Amang the simmer flowers.
But happiness can never reign
Till Gospel glories shine
Ower the world, an' men ha'e learned
To lead a life divine.
If Socialism here below
Improved the human mind,
We'd hear a vulgar language flow
A little mair refined.
But Socialism may spout an' try
To equalise beneath the sky;
There's one thing since the world began,
We've had the poor an' wealthy man,
An' I'm convinced such things shall be
Till time sinks in eternity.

SONG DEDICATED TO MY BONNIE LASSIE KATE

M y winsome dear dear lassie is charming an' gay,
Y oung, sweet, an' blooming like the flower's o' the May.

B lithe is the blink o' her bonnie black e'e,
O h! she's the lassie that I'm to gang wi';
N ae lass in the parish like her I can see,
N eat, handsome, modest, an' ardent an' free;
I 've kent Katie now for three years or mair,
E nrapturing joys wi' her I now share.

L ads in Lochgelly wud like weel to get
A heart-easing smile frae my rosey pet;
S orow an' trouble I'll ne'er see again,
S ince Kate has promised that she'll be my ain;
I mpressed by my kindness, my Katie will be
E ver careful to watch an' hover o'er me.

K indly, sweet lammie, I'll tak' you awa',
A fore the New Year comes this length ava;
T hen we'll be happy as lambs on the lea,
E mbracing ilk ither, my Katie an' me.

THE LOMOND HILLS

I love to view the Lomond Hills
When they are white wi' snaw,
I love the bonny Lomond Hills
When summer breezes blaw.
When summer decks the trees wi' green,
An' gowans on the lea,
Ah! then it is a lovely scene,
The Lomond Hills to see.

I love to roam her flowery plains,
An' hear the birdies sing
Their lovely harmonious strains
That ushers in the spring.
Let others boast o' hills an' glens,
An' mountains wild an' free,
My native place, my rural dens,
The Lomond Hills for me.

'Twas there my father toiled for days
In blasting the limestane,
An' near repose the silent clay
O' dear friens now gane hame.
'Twas there I first breathed native air,
Near Lomond Hills so high,
Now a' my wish is to lie there
When'er I come to die.

MY FALSE LOVE

My soul can never love again,
A maiden false as thee;
No other maid will give me pain,
Since you have slighted me.
When basking in your sunny smile,
My soul believed you true,
But now falsehood, deceit, and guile,
Belongs to such as you.

You've made my world a wilderness,
And left me in despair,
My grief is more than I'll express,
To you - oh! fickle fair,
Still lovely maid I wish you well,
May happiness be thine;
In tranquil moments you must feel
For this lone heart of mine.

SONG DEDICATED TO MY ANNA WILLIAMSON

M odest an' handsome, charming an' fair,
Y outh's wi' my Anna, what do I want mair.

A mang a' the lassie that I daily see,
N ane but my lassie has charms for me;
N othing like her my affections can win,
A maiden o' beauty, a hater o' sin.

W ordly cares an' vexation I time
I n the presence o' this bonnie lass o' mine;
L ang frae her sweet bosom I'll draw
L ove so delicious to keep grief awa',
I ts now mony years since young Anna I saw
A smiling wee lassie baith winsome an' braw;
M y heart's entranced wi' the love o' her e'e;
S upremly blest wi' my lassie I'll be;
O n the rolling waves o' life's stormy sea
N othing but death can part Anna an' me.

LINES TO MY CRITIC

In my garret ha' I sit, smoke, an' blaw,
An' string up my songs in the night,
But little I care for great learned jaw
That says it is blethers I write.

Common sense o' grammar are very good
If language is holy an' pure,
But educational men are whiles rude,
An' use words that are hard to endure.

The world's display o' rhyming power now
Disna show a Shakespeare an' Burns;
Our grand Scottish bard wha followed the plough
The hearts o' his countrymen warm.

My elegant critic go on in your ways,
An' stigmatise my simple rhyme,
You should remember in auld Jenny Gray,
I wrought before school boards did shine.

Few schools ere I saw in days now awa';
Poverty was high in langsyne,
But nothing care I for your critics high
In knowledge an' language sublime.

So lang as I have the lasses so braw
I'll flourish an' write in my prime,
For weel do I ken the sweet creatures a'
Are fond o' this nonesense o' mine.

I've heard critics say our church to them now
Is just superstion an' gloom;
It never had men that could be compared
To Bolingbroke, Voltaire, an' Hume.

CHRISTIAN MARTYRS

Where is the land that can boast
Like ours of glorious names;
Our island home has the most
Who died in barbarous flames;
The gentle Cowper tells how
Our Scotch heroes had striven,
Till flames o' persecution
Chased them up to heaven.

YOU'LL REMEMBER ME

Severely frowned my Colonel when
He read my drunken crime,
For gettin' fou wi' Sandy Blane
On dirty Gin an' wine,
An' drunk upon the Barrack gate
The yestreen at half-past three;
Such punishment you now shall have
That you'll remember me.

Four times this year you have appeared
Before me at this board;
But now you'll have the punishment
My influence can afford,
When up in Wind Hill's gloomy cell
No cursed drink you'll see
But when you carry shot and shell
You will remember me.

I'm sorry to see one like you
A slave to drink already;
You should have been a sergeant noo
Respectable an' steady,
But here you are a black disgrace
To the gallant corps an' me;
If from the drink you would but cease
A sergeant soon you'd be.

MY GALLANT REGIMENT

Although my hair is waving white,
And shoulders turning bent,
I'll ne'er forget the days so bright
In the seventy-first I spent;
While I'm able to breathe and move,
And eat my humble crust;
I'll sing in praise of the corps I love,
The Gallant Seventy-First.

LINES TO AGNES HUNTER

A wa' wi' the pleasures the world can gi'e,
G ive your heart to what is truthful and free,
N o pure happy peace you ever can find.,
E ngulfed in a soul that's sinful an' blind;
S incere be your path, and pure your young mind.

H onour all good things that's fair to your view;
U nburden your cares to friends kind and true;
N ever forget that our home is not here;
T ake my advice, truthful, plain, and sincere,
E ach day may your pathway be bright and clear -
R eligion when pure shows nothing that's drear.

VALE O' MY CHILDHOOD

Sweet vale where I wandered a wee happy child,
'Mang the murmurin' streams an' flowers bloomin' wild;
But though lang I roved in a bright sunny clime,
In fancy I heard the auld kirk's solemn chime.

Since I left the scenes o' my childhood -
The burn, the meadows, an' flowry green wood,
Nae foreign scenes were sae radiant as thine,
Where I pu'd the sweet gowans in the bright langsyne.

Thy green rural beauty my heart still reveres,
I behold thee still through the dim mist o' years;
An' my heart gi'es a sigh, for mony are gane
To the lonely grave since I left my auld hame.

I see the wee cot where my dear mither dwelt,
An' the bright hearthstane where in prayer we knelt -
Where I learned my hymns for the Sabbath School,
Where I sat near the fire on my wee creepie stool.

But now I only mourn - those sweet halcyon days
Will never mair return to cheer my aged ways;
But a' the strength o' memory will languish an' fail,
When I forget my smilin', my bonny native vale.

MY AIN LOVING LASSIE

Let our local bards sing o' our learned men,
The socialist, whig, or high tory,
But the only bit sang that I'll ever pen,
Is to the young lass in youth's glory;
Through the quietness o' night when nature is still,
An' the bright stars are a' twinklin' doon;
Oh, then o' pure love I hae my sweet fill
Frae the rose o' our braw burgh toon.

When Clune burn wimples by bank, shaw an' brae,
The sweet glories o' nature we view;
An' crack ower the joys o' life's golden day
When the pleasures o' young hearts are true;
There's nane could resist her sweet charmin' ways,
An' the light o' her love speaking eyes;
Nae vulgar sang can be sung in praise
O' the beauteous sweet lass I prize.

When gloamin' is hushed to gentle repose;
An' the roughs frae the Main Street are gane;
'Tis then pure love to my lass I disclose

Near the tap o' our handsome School Lane;
In this world o' ours o' pride, sin, an' gloom,
I'd like to see righteousness shine;
An' ilka sweet lass in purity bloom
Like the rosebud wha soon will be mine.

TEENIE

Air - "When Ye Gang Awa', Jamie."

I am gaun awa', Teenie,
 Far frae thy sweet smile, lassie,
I'm gaun frae thee across the sea,
 An' bonnie Scotland's Isle, Teenie.
But I'll remember still, Teenie
 The happy days are gane, lassie,
 The sunny days on our green braes,
That we hae spent at hame, Teenie.

When in a foreign camp, Teenie,
 Nae pleasure there for me, lassie,
My heart will baith be cauld an' damp,
 While far frae hame an' thee, Teenie,
Though foreign dames are fair, Teenie,
 They'll win nae smile frae me, lassie,
Nane o' them can break the chain
 That links my soul to thee, Teenie.

Oh, for that day to kneel, Teenie,
 Before high Hynen's shrine, lassie,
I canna tell you what I feel
 In this burnin' heart o' mine, Teenie,
Let's set our thoughts abune, Teenie,

The world's wicked ways, lassie,
An' then although we're far awa',
God shall brighten up your days, Teenie.

BE KIND TO THE BIRDIES

Dedicated to the Bairns.

Be kind to the birdies
Sin' Simmer's awa',
There's little food left now
To cheer them ava.
Cauld Winter is comin'
Wi' frost, Hail, an' snaw,
While sparrows are hoppin'
Upon the stane wa'.

Ye dear little bairns
Wha's fond o' their sang,
Drap a crumb on the street
When to schule ye gang;
They'll cock up their wee nebs
In your faces braw;
Then be kind to the birdies
My sweet bairns a'.

An' kindly hoose wives,
In Winter you've seen
At your door a sparrow
Wha felt hunger keen;
When the wee nips o' crumbs
Frae your table fa',
Mind sparrow, and robin
An' blackbird, an' craw.

Our dear robin red breast,
When Simmer is here,
At our doors an' windows
He'll seldom appear,
Let's be kind to the birds
In their dreary lot;
They'll sing bright sangs again
When Winter's forgot.

OUR COUNCILLORS NINE

Air - "Nae Luck Aboot the Hoose."

Oh, dinna say a word ava,
For we are happy noo,
For weel we ken we hae nine men,
A' earnest brave an' true;
Eloquent speeches they can mak',
In words baith smooth an' braw,
So we ratepayers ought to tak'
A pleasure in them a'.

Chorua -
> In our prosperous burgh here,
> May health an' beauty shine,
> Decisive language ne'er appear
> Among our councillors nine.

Our taxation they'll reduce,
An' gi'e us happy cheer,
When frae Lochornie we can use
The water pure an' clear.
Sewage fumes will flee awa',
Without unpleasant smells,

An' ilka drain be fragrant as
The roses in the dells.

Economy shall rule the day,
The Police rates come doon,
An' just a bright halfcroon to pay
For fechtin' in the toon;
A slaughter hoose to please the e'e,
Its like is far frae here -
A bonnier hoose ye canna see
Wi' windows shinin' clear.

Noo dear frien's baith great an' sma',
Our taxes high hae been,
But let us do our level best
To keep our burgh clean.
The piper maun be paid ye ken,
Whether we dance or sing,
Ha'e patience till out rulin' men
Improvements in May bring.

.

LINES DEDICATED TO JOHN SIMPSON

T o the critics who say that my knowledge is small,
O h! never can know my soul's feeling at all

J oy and peace be thine dear friend,
O n tempestuous sea;
H eart felt sorrow here below,
N e'er be known to thee.

S ince home I came to our bright land,
I 've found thee kind and true;
M emory lingers o'er the hours
P leasantly spent with you;
S can vicious men with prudent care;
O f such young men I pray beware;
N othing good with such you'll share.

THE DAYS THAT'S AWA'

Kindly Addressed to Joseph Wilson.

Oh calm lovely night wi' thy bright beamin' moon,
Shinin' sae sweetly through my cauld attic room,
While here I sit lonely when gloamin' shades fa',
Pensively musin' ower the days that's awa'.

In far-awa' lands I saw grandeur sublime,
But ne'er saw a land like the land o' langsyne;
Where happy I wander'd by bank, rill, an' shaw,
But noo I am dreary - those days are awa'.

In life's sunny morning how beauteous an' fair,
Were the lang simmer days that come back nae mair,
The bright springtime o' youth nae cares had ava,
But pure joys are gane wi' the days that's awa'.

In lang winter nights wha was blither than me,
Nae cares at my heart, nor tears in my e'e,
Oh; little I cared then for wind, frost, or snaw,
In yon bonny sweet days that's noo far awa'.

How happy I'd be cud I only obtain
A vision, a dream o' those bright days again,
To meet wi' the dear frien's, the lovin' frien's wha
Cheered up my young heart in the days that's awa'.

Dear land o' my fathers, my ain parent earth,
Renown in the annals o' valour an' worth;
I'll love my dear land while a breath I can draw,
Though noo I'm lamentin' the days that's awa'.

TO MARY

Dear Mary, I oftimes wonder
If ere you think of me,
Since we were parted asunder
By cruel land and sea;
Cheery as birds in morn of May,
We wandered long ago,
Where rippling Fitty sings all day,
And the pure gowans grow.

Since these calm days thine eyes have shone,
Around me everywhere;

Far away in the torrid zone;
I've seen thy image there,
The luscious breath of thy rosy mouth,
I've kissed in my fond dreams,
While wandering in the sunny south,
On the banks of bright streams.

Still in my wanderings Mary,
Thine eyes my steps illume;
Remembrance of thee I'll carry,
'Till I rest in the tomb;
Although my cheerless life's now fraught
With cares of life's rough sea,
I would rejoice in the thought
That Mary minds of me.

THE LADY KILLER

*"Oh Heaven put in every honest hand a whip
To lash the rascal naked through the world".*
SHAKESPEARE.

An ignoramus, a Punchinello,
A presumptuous fool, a cowardly fellow,
Who thinks that every female, foot and limb,
Were only made to be bestowed on him;
Cursed be his pride, his vulgar mean conceit;
Just hear him tell how females on the street,
For love of him would kiss his dandy feet;
He wins them by his brilliant conversation;
There's few can stand before the fascination
Of his alluring words; this low cotquean
Makes female virtue pale before the beam
Of his amorous eye; maidens in their bloom

In prostration fall before the vile baboon.
Speak of a woman; the bombastic fool
With impudence and presumption cool,
Tells he alone the female heart can rule;
The glance of his bright lady-killing eye,
Has ruined thousands, and made hundreds die;
To hear him speak of conquests he has won,
Of homes destroyed, and young maids undone.
You'd tremble for the safety of the world,
When the lady-killing flag's unfurled,
Maids from virtue's pinnacle are hurled
To the gulf of infamy; no more to rise,
And be a wife to cheer a husband's eyes;
Matrimonial fights and domestic sorrow
Are attributable to this lying hero;
He laughs and tells that all married men
Shun his presence as they would the devil's den.
Lady killer, thou art a living lie -
A thief, a scoundrel, and a spy.
Yea, language fails me to tell what thou art -
A painted sepulchre with a rotten heart,
All men who know thee shall always be
Ashamed to breathe immoral air with thee,

CHARGE OF THE DRY BRIGADE

Half a gill, half a gill,
Is what we want here,
But a quart you must fill
Of Younger's best beer -
None of us are dismayed,
We of the dry brigade,
But your cold lemonade
We can't guzzle now.

Then forward they all ran,
Each eager to steal a dram
Of Cameron whisky;
Their's not to make reply,
Their's not to reason why,
Their's but to steal and cry
Make our hearts frisky.

Tumblers to the right of them,
Tumblers to the left of them,
Tumblers in front of them,
Were crushed in the war,
Then Bung did shout and roar,
Scoundrels pay up your score,
And never be seen more
At my shining bar.

The three loafers stood there,
With their pockets all bare,
Not a tanner to spare,
Among the brave three;
Right through the bar they broke
'Mong glasses and whisky smoke,
But they found it no joke,
When fined for their spree.

To wild words they gave vent,
When to the door they went,
Their impious lips soon sent
Forth volleys of thunder;
But the Bailie, good man,
Made them pay for their dram,
Justice and mercy with him,
Without any blunder.

Now they have time to think,
O'er their wild pranks in drink,
By charging the bottle;
Now each drinker declares,
To leave public-house snares,
With its heart-breaking cares,
And join the teetotal.

THE GUILELESS LASSIE

Rabbie sings o' lassies so braw,
And Moore o' his girls so sweet,
But in Fife you'll no find ava,
A lassie like mine so complete.
Beauty shines frae her lovin' e'e,
While her voice has music divine;
Where is the lass on Scotland's lea,
To match this Scotch lassie o' mine.

Fragrance blooms on her rosy cheek,
And love in her bosom reigns pure,
Her words are sweet, modest, and meek,
Although she belongs to the poor.
High born dames are nothing to me,

I admire what's pure an' sublime,
In the young lassie wha soon will be
The true bosom wifie o' mine.

Statesmen may brag o' their foreign dames,
They've nane like my bonny Bella,
Wha sings our poet's sweet melting strains,
In a voice delicious an' mellow.
Soon she will share my domicile,
And make me blythsome an' happy,
Where I'll enjoy her sunny smile
Without the aid o' a drappy.

EPIGRAM

There lives in the Kingdom o' Fife,
A little auld man an' his wife,
Wha drinks a' their means
In private shebeens,
Then live in contention an' strife.

MY BONNIE IRISH KATE

I love sweet Erin's flowery plain,
The land o' emerald green;
For there eternal grandeur reigns,
And beauty rules the scene;
But beauteous though her scenery be,
My soul it can't elate,
Like a blink o' that lassie's e'e,
My bonny Irish Kate.

Lord Byron's pen would powerless be,
To paint her peerless charms;
The world's wealth I'd freely gi'e,
To clasp her in my arms;
Two lonely hours I stood last night,
Close by the auld kirk gate,
Without a soul enrapturing sight,
O' bonny Irish Kate.

She's fairer than the blushing morn,
But what is that to me,
Since I must wander here forlorn,
And happy never be;
This lovely maid has made me undone,
Oh! cruel is my fate,
I Ne'er can be the chosen one,
O' bonny Irish Kate.

THE FOUR TUB BRAE

Meet me at the Four Tub Brae,
Collier Davie, collier Davie,
Meet me at the Four Tub Brae,
My gallant dainty Davie.

And we'll go be to the Minair,
Where forty tubs we'll houk or mair,
And mak' the brushers a' to stare,
My gallant dainty Davie.
Meet me, etc.

If they but gi'e us tubs an' cleek,
We'll mak' our forty bob a week,
In spite o' a' the powther reek,
My gallant dainty Davie.
Meet me, etc.

For managers we dinna care,
Oncost bawbees they can spare,
We never leave our places bare,
My gallant dainty Davie.
Meet me, etc.

In Jenny Gray, or Mary Pit,
We dinna smoke an' lazy sit,
But struggle hard for what we get,
My gallant dainty Davie.
Meet me, etc.

When the simmer days are lang,
Hame to the fragrant fields we gang,
To hear the birdies cheery sang,
My gallant dainty Davie.
Meet me, etc.

When frae the dark pit we repair,
To sniff the caller simmer air,
We kiss the lasses sweet an' fair,
My gallant dainty Davie.
Meet me, etc.

May sorrow dim nae lassie's e'e,
While sailing ower life's troubled sea,
For they are fond o' you an' me,
My gallant dainty Davie.

ACROSTIC ARRANGED IN ALPHABETICAL ORDER

A For Anstruther, where Chalmers was born,
B For Buckhynd, a toon ne'er forlorn,
C For Cupar, where lawyers are mony,
D For Dunfermline, wi' dear lasses bonny,
E For Earlsferry, now rusty by time,
F For Falkland, where kings ruled langsyne,
G For Guardbridge, where they mak' paper fine,
H For Haughmill, near the Cameron Brig,
I For Inverkeithing, aye handsome an' trig,
J For Jamphlars, where they're sinkin' for coal,
K For Kirkcaldy, where Forth's waves do roll,
L For Lochgelly, wi' its laureate sublime,
M For Markinch, wi' big cabbage an' swine,
N For Newport, near the grand river Tay,
O For Oakfield, where they send coals away,
P For Pathhead, ance famed for the loom,
Q For Queensferry, where wee garvies soom,
R For Rosewell, on the braes o' Lochore,
S For Saint Andrews, o' learning and lore,

T For Torryburn, a place I've never seen,
U For Urquhart, wi' its fields waving green,
V For Valleyfield, a wee clachan indeed,
W For Wemyss, wi' its Unionist creed,
X For X-cellent, the places I mention,
Y For Yoofield, not worth my attention,
Z For Zetland, the Lord O' Lumphinnans,
& Soon may the miners enjoy big winnings

TO THE SCHOOL BOARD ELECTORS

Prudence, caution, judgement, and calm deliberations ought to
distinguish the aspirants for School Board honours.

Schule Board Electors o' oor toon,
The election day is comin' soon;
May we find men wha winna froon
At ane anither.
But honour, grace, an' sense illume
Ilk lovin' brither.

Backbitin', scolding, declamation
Should ne'er be heard where education
Glorifies our dear Scotch nation
Richt through an' through;
Let us get men, tho' low in station,
To please us noo.

Seven gude men we, weel can find
O' common sense an' manners kind;
The men that's feckless leave behind,
An' cling to those
Wi' intellectual strength o' mind,
An' no oor foes.

A Schule Board Member ought to be
Frae parasitic wheedlin' free,
An' scorn the tongue o' flatterie
Frae lad or lass,
Although at times he may, like me,
Enjoy a glass.

But dinna let a stranger in
Wi' narrow soul an' scant o' tin;
Men like mysel', no worth a pin,
Can naething do,
But wi' the new Board let's begin
Wi' members true.

I hope the next new Board we see
An' honour to the toon will be,
A fort o' love an' harmonie
Surround the Board,
Like pleasant saints may they agree
In sweet concord.

Where is the bard can charge my pen
Wi' scrbblin' lees 'gainst public men?
I ha'e my fauts, ah! weel I ken,
But no wi' me
Bides the shame o' leein' when
I come to dee.

Oor new Board will soon appear,
A few mair days will bring it here,
If a' gude men wi' love sincere
I'll sing their praise
An' mak' their fame on wings career
Ower Scotland's braes.

Noo, the members that's to be,
May they hae muckle propriety
Until the day they come to dee
That they'll in Heaven
Sing amang the angels free
That - we were seven.

NELLY O' COWDENBEATH

Beauteous fairy, smiling Nelly,
Where is the lass like her;
Her sweet voice sae sweet an' mellow
Does my affections stir.
Sir Walter Raliegh sang o' ane
They ca'd a virgin queen,
But the lassie that I lo'e
Her equal's never seen.

Chorus

> *The world canna gi'e me pain,*
> *Nor winter mak' me chilly,*
> *When to my bosom I can strain*
> *My gentle, loving Nelly.*

'Tis only bards like Robbie Burns
Wud ha'e the power to write
O' beauty in her glancin' een,
That shines like stars at night.
The rosy smile upon her lips
The fragrance o' her breath,
Draws me frae my native haunts
To her in Cowdenbeath.

I'm no a bard o' much regard,
An' ne'er expect to be,
But I can tell when lowin' love
Beams in a lassie's e'e.
When gowans deck the fragrant heath,
An' simmer comes again,
The fairest lass in Cowdenbeath
Will surely be my ain.

No muckle knowledge I possess
O' Radical or Tory,
But like them baith I glory still
In Scotia's ancient story;
But flee frae me, blind politics,
An' welcome early death,
If I'm to lose my hearts desire,
My rose o' Cowdenbeath.

There's rhymers fain wud like their fame
To bloom beyond the urn,
But I'm content wi' Nelly's name
To live near Buckie Burn.
Nae worldly care, domestic strife,
When we're joined together,
We'll then enjoy a tranquil life
O' bliss wi' ane anither.

AULD CUDDY NEIL

A wonderfu' body wis auld Cuddy Neil,
He cud sing a sweet sang, an' dance a Scotch Reel,
His pleasant face cheered the schule bairns weel,
When doon oor lang High Street cam' auld Cuddy Neil,

An' Jenny, his wife, selt bread through the toon,
Wi' her snaw coloured mutch an' stripit short goon
Penny scones, farthing bakes, she had in a creel,
A real cheery helpmeet had auld Cuddy Neil.

Through green Fifeshire he taen mony a turn,
Frae the East Nuke o' Fife, wast to Torryburn;
The cacklin' o' hens, an' the young grumphies squeal,
Wis music we whiles heard wi' auld Cuddy Neil.

Fine country fresh eggs he wud bring frae Kinross,
An' tautties that grew north in Scotlandwell moss,
An' big thumpin' carrots a pleasure to peal,
Cam' into Lochgelly wi' auld Cuddy Neil.

A kindly smart bodie aye honest an' clean,
A stranger to onything vulgar or mean,
But those wha wud cheat him roosed up the deil,
When trying to bargain wi' auld Cuddy Neil.

Braw red-checkit apples, pears, candy, an' jam,
An' grand cauliflowers, Scotch onions an' bran,
Whitenin' an' saut, ochre, blacklead, an' keel,
Were selt to our mithers by auld Cuddy Neil.

The world's nae better, o' that I've nae doot,
Since our ancient frien' trauchled here roond aboot,
But noo he's awa' to the Land o' the Leal,
The honest auld hawker we ca'd Cuddy Neil.

THE HEROINES OF BURNS' SANGS

Oh, where is the bard like him that's awa',
Wha sang o' Scotch lasses bonny an' braw;
To mention their names wud tak' me owre lang,
O' the lasses wha felt the power o' his sang.

Handsome Nell, Jean Jeffrey, Eppie Adair -
He praised these young lasses charmin' an' fair;
And dear Highland Mary, his bonniest queen,
At last she made room for his lovely Jean.

Polly Stewart, Agnes Flemming, likit to see,
Wi' Mary Morrison, the licht o' his e'e;
But Ellison Bigbie, that loved him sae weel,
Frae ither Scotch lasses his heart couldna steal.

Some ither Scotch lasses, high, high in rank,
Ballochmyle's Lass an' Jenny Cruikshank,
An' Charlotte Hamilton, near Devon's stream,
Cam' in for a share o' our poet's esteem.

Montgomery's Peggy, and milk maidens fair,
Ann Rolland, Leslie Baillie, were anxious to share,
The love that fired in his bosom a flame,
That shines owre the world, an' kindles his fame.

Maggie Chalmers, Jessie Lewars, wi' some beauties mair,
Wha bloomed near the Naith and banks o' the Ayr,
Wud ne'er hae been kent had Burns not seen
The enrapturing love frae bright glancin' e'en.

THE QUEEN'S DIAMOND JUBILEE

Respectfully dedicated to our Public Men.

The poets now the world through,
Will tune their sublime lyres,
And sing in praise o' our good Queen,
Whom all the world admires.
We've bards o' beauty, power, an' fame,
Who'll strike their lofty key,
And fire the world with their strain
On the Queen's Jubilee.

Lord Tennyson has passed away,
And other singers too,
But still we have with us to-day,
Some bards of Nature true.
We have in our poetic throng
A Cunningham in his glee,
Who's sure to sing a cheery song
On the Queen's Jubilee.

Although a water fountain here,
May never cheer our e'en,
Perhaps a blooming Public Park
May soon be waving green;
Where lads an' lassies all can roam
'Neath the fragrant flower and tree,
Enjoying the beauties of their home
On the Queen's Jubilee.

In Fife there's not another toon
Surpassing our Lochgelly,
With lasses aye in vernal bloom,
An' many a young fellow,
Who'd leave their native land to-day

And cross the rolling sea,
And fight for her who's reigned to see
Her Diamond Jubilee.

Perhaps from some conspicuous place
We'll see her looking doon
A worthy clock, with honest face,
To cheer our worthy toon.
No miner lad will need to rap
And cry "Come on wi' me";
We'll hear our clock in melodious chap
On the Queen's Jubilee.

Let Jenny Gray, now cease her blaw,
We want her din nae mair,
A sound just fit to frighten craws
That hover through the air;
We'll have a clock whose silvery chimes
We'll sound o'er hill and lea,
In the glorious happy times
On the Queen's Jubilee.

With bowling green, and cricket clubs,
And Volunteers sae braw,
For golfing lads and football players
Weel may our burgh blaw;
So we in gloom shall never stand
Nor sad and sulky be,
But glory in our native land
On the Queen's Jubilee.

May our school Board Members ever be
Just like our councillors nine,
All jolly fellows, proud to see
Our burgh in beauty shine;
I hope our Public Men will dine

In friendship pure and free,
And sing a sang for auld langsyne
On the Queen's Jubilee.

No land like ours can e'er be found
Mair kent to fame and glory,
Since that bright morn in June was crowned
Our gracious Queen Victoria;
Although a sma' bit laddie then,
Until the day I dee,
I'll sound my lyre, though puir the strain,
And praise her Jubilee.

JEMIMA

When the sweet summer sun
Has gane to its rest,
Behind yon bright cloud
On the broo o' the West,
An' the twinkling stars
Shine forth in the sky,
O, then to thy presence
Jemima, I'll hie.

When gloamin' shadows
Fall dark on the scene,
We'll meet in the meadows
'Mang flowers wavin' green;
What transportin' bliss
We'll experience, when
We pree the sweet kiss
In Kirkie's calm glen.

The pure roes bloomin'
On Clune's bonny broo
Are scentless, Jemima,
Alangside o' you;
Summer flowers in their beauty,
Nae sweeter can be,
Than my bonny lassie,
The pride o' my e'e.

EPIGRAMS

I ken an auld man in Lochgelly,
Wha sailed for years o'er the billow,
But now he is auld,
Grey, crabbit, an' bald,
A cankerous sort o' a fellow.

You offer a pound for a rhyme, sir,
Here's one that's rather sublime, sir,
Lord Byron and Scott,
A better ne'er wrote;
So send me the money in time, sir.

A LOYAL ACROSTIC

T he land of Scotland, the land of our birth,
H onour, fame, and glory is ours,
E urope failed to make old Scotland tremble,

Q uietly we conquered great savage powers;
U nder the banners of Wallace and Bruce,
E ngland was our great southern foe;
E nmity then brought to Caledon
N othing but poverty and woe.
S ince the Union taen place we are happy,

J oined now is the thistle and rose;
U nder the rule of good Queen Victoria
B ritian fears no foreign foes;
I nnocent youth, and men grey and hoary,
L ive in loyalty to our Scotch Queen;
E ncirling the world, the fame of her glory,
E arth her equal never seen.

MY ALPHABET O' BONNY LASSES

A for my Annie, fair, tranquil, and sweet,
B for my Bella, with charms complete;
C for my Clara, who makes my heart swell,
D for my Dinah, who loves me real well;
E for my Emma, who lives near Lochore,
F for my Fanny, who watches my door;
G for my Glenie, who works on Cartmore,
H for my Hannah, a sweet flower to pree;
I for my Isa, with dark rolling e'e,
J for my Jeanie, who smiles upon me;
K for my Katie, the pride o' the toon,
L for my Lizzie, a pure rose in bloom;
M for my Mary, whom none can trepan,
N for my Nellie, who loves an old man;
O for my O'neal, who lives near the square;
P for my Peggie, fat, forty, and fair;
Q for my Queen, the best o' them all,
R for my Robina, proud, graceful, and tall;
S for my Susan, who scorns my pride,
T for my Teenie, who walks by my side;
U for my Ulenia, who sounds high my praise,
V for my Violet, who warbles my lays;
W for my Winnie, a flower in her prime,
X antippe sourness has no lass o' mine;
Y outhful and bonny with love flowing o'er,
Z ael's in their hearts for the bard they adore;
& now I have finished my twenty-three names
O' bonny Scotch lasses, the pride o' our hames.

LOCHGELLY JUBILEE BONFIRE

22nd June, 1897.

Let Saxon toon's tell the glory
O' Queen Victoria's fame,
But listen' an' hear the story
O' our Lochgelly flame.
Let learned critics boast an' brag,
An' say our minds are shallow,
But Scotland's greatest fire to-day
Was kindled in Lochgelly.

The fire they had in Cowdenbeath
Their streets could not illume,
But our great fire on fragrant heath
Made stars to sink in gloom.
Frae Dover toon to Inverness
Our loyal fire was seen,
In glorious light on Tuesday night,
When we a' praised our Queen.

Though poor in wealth, we're rich in fame,
The men o' dear Lochgelly;
We lit a fire that sent a flame
Far ower the stormy billow.
Awa' where foreign rivers roll
Auld Scotland's sons wud stand
An' see the light that waft their thoughts
Back to their classic land.

Let Edinburgh hide her head
And close her loyal een,
For Page's birth-toon made a fire
That shone ower Aberdeen.
When the flames ascended high

Beyond the clouds o' heaven,
Our Lochornie's streams ran dry,
Loch Fittie, an' Loch Leven.

The rabbits on Benarty Hill
Shook a' their fuds wi' fear,
While snakes an' hares forsook the plains
As our great flames rolled near.
The blackbird on the Hill o' Beath
Refused his sang so mellow,
For scorching flames caused his death
Frae fires in famed Lochgelly.

The mushroom village in the west
May fill its streets wi' cheers,
But we've a corps it never had
To match our Volunteers.
An' councillors too, wi' spirits bright,
In friendship did convene,
An' spoke wi' eloquence that night
For Scotland's Stuart Queen.

We have a paper that reports
Our follies an' our fines,
To scurrilous language ne'er resorts
Our ain "Lochgelly Times".
The bailies a' I ken them well,
They've proved real friends to me,
I hope to sing their praises again
At the Queen's next Jubilee.

Before our bonfire blazing bright
Our prize band played in tune,
That filled our maidens with delight
Amang the yellow broom.
The strangers here do a' admire

The toon they cam' to see,
But they will mind our great bonfire
On our Queen's Jubilee

Lochgelly is nae upstart toon,
She has bards not a few,
That sends Lochgelly's fame aroon'
The world's oceans blue.
The Cartmore bard, whose strains are heard,
Delicious, sweet, an' true,
An' we have councillor Williamson,
Mackie, an' laureate Hugh.

I'm often called just what I am,
A kind o' Scottish Tory,
But proud o' Burns an' Willie Tam,
An' our national glory.
Though aged now, I'm proud to say
A soldier I have been,
An' had the honour to present
My arms before the Queen.

Now lads an' lasses, young an' gay,
An' bonnie bairns a',
I'm sure you'll mind the Birnie Brae
When Pindar is awa'.
An' when like me you're auld an' grey,
An' tears may dim your een,
You'll have a pleasant word to say
In memory o' the Queen.

DANDY JO

They call me Dandy Jo,
But none can tell the grief,
That make my tears to flow,
And cannot find relief;
I am sad and lonely,
I'm dying inch by inch,
For my heart loves only
My pretty Irish wench.

She promised to meet me,
Down by the Parish Church,
But ran off with Sandy,
And left me in the lurch;
The next time I met her,
She made me sigh and sab,
Clinking through the Drill Hall,
Along with Sergeant Rab.

Love's unclouded sunshine
Illumed my early days,
When dancing with Helen
On Tollie's fragrant braes;
Gloomy thoughts are on my brow,
'Tis very hard to wrench
My heart away just now
From my sweet charming wench.

Adorable dear maid,
When I am dead and gone,
Raise above my silent head
A lump of granite stone,
And let the world know
The love I had for you;
You'll ne'er find another Jo,
So Dandy, kind, and true.

MAGGIE O' INCHGA' MILL

The sun has dipped his head behind,
Benarty's glowing hill,
While nature like a sleeping child
Is lovely, calm, and still,
The queen o' night reflects her beams
O'er Contel's gentle rill,
When I met my sweet Maggie Gray,
The pride o' Inchga' Mill.

My pretty queen is seventeen,
Sweet, fair, and sprightly gay,
A bonnier lassie ne'er was seen
Than my young Maggie Gray,
To meet her on the gowan lea
My heart wi' love runs o'er,
She is a goddess pure to me
To worship and adore.

When other lovers round you come,
My bonnie Maggie Gray,
To their pleading love prove dumb,
For mine can't pass away,
Withoot thy smile, my Maggie dear,
The world's grief must fill
My faithful heart and leave it drear,
Sweet maid o' Inchga' Mill.

KATIE O' TORBANE

Let England boast o' her fair dames,
Erin her virgins pure,
Gi'e me the ane my heart inflames,
My bonnie Scottish flooer.
She dwell where bloomin' sweets adorn,
Her smiling, cosy hame,
An' purer than the simmer morn,
My Katie o' Torbane.

Her lovin' smile has made me blessed,
An' cheered this heart o' mine,
When her gentle form I pressed
In blissful days langsyne.
When mingling in the clash o' arms,
Across the rolling main,
I pondered on the peerless charms
O' Katie o' Torbane.

Her beauteous face, her graceful mien,
An' love devouring eyes,
The world her equal hisna seen
Since Eve left Paradise.
Were I to roam the world through
A lassie I'll find nane
To match my rose sae sweet an' true
That blooms in auld Torbane.

THE DRUNKARD'S WAIL

I am weary, sad, and lonely,
A plague beneath the bright blue sky,
My desire is to have only
A quart of beer when I am dry.

Here on earth I pine in anguish,
When sober I am in despair;
Then, kind friends, don't let me languish,
When a drop would banish care.

I have a weakly constitution,
From whence all my misery springs;
And my soul's steep'd in pollution
With the sin that whisky brings.

O'er the drink's intoxication,
I oftimes thought my life sublime,
But a mortal reformation
I rather fear can ne'er be mine.

Where is the power so effectual
To move the hearts of drunken men?
Potent, strong, and intellectual,
Oh; give to me a little then.

The foolish drunkard do not spurn,
Give him something his soul to cheer,
Do not let him lie and mourn
For one small glass of bitter beer.

If my eloquence and pleading
For Cameron whisky can't prevail,
You can plainly see I'm needing
A glass of Bass's sparkling ale.

Friends be generous, kind, and trusty,
Extend your kindness now to me,
For at present I am thirsty,
I'll even take your last bawbee.

TIME FLIES

Come back bright golden days o' youth,
Come back again to me,
An' bring wi' you the fragrant dew,
The roses an' the bee,
Auld age is sad, my life's forlorn,
I'm fu' o' misery,
Oh, for a glimpse o' life's young morn,
When innocent an' free.

Come back to me sweet pleasant streams,
Come back pure love an' joy,
An' fill my soul wi' pleasure sweet,
The same as when a boy.
For noo I'm weary wi' the gloom
That roon' my path hae sprung,
The simmer flowers now want the bloom
They had when I was young.

Come back to me sweet childhood's hours,
Come back bright cloudless skies,
Come back - Oh, odoriferous flowers,
An' ease my heart o' sighs;
Vain wish - Alas! those happy days
Will ne'er return again,
Youth come but once, an' then auld age,
Wi' troubled thoughts o' pain.

APPENDIX

NOTE TO THE APPENDIX

The following pages are included so that readers may enjoy Pindar's scrap-book of newspaper cuttings, which turned up among the Alex Westwater papers given to me by Mrs Jenny Mitchell. The compilation appears to have been by the poet himself, and the cover, written in pencil, simply states his *nom de plume*, 'Pindar'.

The scrapbook consist of a miscellany of poems and articles clipped from *Cowdenbeath & Lochgelly Times & Advertiser* and glued on to the pages of a small notebook. It is reproduced here in a much larger format for ease of legibility and no attempt has been made to edit or re-arrange, as the scrapbook is the work of Pindar's own hand, reflecting not only the tone of the local press and the community of his time, but also Pindar's engagement with his fellow citizens.

On a final note, I hope that readers will delight in the local wit and humour that is as fresh today as it was all those years ago.

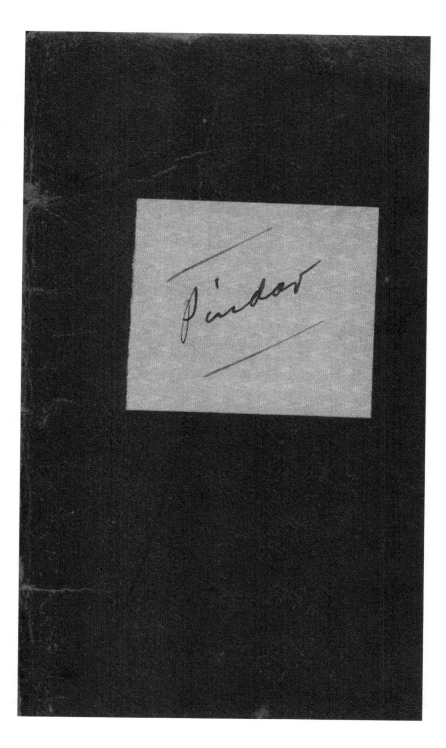

JoHN PINDAR.

(By a Personal Friend and Admirer.)

Lochgelly has given birth to many distinguished sons — notably the late Professor Page, whose works on Geology are of world-wide reputation, and which are a great help to the student trying to fathom the mysteries of creation, as well as to those who have drunk deep of the grandest, most stupendous, and solemn truths about the world we live in, revealing, as the Science does, the immensity of the works of the Great Architect of the Universe. In addition to that great philosopher, the Burgh has given birth to many sons who, in different spheres of life, do credit alike to themselves and to the village that gave them birth. The missionary field and the ministry at home have both been enriched by them ; and, if none have proved a John M'Neill, they have, at least, wagged their pows in the pulpit with a considerable amount of success. But, notwithstanding all this, it has been reserved for John Pindar, poet-laureate of his native village, to be enshrined in the hearts of the people as the Grand Old Man of whom they can truly say, " We are all proud of him." Our G.O.M. has heard

> " The cannon roar
> Nearer, clearer, deadlier than before "—

having served Her Gracious Majesty for 21 years ; and when in his war paint, his broad massive shoulders and his martial bearing proclaimed him every inch a soldier. Well does the writer remember with what impatience he used to wait for the *Fife News* turning up, so as he might devour his life, which was then appearing there week after week, written by himself when still in the Service, and which was afterwards re-printed in book form. On a recent visit to his domicile in

Main Street, the writer found him perusing one of his favourite authors. It is needless to say that Scott, Burns, Shakespeare, Browning, Tannahill, and other minor poets find a place in his small but select library. We even got a peep of the "Vestiges of Creation," which showed that he also takes an interest in those great problems which perplex the minds of so many distinguished men. His otherwise dingy room is adorned by some nice portraits. Prominent amongst them is one of Lord Beaconsfield—

> " A statesman
>   Who knew the seasons when to take
>   Occasion by the hand and make
>   The bonds of freedom wider yet."

Pindar is now on the shady side of fifty; but by reason of physical infirmities is unable to follow his occupation of working in the mines; but he still sings in a cheery strain :—

> Although I'm getting old and grey,
>   Hardship I winna mention ;
> I'll do my best, from day to day,
>   To live upon my pension.

Which I sincerely hope you will, John, but with only one shilling per day I am afraid you can't afford much of the luxuries of life.

Our friend has still a fresh and healthy complexion, with a shrewd cast of countenance ; and when he is relating the latest joke about some village worthy, his face is lighted up by a pair of waggish eyes that make one realise that

> "Old age, what is it but a name
>   For wilder joys departed?
> For we shall be for ever young
>   If we are loyal-hearted."

In politics he is a staunch Tory, as most old soldiers are who have seen the greatness of the mighty Empire on which the sun never sets, and, therefore, realises that a strong Foreign Policy is necessary for the welfare of the United Kingdom, as the trade follows the flag ; and as it would be difficult to take up the map of the world and say here Radical Foreign Policy has done good, so he

dislikes the party that believes in peace at any
price abroad, and that truckles to anarchy at
home. He is also a loyal Free-Churchman ; but
has no sympathy with that crusade against the
Auld Kirk, as he considers that Disestablishment
and Disendowment are nothing short of barefaced
robbery, and he is disgusted at the suggestion that
all that is required is a two hours' Parliamentary
discussion to dispose of our National Zion. When
worshipping abroad in some grand edifice, of
which its very magnificence filled him with holy
awe, he still yearned for the simpler Presbyterian
forms of worship of his native land, and
exclaimed—

> Oh, for a sound o' a Sabbath bell
>   On the calm, sweet summer gale—
> The same as I heard in years gone by
>   In the sweet toon o' Glenvale.

But the following will prove he is no religious
bigot—

> And this is Malta, don't you hear
>   The chapel bells already ringing,
> And see the candles burning clear,
>   And grey-hair'd priests around them singing.
> Altho' grim-featured superstition
>   Reigns o'er Malta's barren plain,
> A holy, pious, pure petition
>   Ne'er went up to heaven in vain.

The subject of these remarks is a master of pathos,
as every one knows who has read his " Autobio-
graphy." It has brought the tears to many a
fond mother's eyes as she thought of her own
darling son away in a distant land. The writer
has seen the tears trickle down the cheeks of a
household as they read the simple nursery ryhmes,
which the soldiers preferred to the more classic
works of a Tennyson or a Browning, as it brought
to their memory the happy days enjoyed round
the hearthstone away in the dear old home.
Like every patriotic Scotsman he has intense love
for the land of the mountain and the flood, and
although he was for many years on a foreign
shore, he never forgot the land of his birth—

> Sweet isle o' the ocean, my soul clings to thee
> Wi' the purest devotion whare'er I may be ;
> Tho' noo I maun wander in lands o'er the sea,
> My dear fatherland is the licht o' my e'e.

Or again—

> Lang years ha'e gane by sin' I left my dear hame
>   An' the friends o' my early days ;
> But noo I'm at hame, an' nae mair will I roam
>   Awa' frae my sweet native braes.
> Though ance on the blood-stained field I did lie,
>   Surrounded by comrades slain,
> It's noo, thank God, I am able to cry—
>   Is this bonnie Scotland again?

And what hard heart would this not melt—

> Sweet to see one's native land
>   After many wandering years,
> And grasp the kind, familiar hand
>   Of parents smiling through their tears.

The patriotic spirit infused throughout the story
of his life has made many young aspirants for
military honours enter the service of their
country. It was, indeed,

> "A tale to stir the blood of generous youth,
> To rouse the heart, to call forth daring deeds."

His patriotism is well displayed in the following
verse from his Centennial Song addressed to his
old regiment on its hundredth birthday—

> The spirits o' our forefathers
>   On yon celestial shore
> Would frown upon a craven heart
>   In their distinguished corps.
> To us they have bequeathed a name
>   Of glory and renown,
> Achieved on fields o' storied fame
>   For Country, Queen, and Crown.

Although long a wanderer in other lands, his sym-
pathy has always been with the class from
whence he sprung — namely, the hard-working
miners—

> Oh, where will you find a hero like him,
>   Toiling awa' in his cavern grim ;
> So arduous his work, he scarcely gets time
>   To drink his cauld tea in the gloomy coal mine.

As for his Love Songs they are legion, and one
can hardly realise that he is still an old bachelor
and can yet breathe forth such pure devotion as
this—

ELLEN O'KEEFFE.

> Alas ! we must sever, dear maiden, for ever,
>   While tears like a river now flow from my eyes ;
> Since I saw thy sweet face in thine own native place,
>   My heart has been nought but a fountain of sighs.

Wherever I roam now, far from thy sweet home now,
  Nothing is left me but sorrow and grief ;
Where'er I may wander 'mong beauty and grandeur,
  On thee I must ponder, sweet Ellen O'Keeffe.

Thou art brighter by far than the pure morning star ;
  And may sorrow ne'er mar thy passage through life—
May angels defend thee, and blessings attend thee,
  And husband befriend thee when thou art a wife.

I must soon roam again far beyond the dark main,
  While my tears are all vain, thou young rosy
    thief ;
Ah ! a sweet thief thou art, thou hast stolen my
    heart—
  And in sorrow we part, sweet Ellen O'Keeffe.

The poet has a great love for children, and his
old house is often brightened up by the rosy
smiles and innocent laughter of childhood.   Could
any Benedict match these lines from an old
Celibate—

Children are the poetry of life—
  I love to see them on a mother's knee,
I love the music of their tiny strife,
  The rattling noise of their childish glee.

But John is both reared and loved, and is quite a
master of "Flouts and Gibes and Jeers," and
many a would-be swell has squirmed under the
lash of his stinging satire.   The following is a
verse from his latest satirical poem—

Wha rules supreme in auld Lochgelly
Wi' mind so big, and brains so shallow,
And ca's an honest man a *fellow* ?—
                                    The Masher.

I am surprised that Pindar's Poems have not ap-
peared in a collective form, for many of his ad
mirers would be anxious to procure a copy, as he
has no ordinary hold upon the affections of the
people.   Many other minor poets have lived to
see their works in book form, and the next time
I take up my pen may it be to pass an honest
criticism upon the "Children of his Brain."   I
will now conclude with the words of a brother
poet :—

"Fareweel, John Pindar, aye mind sellie,
May ye ne'er want for back nor bellie,
But aye a drap to keep ye mellow
                      Wi' song divine—
As Poet-Laureate of Lochgelly
                      Lang may ye shine."

We have this week received the following verses from John Pindar, which bear testimony to the above estimate by an admirer :—

MY AULD SWEETHEARTS.

I mind when I was a young man,
  Some thirty years ago,
My heart was like a simmer day,
  Without a shade of woe.
The gladsome days o' auld langsyne
  Come never back again ;
The present has owre muckle grief,
  The past not much of pain.

But wi' the bonny lassies dear,
  I've spent delicious hours ;
The world wud be dark an' drear
  Without the blooming flowers.
I'll ne'er forget sweet Bella Gray,
  An' lovely Mary Swan,
An' smiling Jane, wha cheered my heart
  Ere sodger days began.

An' when I roamed through Erin's Isle,
  My heart was ne'er forlorn ;
For then I busk'd in the bright smile
  O' little Bridget Horne.
In Erin's land I always had
  Some soul-entrancin' thief
To steal my heart, like Mary Quin,
  Or blue-eyed Nell O'Keeffe.

An' when afar, in other lands—
  In Malta's sunny clime,
I had my Teenie Gammie there
  An' rosy Caroline.
Oh, some o' those dear lassies now
  Are silent in the grave ;
An' some, I ken, are, like mysel',
  Still battling on life's wave.

Now a' the sweethearts I can get
  (But this I shou'dna tell)
Are auld, an' frail, an' toothless—
  Just something like mysel'.
I've often been invited in
  Wi' some auld maid to dine ;
But that is when I ha'e the tin,
  Aboot the pension time.

I little thought in life's young days,
  When wi' the lassies roamin',
That I wud miss their cheery smile
  To bless life's cheerless gloamin'.
I feel auld age now coming fast ;
  An' early friends are gane ;
While I maun shelter frae the blast
  At a bachelor's hearthstane.

JOHN PINDAR.

IN MEMORIAM.

Rest, warrior, thy battles now are o'er
On Crimean plains and India's coral shore.
Boldly thou fought up Alma's rugged height,
Engaging all the power of Russia's savage might—
Regiments, French and British, assembled there
To crush the power of the Russian bear.

Battles fierce were ofttimes waged before—
At Waterloo, Vittoria, and Cawnpore ;
But of all battles fought without a plan,
None e'er rivalled bloody Inkermann.

JOHN PINDAR.

COWDENBEATH *V.* LOCHGELLY.

Let auld Lochgelly hide her head,
   An' brag an' blaw nae mair
Aboot her poet-laureates,
   An' streets so bright and fair.
Auld Pindar lang has done his best
   To mak' his burgh shine ;
An' Poet Hugh has praised her too
   In language neat an' fine.

Cowdenbeath has factories grand—
   Forbye a reading-room,
To cheer the heart an' free the mind
   Frae ignorance an' gloom.
Although our burgh's in a vale,
   Our lads ha'e sense an' skill
To equal those wha craw so loud
   Upon the Birnie Hill.

The water for their daily use
   Flows frae Lochornie burn,
So fu' o' heather, peats, refuse,
   As mak' a saint to mourn.
It canna match the pure, bright stream
  - That flows through Cowdenbeath—
A stream that mak's our maidens fair,
   An' sweetens a' their breath.

I ken my sister east the way
   Is fond o' social rank ;
I think she'll live to rue the day
   She built her ugly Tank.
A fearful-looking thing indeed—
   As black's a houdy craw—
An' stands so high that Bobby's horse
   Can never drink ava.

Noo, hide your head, Auld Burgh Toon,
   You canna shine wi' me,
For I have three hotels for those
   Wha love the barley bree ;
An' I have food an' clothing too
   For ilka lad an' wench ;
We'll ne'er want siller while we have
   A *Fortune* on the Bench.

Cowdenbeath.   L'ALLEGRO.

VERSES FROM AN UNKNOWN FRIEND TO JOHN PINDAR, LOCHGELLY.

An unknown Friend and Brother Bard,
Wha's neither blate nor easy scar'd –
Since first thy strains he chance-ways heard
 He's grown much older ;
But still does hold the same regard
  For valiant soldier.

You've stood the brunt of fire and steel,
Made your opponents a' to reel ;
Yon savage hordes as black's the Deil,
  Wha hid like snakes,
Did 'mongst the grass themsel's conceal
  To avoid your " *paikes.*"

Cheer up, brave soldier ; when we meet,
If *chance* direct our wandering feet,
Be 't on the highway or the street,
  Gin' ye'll receive it,
We'll ha'e a drap, to mak' us fleet,
  O' real Glenlivet.

Whate'er the temp'rance folk may say,
I've nae objections—ne'er says nay ;
I only wish for a' fair-play,
  And much less clatter—
Enough's as guid's a feast, folk say,
  Be't wine or watter.

I'll wager, John, on India's plains,
Where heat is high, and seldom rains—
Of Lochore's stream, that aye retains
  Its virtue still,
Ye wad ha'e gi'en part o' your gains
  For half-a-gill.*

For, weel, men ken drouth's ill to bide ;
Hunger comes next—it winna hide ;
So, ne'er a soldier lad deride,
  He whiles feels baith,
And a' his country's claims decide,
  Or meet his death.

Fareweel, John Pindar, aye mind sellie ;
May you ne'er want for back nor belly,
Nor a wee drap to keep ye mellow
  With song divine ;
As Poet-Laureate of Lochgelly
  Lang may ye shine.

    A FIFE MILLWRIGHT.

Dysart, 4 July 1890.

TEENIE BAIN.

Let Cowdenbeath blaw o' her lasses sae braw,
  Wi' their red cheeks like roses in June—
They a' maun gi'e place to the sweet, modest grace
  O' my Teenie in Lochgelly toon.
She sings like a lark round my cheery hearthstane,
  Her heart is confidin' an' warm ;
She lichtens my care, an' my sorrows she shares
  In this vale o' sunshine an' storm.

This canty, this bonnie, sweet wifie o' mine
  Is a radiant sun in my hame ;
The blink o' her e'e gi'es me pleasures sublime—
  She's the world to me, Teenie Bain.
Now I whistle an' sing, because I ha'e won
  A bright lassie wha mak's me her care ;
There's nae toon in Fife that can show such a wife
  As my Teenie, sae thrifty an' fair.

When hame frae my wark in the gloamin' I come
  To my housie, sae tidy an' nice,
What a heaven o' bliss to get a sweet kiss
  In the fauld o' our ain paradise.
Her bright, sunny smile drives awa' care an' gloom—
  Nae wonder I'm fond o' my dearie ;
I've nae cause to wish for the peace o' the tomb,
  For Teenie is aye blythe an' cheery.

Lochgelly, 1891.   JOHN PINDAR.

DEDICATED TO JOHN PINDAR,
NENT "OOR BRAW BURGH TOON.

Losb, Pindar, but it pleased me fine
Tae get my *News* and scan yer rhyme,
As aft I've daen frae time tae time
　　　　In bygane days,
When on a foreign shore and clime
　　　　You'd tune yer lays.

Then, but a laddie, prood I'd read
Your lengthened strains wi' muckle speed,
Till aft I'd fairly lose my head
　　　　An' wonderin' seem
Tae think hoo mony a warlike deed
　　　　Ye mun ha'e seen.

'Twas then frae "Malta's" shore ye penned
In honour o' the folks ye kenned;
Or o' the days ye used tae spend
　　　　When but a loon,
Whan youthfu'-like yer steps ye'd wend
　　　　Ayont the toon;

Or where "Orr's Water" rins sae clear,
Its banks, yer muse aft led ye near;
Or dreamin', aften ye wad spear—
　　　　Hope on the wane—
If joyfu' ye wad ever mair
　　　　Return again.

Fate wist it sae, and sae again
Auld Time did grant yer wish fu' fain;
And noo secure frae yont the main,
　　　　Frae wind or storm,
We hail yer pleasin' hamely strain
　　　　An' stalwart form.

Oor village then 's a Burgh noo,
O' Councillors we ha'e enew;
But, mind, there's wark for a' tae do,
　　　　Frae Bailies doon,
Tae mak' the grievances but few
　　　　In "Oor Burgh Toon."

An' that she should be trig an' braw,
I'm shure it is the aim o' a';
Wi' water pure for cot and ha',
　　　　Or aunty's tea—
Ye winna get her match ava
　　　　By land or sea.

"Lang may the Councillors we choose
Be men wi' wisdom in their views;"
And ev'n should some court the muse,
　　　　Or lecture "Burns,"
We'll gladly sit and list the news
　　　　When Spring returns.

Then lat each dae the best he can
Tae keep oor Burgh in the van ;
An' should at times a helpin' han'
      Sic labours croon,
'Twill dignify thro' a' the lan'
      " Oor Burgh Toon."
Lochgelly is extending, more and more ;
To the west we will soon add Number Four,
And when that's built up, we will take in Lochore
    Later on ! Yes ! later on.

Our leading Bailie is up to Dick,
Of our Commission he is the pick,
   A to the bench we'll have him stick,
     Both now and later on !

  ne U.P. Literary Society has been a success,
It may yet help to lift Parliament out of distress,
For t' members' ambition we cannot suppress,
     Either now or later on !

Each of them burns with intellectual fire,
And when Balfour and Goschen think fit to retire,
Some may step into their shoes, and even rise higher
    Liter on, very much later on !   X.

DEDICATED TO "L'ALLEGRO" ANENT "COWDENBEATH *V.* LOCHGELLY."

"Let auld Lochgelly hide her head,"
    Losh, Pindar, dae ye hear that?
He surely thinks her poets dead,
    That flesh an' bluid can bear that.
Na, na, my lad that winna dae ;
    Though frae yer heart ye've cuist her,
We'll sing her praises while we may,
    In spite o' a' yer bluister.

Nae wonder that ye hide yer name,
    An' *nom- lume* it " L'Allegro,"
For question, if I kenned yer hame,
    I'd find you were a negro,
Tae scorn oor guid " Auld Burgh Toon,"
    An' a' that in it dwell, sir ;
Sae hide yer ain head, saucy loon,
    Her worth I'm loath tae tell, sir.

But Cowdenbeath, though young she be,
    Wi' Bailies, rich an' rare, sir,
I doot will hae tae wait a wee
    Or e'er she can compare, sir,
Wi' her, wha's kent the world o'er
    For pith, an' lear, an' sense, sir ;
Lochgelly never yet, did cower
    Tae arguments sae dense, sir.

Dae ye no ken that 'Page did find
    His cradle bed an' home there ?
And science led his noble mind
    To study many a stone there ?
An' mair than that, " oor Burgh Toon "
    Can point wi' honest pride, sir,
To mony a gracefu' weel-faured loon,
    Wha's been our country's guide, sir.

And 'midst the din an' clash o' arms,
    And war's unbridled clamour,
In death's pale presence, wild alarms,
    We've watched, while eyes would glamour,
For then we knew, 'neath world's gaze,
    Our sons would nobly stand, sir,

Until the victors' well-known praise
  Did stream through a' the land ·fr.

Then, auld Lochgelly, cock yer head !
  Yeu've beat your rivals fairly,
In maist things aye ye tak' the lead,
  Surpass you, they dae rarely ;
And while yer poet-laureates bring
  A tribute frae the altar,
Your beauties we will ever sing
  In strains that never falter.

  20 High Street,   ALEXANDER HUGH. ·
Lochgelly, 6th March, 1891.
            *David Page, geologist.

LOCHGELLY *V.* COWDENBEATH

You're vext to think I stand aboon
    A mushroom thing like you ;
Your prosperous days are nearly dune,
    While strength sits on my broo.
Because you are a Burgh noo,
    You cock your head fu' braw ;
I dinna think you're justified
    In settin' up your jaw.

I stood upon this lofty hill
    Ere such as you was born ;
But, like some bairns that I ken,
    You like to blaw your horn.
I'll be vigorous, strong, and gay
    When you're forgotten clean—
A few years hence, and folk will say,
    Has such a Burgh been ?

The mineral wealth that 'neath me lies
    Will last for ages yet ;
I dinna think you'll ever try
    To sink another pit.
For I believe, frae what I hear,
    Your coals are nearly dune ;
'Tis then you'll come to me for coals
    To feed your factory lum.

To tell the truth, I dinna like
    To blaw aboot mysel' ;
But for pure health and cleanliness
    Here Royalty might dwell.
Nae stumbling in the dark at night
    Through bonny streets like mine ;
You dinna ha'e the clear gaslight
    To mak' your beauties shine.

You brag aboot your hotels fine ;
    But let me tell you here,
I dinna need the aid o' wine
    My honest heart to cheer.
I've libraries for my thoughtful men
    And pretty smiling dears ;
I have five halls, four kirks, a band,
    And gallant volunteers.

May happiness and plenty fill
    Your heart, and cheer your e'e ;
But while I stand upon a hill,
    You must look up to me.
Frae Frosty Hill to Cowdenend,
    Your beauties are but few ;
Be proud to think I condescend
    To notice such as you.

Lochgelly, 1891.   JOHN PINDAR.

THINGS I LOVE TO SEE.

I love to rest
On the side of a hill,
Listening to the flow
Of a silver rill.

I love to lie
In a rural shade,
To gaze on the sky
And the stars o'erhead.

I love a green glen
And a calm retreat,
And sweet flowers blooming,
The air perfuming
With fragrance sweet.

I love to see
The summer lea,
With gowans so bright
In the pure sunlight.

I love to view
The grass wet with dew,
And hear birds singing,
And Sabbath bells ringing,
And see flowers springing
On Birnie's broo.

I love little girls,
With teeth like pearls,
With hair in curls
Hanging down their cheeks.

I always rejoice
To hear little boys
Making a noise
In their sportive freaks.

I love to see
On its mother's knee
A laughing child,
Though wayward and wild.

I love a bonny lass
Treading over the grass.

I love a funny joke,
And an evening smoke,
With a pleasant friend,
Where none dare intrude
Wha are vulgar and rude,
At my own fire-end.

I love an old man,
With his hair so gray,
Going to the church
On the Sabbath day.

I love an old woman,
With her daughters fair,
Wending their way
To the house of prayer.
In the world I love to see
Piety and humility.

Lochgelly.   JOHN PINDAR.

DEATH OF MR DAVID YOUNG.—We regret to
record the death of an old and worthy friend—
Mr David Young, South Street. For more than
a generation Mr Young acted as correspondent to
the local papers, and was always very attentive to
the *Fife News.* It is only about two years since
he ceased, on account of age and infirmity, to
supply us with Dysart news. But since then a
poetic effusion of his has occasionally appeared,
called forth by the productions of his brother
poet, "John Pindar." Mr Young, who had
reached the ripe age of four-score years, was an
intelligent, public-spirited townsman, and was
highly respected for his honest, upright character.

LOCHGELLY.

IT rarely happens that a small room in a
country town contains as much talent and
ability as Mr Dunsire's did on Burns' Night.
As a matter of course, the poets were there, as
already noted and partly quoted in last week's
Advertiser, but the half has not been told. Th
village warriors and statesmen were there, a
their inevitable adjunct, "the candid frie
who twitted them on the tank question,
their cantrips on the Birnie Brae. The long service,
the short service, and the volunteers were repre-
senttd, so were the ranks of officer, non-com-
missioned officer, and private in the army. The
editor of the local newspaper and correspondents
of other journals took part in the programme,
and it need not be wondered at that the proceed-
ings were an unqualified success. The toasts were
honoured with enthusiasm, "The Queen," by
the Chairman ; "The Army" was responded to
by Messrs Pinder and Henderson, "The Memory
of Burns," by Mr Pinder; "The Scottish Poets,"
by Mr Moody, who also linked the names of
Peter Pinder and Alexander Hugh to the toast.
Mr Moody gave some telling extracts from the
Scottish poets—Burns, Tannahill, and Scott.
The village poets, Pinder and Hugh, were
quoted at length, and the hope was expressed
that the time was not far distant when a volume
of Pinder should be placed on the shelf alongside
that of Burns.   "Sweet Isle of my Soul" was
beautifully rendered by Mr Moody ere he
assumed his seat, and the author, Alexander
Hugh, rose to reply He referred to the pleasure
the occasion had afforded him of meeting for the
first time in a social capacity a brother poet,
whom he had so long admired and venerated,
and hoped that the meeting held there that
evening might result in the formation of a Burns'

club in Lochgelly. We give the promised quotation from this poet which the meeting was privileged to hear from his own lips :—

"The Town and Trade of Lochgelly" were honoured, "The Press," coupled with the name of Mr Denny, who suitably responded. The musical element was well sustained by Messrs Anderson, "There was a Lad ;" "O' a' the Airts," by A. Hugh ; "The Cottage where Burns was born," by Mr Gary ; "My Nannie, O," R Milne ; "The Lea Rig," A. Anderson ; "Mary on Heaven," Mackenzie ; "Flow Gently Sweet Afton," A. Hugh ; "Scotsman Born," Penman ; "Dinna ye hear it," T. Denny. The comic element was supplied by Mr Henderson who sung "Rock the Cradle." Before the meeting came to a close a motion was proposed and adopted "That a Burns' Club be formed in Lochgelly, and that Messrs Peter Pinder and A. Hugh be appointed joint poets laureate for the Year." The usual vote of thanks closed a well spent evening.

Poetry.

LOCHGELLY'S SALUTATION TO HER YOUNG SISTER.

Though I stand high, oh ! dinna think
   I'll ere look doon on you ;
Although we're foolish whiles in drink,
   We're faithful friends and true.

May wark amang us aye be rife,
   And happiness wi' us dwell ;
Twa bonnier toons are no in Fife,
   Although I say't mysel'.

For our young intellectual men,
   We have a paper, too ;
Let's raise its circulation till
   It's kent the world through.

Our village Miltons now can sing,
   And chant their strains sublime ;
May they fresh honours to us bring,
   And make our beauties shine.

Now, sister dear, ye ken we stand
   Aboon our low compeers ;
Now, strive to get a good brass band
   And gallant volunteers.

Then ne'er a foe would cross the Firth
   To our bright Fifian shore.
Except to find in Scottish earth
   A grave for evermore.

                          S. P. T.

S. P. T,

------◆◆------

T he little paper published here,
H as many friends I know,
E xtending aye its useful sphere

A mong both high and low ;
D evoted aye to learning cause,
V igorous may it be ;
E ncouraging hands and cheering hearts
R ight brave and manfully.
T here's nothing mean shall e'er be seen
I n any column of thine ;
S upport it then and make it shine,
E ffulgent over glen and heath,
R ound Raith, Lochgelly, Cowdenbeath,

S. P. T.

------◆------

EVENING.

The silvery moon is beaming
    O'er the evening's birth ;
And twinkling stars are streaming
    O'er the silent earth :
Nature's hushed in calm repose,
    And bright the jewelled sky ;
Here, where the murmuring Fetty flows,
    Oh ! let me dreaming lie.

S. P. T.

LOCHGELLY.

ST PATRICK'S DAY.—Once again the Lochgelly Irishmen's concert was a success. Good as last year's was, this has outshone it in talent and go. Miss Simpson made her debut as pianist and accompaoist, and was warmly applauded. The choir sang two glees, giving their friends a great surprise, who did not expect them to do so well. Messrs J. H. Hitton, Tom Kelly, and J. Donachie did well and gave great pleasure to the large and enthusiastic audience. Miss Rippon made a fair show with the violin.

WHAT THE LOCHGELLY FOLK ARE SAYING.— That the Berry Street squeaker is powerless to silence the strains of the South Street fiddler. That the mantle of Godfrey has not descended upon his musical shoulders. That the old blind fiddler will be able to secure a crust of bread in spite of a thousand amateur horn blowers. That the ratepayers are highly satisfied with the creditable manner in which the School Board have discharged their responsible and onerous duty. That the talent and intellectual ability displayed by the present Board should guarantee its return for another three years. That the ratepayers should be invited to be present at the financial deliberations of the Board. That their presence would strengthen their hands and cheer their hearts. That the architectural beauty of the new Volunteer Hall will entirely eclipse the ecclesiastical grandeur of the church about to be erected in the valley. That, if the new burgh had waited a little longer, she would have been embraced within the arms of the burgh on the hill. That our streets are just as clean as they should be, considering the conspicuous position we occupy in the eyes of the world. That the Binnie Brae has been examined by a distint guished pathologist for the purpose of erecting a hydropathic establishment. That our genial and bracing atmosphere is attracting many visitors from southern lands. That Lochgelly is going to lose Dr Nasmyth, where he is so highly respected and esteemed for his charitable, generous, and kind consideration, especially for the poor. That—

Auld Lochgelly liked weel,
Whether at night or morn,
To hear the doctor's cheery voice,
And see his manly form.

Poetry.

A NEW FIRE MACHINE.

Dedicated to Councillor Leitch, Dunfermline

A strange contrivance here has been,
The like before was never seen,
Your father's made a new machine
    For burnin' coals ;
Within its head it has twa een
    Like twa red holes.

It flings the Forth Bridge in the shade,
The Effiel Tower by Frenchmen made,
This new machine can toast your bread,
    An' fry red herrin' ;
An' burn your fingers, too, when laid
    Upon the iron.

Parriach, muslin, kail, an' brose
Can a' be cooked upon its nose,
Which looks at times as red's a rose
    On simmer's lea ;
An', oh, it masks a splendid dose
    O' *Beveridge* tea.

It mak's dear Nannie's fryin' pan
To fry at ance a p'und o' ham,
Forbye, it cheers you o'er a dram
    When burnin' bright ;
Come to our burgh if you can,
    An' see the sight.

This strange machine does now illume
The darkness o' your father's room ;
Castmetal, stanes, sma' coal, and coom

It can devour,
An' sends the reek right up the lum
Wi' ten horse power.

Your sailors, sodgers, grenidiers,
Grocers, drapers, an' volunteers,
Town Councillors, an' engineers
     Will hide their head,
When ance they see the thing so queer
     Your father's made.

So I expect you very soon
To visit our new burgh toon,
I doubt your heart will tum'le doon
     When ance ye view,
A real, substantial, solid boon
     For housewives noo.

When heated up, an' in full blaw
It disna need yer coals ava ;
A wee bit stick, a spunk or twa
     Does well enough
To keep it for a week or so
     In constann puff.

Before you come within the door
You hear the noice like breakers' roar
Alang auld ocean's rocky shore,
     But you'll sing domb,
To see the reek in clouds galore
     Gaun up the lum.

MY AIN DEAR WIFE.

Do ye mind the sunny days langsyne,
    When you, a country maid,
First vowed an' promised to be mine
    In Pirnie's hazel shade.
Now mony fleeting years we've seen
    Since first I did admire
Your guileless heart an' witching een—
    My cheery wife Dunsire.

Though forty years ha'e pass'd since you
    Became my loving wife ;
You've been to me affectionate, true,
    The pleasure o' my life.
For to secure the world's wealth,
    We never did aspire ;
Content, while God hath gi'en us health,
    My modest wife Dunsire.

Throughout our lengthen'd pilgrimage,
    The tear has filled oor e'e ;
But a' our trust's in Him wha rules
    The earth, the sky, an' sea.
We've aye a dud our backs to cleed—
    A pantry, house, an' fire ;
There's little mair in life we need,
    My pleasant wife Dunsire.

We've twa braw sons at our hearthstane,
    An' ane far ower the sea ;
While twa bit lasses bless our hame
    On Fifeshire's pleasant lea.
Twa wee pet lambs frae us are gane
    To join the angel choir ;
We'll meet them in the fauld aboon,
    My ain dear wife Dunsire.

Although upon life's troubled sea
    We sair an' hard ha'e fought ;
We aye ha'e been contented wi'
    Our present humble lot.
Soon frae this lowly vale o' life
    We'll rise to worlds higher ;
Oh, never mair, we'll part when there,
    My bosom wife Dunsire.

JOHN PINDAR.

Lochgelly.

WHAT THE LOCHGELLY FOLKS ARE SAYING.—
That a place on the School Board must confer
great glory and reputation upon the aspirants,
seeing that so many are seeking that distinguished
honour.—That Edinburgh could hardly show
such a gallery of eminent candidates.—That
poets, philanthrophists, publicans, and philos-
ophers are in the field —That the ratepayers will
have sense and judgment to reject all those who
are likely to increase School Board expenses.—
That bachelors and ancient maids should be ex-
empted from a tax which confers no benefit upon
their offspring.—That common sense and intelli-
gence was more in fashion in the days of our
grandfathers than now.—That a boy who has
passed the 6th Standard can smoke, drink
Cameron Brig, and carry a gold rigwodie across
his breast now is considered to be a man —That
school teachers will never be able to raise the
moral and spiritual instincts of children unless
supported by a parental example set to the
children at home.—That no School Board should
be without a clerical member.—That a secular
spirit is too predominent in public schools in the
present age.—That the young have minds to
be convinced, sympathies to be aroused, and
affections to be warmed.—That we should keep
them in mind of the glorious heritage left us by
our covenanting forefathers.—That every rate-
payer should refuse to listen to any candidate
who would prohibit the Bible from being publicly
read in schools.—That every candidate for School
Board honours should by his walk and conver-
sation show a bright example of spiritual and
moral rectitude to the young generation.—That

The seven successful candidates should
  Do their best endeavour
To make our children truthful, good,
  Honest, pure, and clever ;
And may they always bear in mind
  That a moral education
Will make our children to be
  The glory of our nation.

WHAT THE LOCHGELLY FOLKS ARE SAYING.—
That the musical entertainment given by Mr
Lumsden in the City Hall on Tuesday night was
a musical treat seldom enjoyed by a Lochgelly
audience.   That the singing of "Scots wha
ha'e," by Miss Stockwell, has aroused the
patriotism of many of our young men.   That a
great increase in numbers of the local Volunteers
must be the result.   That the brilliant wit and
comic expressions of "Souter Johnnie" and
"Tam o' Shanter" will keep the Lochgelly folk
laughing till the next census is taken, if not in
the "Land o' the Leal."   That many of the
audience were disgusted by the exhibition of
clay pipes in the mouths of many young men.
That, if less smoke and more brains had been
shown by them, the atmosphere in the hall
would have been more pure and genial for the
delicious warblers, whose songs are still ringing
in our ears.   That Lochgelly young men are
distinguished for their chivalrous devotion to
the fair sex.   That the smokers, who perfumed
the hall with the Virginian weed, must be a
recent importation from lands where women are
held to be soulless things.   That the various
church choirs in the burgh should have dignified
the concert with their presence.   That the
power, beauty, and strength of song filled the
City Hall on Tuesday evening.   That, if our
choirs would be more energetic, and attentive to
their musical instructors, our churches would
present a cosy appearance on the Sabbath day.
That the poet Collins calls music a heavenly
maid.   That the master minds of the world
have been swayed and entranced by the melody
of the divine art.   That, if more attention were
given to the cultivation of music among the
people, their aspirations after the grand, the
beautiful, and true in nature would raise them to
a position akin to the angels.   That refined
musical concerts for the people would do much

to leesen their desire for the false and captivating attractions of the intoxicating cup. That Markinch, with her Herculen cabbages and other wondrous things in nature, cannot match the cow which gave birth to twins in our neighbourhood the other day. That our worthy and respected Provost Jim has been classed by "Tam o' Shanter" among Scotland's great men —Shakespeare, Bruce, Maggie Lauder, and William Wallace. That this is a credit to the burgh, which prides herself on the number of her large hearted citizens. That every one wishes well to our friend, the Provost. That—

> Lang may he live to ring the bell,
>   And cheer us with his sang ;
> And to oor thrifty housewives tell
>   Lochormie's aff the fang.

———:o:———

IN MEMORIAM.

M. C., who died suddenly at Lochgelly,
2nd March, 1891, aged 69 years.

The winter is past, and sweet flowers are springing,
  And clothing the vale, the mountain, the lea ;
While Nature's bright songsters are sweetly singing
  Their melodious songs from valley and tree.
Summer may come in her pride and her glory,
  But winter must reign in this bosom of mine
The receptacle of grief, pain. and sorrow,
  Till we both meet again in a happier clime.

I think of thee, wife, in my now lonely room,
  So dreary and dark since thou went away,
For, thy bright, cheery smile no more will illume
  My path through this vale of human decay.
We've roamed the world for long years together :
  Separation, dear Margaret, cannot be long,
When we'll meet again and enjoy each other
  In the land immortal in beauty and song.

J. P.

THE POET.
A BURLESQUE PARODY.

Canto first.

High in a garret in the burgh dwelt
  A wretched poet, by the nine inspired,
Whose body oft the pangs of hunger felt,
  Whose mind sublime poetic raptures fired.

His garb was mean, and many a rent,
  Expanding, fluttered in the wintry storm;
His lean legs and his grim glengarry lent
  A two fold horror to his martial form,

A cupboard, moth-eaten, which had cost
  Some half-score shillings, his all enclosed;
One cobweb'd bed and table he could boast,
  This where he ate, and that where he reposed.

No smiling wife adorned his lonely house,
  His fire to light, and give him tea at morn;
His sole companion a wretched muse,
  Which earned for him contempt and scorn.

Indulging fancy's visionary height,
  Or rapt in ecstacy of thought sublime,
Oft would he sit and muse the live long night,
  Scratching his head to find a wretched rhyme.

Dark was the night, and loud the tempest's howl:
  Through broken tiles the rushing torrents fell:
No whisky smiled to cheer his drooping soul,
  No beefstake pie his hunger to dispel.

"Wretch that I am," exclaimed he in despair,
  "Dead to myself, and to the world lost,
Wasting my sweetness on the desert air,
  While Tennyson enjoys his tea and toast."

THE POET.

A BURLESQUE PARODY.

Canto Second,

The laugh of fops, the masher's cruel scorn,
   The critic's malice, and the fool's disdain
Have in my bosom planted many a thorn
   To wound my peace, and fill my soul with pain.

The gay companions of my happier days,
   Who were wont my effusions to admire,
Are drinking now, and singing in the praise
   Of other bards, who tune the Elysion lyre.

Oft at my board I've seen them joyful sit,
   Devour my beef, and call my mutton fine,
While each fond heart seemed to imbibe my wit,
   As open mouthed they gulfed the best of wine.

No more the muse with fascinating power
   Shall bind my reason with her dazzling train,
Nor o'er the tallow-lamp at midnight hour
   Call forth the wild effusions of my brain.

The pleasant bard, who sings in Knowledge Street,
   Has filled my soul with sorrow and with pain;
I cannot sing like him in accents sweet,
   Nor match the grandeur of his moral strain.

And there's another great presumptous bard,
   Who sang of beauteous scenes beyond the billow,
Now trys to claim the big world's regard
   By doggrel verse, illiterate and shallow.

Spurned from the door of grandeur and of power,
   He, who had sung in praise of high and low,
Or seized by bobbies in some evil hour
   For having just a little glass or so.

Cowdenbeath.   IGNIS FABUNS.

WHAT THE LOCHGELLY FOLKS ARE SAYING.—
That the presentation meeting in the Co Opera-
tive Hall on Thursday night was a great success.
—That the reciprocal feeling so beautifully dis-
discussedbetween master and man in Lochgelly is
healthy sign of the times.—That the shrewd
intelligence and practical common sense which
characterises the miners of the old burgh has
long since taught them to give a wide berth to
the levelling down principles of an impracticable
socialism.—That Holland House, in its palmiest
Hays, never witnessed such a display of song,
sentiment, and unrivalled eloquence.—That the
genial-hearted chairman was in his element, and
discharged his duties to the satisfaction of the
brilliant assembly.—That the presentation speech
given by Berry Street would have reflected credit
upon the forensic genius of a Cockburn or a
Jeffrey.—Such an eloquent peroration has in-
vested the name of the Co-Operative Hall with
an imperishable lustre.—That if some of our
School Board candidates had been in possession
of such fervent eloquence, they would have
secured our votes, instead of being sent back to
the shades of forgetfulness.—That a selection of
choice *spirits* kept the meeting in a happy state
of social hilarity.—That love and friendship held
universal sway throughout the evening.—That
every one wishes the Ayrshire laddie a successful
career in the old burgh town.—That he may live
long and make the valley of Cripple Kirkie to
ring with the sweet melody of song, so justly
admired on Thursday evening.—That we all
wish health, happiness, and prosperity to follow
Mr Love to his new home among the bonnie
woods of Blairadam.—That every one felt com-
fortable and happy through an interchange of
brotherly love and kindly feeling.—That no dis-
tracting School Board cases molested the minds
of that memorable gathering.—That

> They were happy a'thegither
> In *Love* and friendship wi' their brither
> *Love* his nature, *Love* his name,
> They shook his hand, then toddled hame.

WHAT THE FOLKS ARE SAYING.—That the School Board election has passed quietly over without leaving a ruffle of excitement behind.— That School Board contests must be the invetable result of depraved human nature.—That after man has reached the sacred height of perfection, and can lay claim to human infallability, only then will contests of all kinds be conducted in an amicable spirit of courtesy and love.—That old and young here are rejoicing at the triumphant return (at the head of the pole) of the venerable Chairman, who has occupied a seat at the Board since its formation.—That he has been indefatigable in his efforts to promote the spiritual, moral, and educational interests, of the people of Lochgelly is known far beyond the confinos of Fife.—That some of the rejected candidates are still young and blooming in the pride of vigorous manhood.—That they can bide their time.—That they will, in the shades of tranquil obscurity, have time to study the eloquent orations of the great Grecian orator, Demosthenes.—That this will help their pronunciation, improve their gesture, and cover a multitude of oratorical imperfections.—That when the next election takes place they will come before the ratepayers with an influence so overwhelming and irresistible as to place them at the extreme end of the pole.—That the rate payers are highly satisfied with the composition of the Board.—That few provincial Boards in Fife could exhibt such intellectual power and administrative capacity for the successful discharge of such onerous and multifarious duties.— That high ratepayers and great employers of labour, if in possession of other indispensible qualifications, are surely the men to look after our interest in a matter of so weighty importance as the education of our children.—That we must do everything in our power to keep up the credit of a school celebrated for its learning and distinguished teachers when School Boards were only looming in the distant future.—That

May grief and sorrow, care and pain,
  Ne'er touch their halian door,
Until we meet with them again
  In auchteen ninety-four.

——:o:——

LOCHGELLY SCHOOL BOARD.

The School Board's elected, an' happy are we
Wi' members respected frae hear to the sea ;
Through oor toon we a' ken that peace an' concord
Will distinguish the men o' the Lochgelly Board.

There's few Boards in Fife has the honour to share
The advice of a wife and the smiles of the fair ;
An' oor ain Grand Auld Man, whom we a' admire,
Will again fill the chair—'tis the people's desire.

Now, parents, there's one thing to strengthen their hand ;
Keep the bairns at school— 'tis a School Board command ;
Education is cheap, an' books in galore
Are blessings unkent to the parents o' yore.

The working-man's bairn can noo toddle roond
The gigantic circle o' science, profoond ;
The bright-faced laddies, now doing their sums,
Will be our great men when the next century comes.

Wha kens but a Newton may rise frae East School—
A Pitt, or a Fox, the great Commons to rule ;
Let's lead oor wee bairns where virtue aye dwells ;
A moral example should come frae oursel's.

                               S. P. T.

WHAT THE FOLKS ARE SAYING.—That the professor of mesmerism at present in our midst has, by the power of his animal magnetism, been instrumental in mesmerising several of our young men.—That the professor had some of his interesting young pupils completely in subjection to the principles of hypnotism.—That while going through the crucible operation many of them were seen to turn black in the face.—That it was necessary to use bucketfuls of Lochornie water and a hundred-weight of Sunlight soap to bring them back to their original colour.—That the mysterious influence exerted by the professor over the distinguished company was powerless to change the emerald complexion of Mr Green.— How that came about can only be explained by natural or physical attributes.—That the professor remained in a garment of floury whiteness while transforming his dupes into the appearance of a sepoy regiment.—That some of them after returning to a conscious state and seeing their faces in a glass began to sing "Good old Jeff has gone to rest."—Some of them have no intention of being mesmerised again.—That the amorous bard who fell over the debilitated *band box* during the School Board polling day, has now recovered and is himself again.—That his head is nearly reduced to its original size.—That he still possesses sufficient brains to immortalise his meeting with such a conspicuous companion.— That we only want a few lawyers now to complete the learned professions in the burgh —That another doctor is coming to the village to practise the Therapeutic art —That learned men are required to look after the three afflictions of human nature.—That it was said by Sir Walter Scott, that ministers lived by our sins, doctors by our diseases, and lawyers by our misfortunes.

—That the old familiar faces are passing rapidly
away from our midst.—Last week was laid in the
grave all that is mortal of David Penman, mer-
chant, South Street, revered and loved by a large
circle of friends, he has passed away to the
Father's house of many mansions.—That much
sympathy is felt for his widow and family, who
are left to mourn their irreparable loss.—That

> " His memory long shall live alone
>   In all our hearts as mournful light,
> That broods above the fallen sun,
>   And dwells in heaven half the night."

TO OUR BOYS.

WHAT THE LOCHGELLY FOLKS ARE SAYING.

That we should try to improve the intellectual and moral endowments of all children over whom we can exercise any influence. That at this season of the year we should teach their young minds to be kind, compassionate, and merciful towards the young nestlings who will soon make our valleys and hills ring with the melody of their artless song. That all instructors of youth, teachers in public schools, and ministers of religion should impress the young and susceptible mind that it is a great sin to steal the eggs and destroy the little birds. That no manly boy with a humane spirit would be guilty of violence towards the little warblers whose songs cheer the gaiety of youth and gladden the heart of old age. That the glorious splendour of summer and the howling winds of winter are made to us more cheerful with the chirping of robin red breast and our ever present sparrow. That all our great poets, Wordsworth, Akenside, Milton, Cowper, Burns, Bruce, and Tannahill, have in their poems and songs inculcated kindness towards the feathered songsters of creation. Just listen to the bard of Lochleven; how beautiful and sweetly he sings about our annual visitant, the cuckoo—

> "Sweet bird, thy bower is ever green,
>   Thy sky is ever clear;
> Thou has no sorrow in thy song,
>   No winter in thy year."

That our national bard, whom all Scottish schoolboys love and admire, blest the sweet thrush that cheered his heart with its song on a cold January morning—

> "Yet come, thou child of poverty and care,
> The mite high heaven bestowed, that mite with thee
>   I'll share."

That Wordsworth, who has been designated "Nature's great high priest," delighted in the presence and in the song of our singing birds. Listen to the following:—

" The birds around me hopp'd and played,
  Their thoughts I cannot measure ;
But the least motion which they made,
  It seemed to me a pleasure."

That all Lochgelly schoolboys must be familiar
with the beautiful lines addressed to a skylark
by the " Ettrick Shepherd "—

" Bird of the wilderness,
  Blithesome and cumberless,
Sweet be thy matin o'er moorland and lea ;
  Emblem of happiness,
  Blest be thy dwelling-place,
Oh, to abide in the desert with thee !"

That an old poet named Pringle was so fond of
the company of birds that he wished for the
wings of one

" To mount where angels be,
  And leave behind this world of sin,
    A little thing like thee ;
I'd mount where golden harps proclaim
    Emmanuel's dying love,
And gladly hail the eternal rest
  Of that pure realm above."

That the pure and sensitive mind of the gentle
Cowper was hurt at the sight of a dead worm.
That all schoolboys should read his great poem,
" The Task," where they will find the following
quotation :—

" I would not number in my list of friends,
  Though graced with polished manners and fine sense,
  Yet wanting sensibility, the man
  That needlessly sets foot upon a worm."

That no schoolboy in the Sixth and ex-Sixth
Standards can be ignorant of Tanahill's beauti-
ful and plaintive song, " The bonnie woods o'
Craigielea."   That they should commit to
memory that sweet verse so dear to the lovers of
our singing Scottish birds—

" Awa', ye murdering, thoughtless gang,
  Wha tear the nestlings ere they flee ;
They'll sing you yet a canty sang ;
  Then, oh ! in pity, let them be."

That genial nature will soon put on her brightest
garments and most illuring smiles. That there
can be no more exhilarating pleasure in the
world than to wander forth by leafy bower and
wimpling stream, admiring the sublime beauties
of external nature. That the hills of the Cleish
and the plains of Cartmore will soon be vocal
with the harmony of little birds, if you, my boys,

are careful not to destroy the young nestlings
now. That all kind-hearted boys in our public
schools will ponder over the foregoing consider-
ations now urged upon their attention. That

When the gentle days of June
Does cheer our hearts again,
We'll hear upon the banks of Clune
Their gladsome, cheery strain.

I S A B E L.

'Twas in the vernal season
O' the sweet breathing spring,
When trees put on their robes o' green,
An' birds began to sing ;
The bonny flowers were blinking sweet
In Lowery's fragrant dell,
When first I saw my smiling lass—
The rosy Isabel.

The orient blush o' simmer's morn,
The roses' sweet perfume,
The fragrance on the breezes borne,
The maiden smiles o' June
Are no so sweet to me as she
On whom my thoughts aye dwell ;
Both day and thoughts are wi'
The rosy Isabel.

When the gentle morn is breaking
Oot owre the waving trees,
An' a thoosand sweet birds singing
Upon the simmer breeze,
Oh ! then the music o' her voice
Comes owre me like a spell,
While in each flower I recognise
The smile o' Isabel.

Her rosy lips are fu' o' smiles,
Her een wi' love are beamin' ;
Her bosom pure like sparklin' dew
Upon the meadows gleamin' ;
An', oh ! she spoke so soft an' sweet,
Her words like music fell
Upon my ear the night I gave
My heart to Isabel,

Lochgelly.

S.P.T

DEAR MISTER EDITOR,—You are at present
devotin' a large portion o' the *Advertiser* to the
communications of these three luikies, " Stultus,"
" Nemesis," and " Nemo." They a' tak' various
views of the licensing question in Cowdenbeath.
Noo, I dinna think ony o' the three has very
muckle influence in the Licensing Boards o'
Fife. Ae thing, I ken that, if they are tee-
totallers, they're no very temperate in their
language, ane to anither. Noo, I may be
wrang, but I dinna think Cowdenbeath has
ower mony public houses. Losh me, we have
seventeen in our burgh, and it tak's them a' to
gi'e proper accommodation, especially when
we ha'e (which is often the case) an influx o'
distinguished visitors from England in search
of health. A nicht or twa syne Bell and me
gaed wast to the Raith to visit our auld friend,
Gig Davie, and get a bit crack about the days o'
lang syne, lang afore railroads and factories had
destroyed the amenities of bonny Cowdenbeath.
Weel, after hain a bit smoke an' a chat at Davie's
hearthstane, we a' daundered doon the length o'
Brunton's Inn. But man, though we had
plenty o' bawbees, there was nae room for us.
We tried other places wi' a like result. So I
gaed across to my auld friend Archie, an' got a
wee drappie o' " Cameron Brig " in a five gill
bottle, when we toddled back. Noo, Mr
Editor, I dinna wish to encroach ower far on
your sublime patience, but oor men in authority
should provide suitable accommodation for Bell
an' me when we gang to see our friends, an' we
didna get that durin' our late visit to Gig
Davie.—Ta, ta, the noo,

                                    AULD CLEERIE.

Lochgelly.

LOCHGELLY.

Mr W. T. Rushbury's talented company gave a grand musical entertainment in the Music Hall on Saturday night to a large and appreciative audience. The sentimental singing of Miss May Rushbury and Miss Flora Donaldson was deservedly encored. The comic element was well sustained by Messrs W. Candlish and J. B. Preston, whose singing was so enthusiastically received as to make the very plaster fall from the ceiling of the venerable hall. We have too few of such grand symphonious concerts. If anything is calculated to elevate the people, and to give them refined and exalted tastes, give them music such as we enjoyed on Saturday night. The music was of a very high class, and as Mr Rushbury is a general favourite in Lochgelly, we wish in our hearts, and that very speedily, "*au revoir.*"

WHAT THE LOCHGELLY FOLKS ARE SAYING.— That the windmill in Main Street has come to grief. That it was powerless to attract the feminine beauties towards the domicile of the cankerous old military bachelor. That he is doomed to waste his sweetness in the atmosphere of forgetfulness. That our burgh, occupying such an elevated position, must be the reason of so many *windy* tales floating about. That the most of them are generally discovered to be on the shady side of truth. That the truth often suffers by allowing the imagination to run riot. That tales and stories being so easily fabricated, shows the splendour of language and the vigour of the inventive faculties so prevalent amongst us. That gossips and scandalmongers are plants of every soil. That such characters should be avoided; they spoil the happiness of the domestic circle, and takes the sunshine and pleasure out of human life. That the suggestion of the Main Street critic that the various bards in the burgh should have their brains analysed

is not necessary. That they have sense to ap-
preciate and a capacity to understand the
magniloquent and bombastic expressions of any
self-constituted judge of poesy. That the glow-
ing sentiments, the sublime and delightful
effusions, which emanate from the fertile brains
of some of our village bards, is a book sealed, a
fountain closed to some of our elegant critics.
That our bards

> Can write grand rhymes,
> At once the boast and envy of the times ;
> In every page—song, sonnet, what you will—
> Show boundless genius and unrivalled skill,
> Impregnable against the critic's puny quill.

That some of our critics would be more at home
in some Zoological Garden. That they would
generate a feeling of wonderous kindness to-
wards the animals of their own nature. That
they are incapable of luxuriating amongst the
sublime beauties of our ethereal poets. That
the smith and the piper are much respected
in the burgh for their many amiable qualities.
That the juvenile poet should be merciful. That
he does not possess a monopoly of genius is
manifest from his unpardonable presumption
and unparalleled stupidity, in trying to stig-
matise the brain work of one of our most dis-
tinguished citizens. That an unassuming
humility ought to characterise the conduct of a
stripling in his teens. That critics breathing
after an immortal reputation in this world
should exhibit great magnanimity of soul to-
wards those whom *they* consider to be deficient
in intellectual power and poetical discrimination.
That a meeting of the poets took place the other
night in the Elysium Hall of Parnassus. That
the few favoured friends admitted within the
immortal portal were electrified to hear verse
after verse rolling forth in tones of sublimity and
grandeur. That it is needless to say that each
bard was more than intoxicated with his own
verbosity. That each considered the sublime
expression of their lips a sure passport to the

happy hunting grounds of Burns and Scott.
That before parting poet Sellie recited with
grand feeling and rolling frenzy of eye Long-
fellow's "Psalm of Life"—

> Lives of great men all remind us
> We can make our lives sublime,
> And, departing, leave behind us
> Footprints on the sands of time.

MAGGIE KIPPEN.

Let those wha like sing in the praise
  O' foreign dames sae braw ;
The subject o' my simple lays
  Does far outshine them a' ;
Across life's wild an' stormy sea,
  My barque wi' her I'd lippen ;
There's nane on earth sae dear to me
  As my sweet Maggie Kippen.

She's kindly, coothie, sweet, an' fair,
  Which ony ane can see,
Wha likes to watch her modest air
  An' bonny laughin' e'e ;
Let thoughtless callans laugh an' stare
  When owre the green we're skippin' ;
You winna fin' anither pair
  Like *me* an' Maggie Kippen.

I like to sing in lasses' praise,
  As Burns did langsyne ;
Although like him I canna raise
  A sang sae sweet an' fine ;
But I ken weel had Robbie seen
  Her through Lochgelly trippin';
He'd match'd her wi' his bonny Jean—
  My ain dear Maggie Kippen.

Lochgelly.   JOHN PINDAR.

MY PITHEAD LASSIE.

Brag o' your fact'ry lasses braw,
  Wi' smiles sae sweet an' fine ;
But nane o' them can match ava
  This bonnie lass o' mine.
My dear lass is young an' bonny,
  An' fair without a flaw ;
Here aboot you'll no find ony
  Like Teenie Waukinshaw.

Her pure, sweet heart is free frae guile,
  The fragrance o' her breath
Does mak' the bonny flowers to smile
  Alang the verdant heath.
Your noble-born dames wad frown
  On such a lass as she ;
She's mair to me than Britain's Crown—
  The pithead lass for me.

When frae her wark she comes at nicht
  Wi' bright smiles in her e'e,
She mak's her mammy's labour licht
  By workin' frank an' free.
The wet pit claes afore the fire,
  She lays them in a raw ;
'Nae wonder that I do admire
  My Teenie Waukinshaw.

I dinna think I'd gang far wrang
  To mak' the lassie mine ;
The lass that works an' sings a sang
  Will mak' her housie shine.
If she wud only say the word,
  I'd dance, an' sing, an' craw ;
An' draw ance mair my guid auld sword,
  For Teenie Waukinshaw.
                              JOHN PINDAR

WHAT THE FOLKS ARE SAYING.—That fifteen hundred souls added to the population of the burgh since 1881 shows our temporal condition to be very prosperous.—That all these hundreds added during the last ten years have failed to fill our churches.—That every man, however depraved his nature may be, still retains the instinctive feelings of the religion of his youth.—That the lapsed masses are not ignorant of the great philosophical problems which occupy the mind of the intellectual world.—That the church is a mental as well as a moral and spiritual improver.—That cultured as well as illiterate sinners should wait on the ministrations of our local clergy.—That some of them are abreast of the scientific thought of the time.—That we look in vain for any decadence in the pulpit and theological ability on the part of any of our ministers.—That sceptical and atheistical plausibilities must give place to the stern realities of a pure and indestructible truth.—That the questionable sophistries of a Voltaire or a Hume can exert little influence upon a well-regulated and reflective mind.—That the men of the present day have intellectual pleasures and advantages unknown to our grandfathers.—That it is a shame in this age of light and leading for any young man to go through the world none the wiser of all the glory and beauty which a benificent Creator hath strewn around his path.—That the pleasure derived from an intellectual perusal of the works of the great and good, who have gone before us and left their monuments of their genius and learning, is a pleasure from which the ignorant are entirely shut out.—That all that has been sung and said by the mighty dead in

byegone ages is to them as the hieorglyphic writing upon the monumental pillars of Egypt—unmeaning inscriptions.—That the young man, who pours over the sanctified genius of a Milton,

or a Cowper, or rivals among the sublime beauties
of Shakespeare, enjoys the greatest pleasure that
knowledge can bestow.—That we enjoy a beauti-
ful smiling world.—That if hatred, envy, and
evil speaking were less known amongst us it
would be better for the peace and happiness of
our braw lads and bonny lasses.—That any
young man who is inclined to exhibit a pessimis-
tical nature should be avoided by every sunshiny
soul.—That young men should embrace every
opportunity for moral and mental improvement.
—That the man who takes no delight in cultiv-
ating his intellectual faculties just goes through
the world like an animal of inferior creation.—
That the language of the bard of Paradise
lamenting the loss of his sight is appliable to
every soul shrowded in the mist of ignorance.

Ever during darkness surrounds me—
From the cheerful ways of men cut off, and
From the book of language fair, presented
With a universal blank of nature's law,
And wisdon at one entrance quite shut out.

That our young men will endeavour to avoid
what is base in human nature, and disdain all
cowardly conduct.—That they ought to rejoice
in the truth and fix their hearts on the simplicity
of her charms.—That to rise above the meanness
of dissimulation should be the aim of young men.
—That the Y.M.C.A. should be patronised by all
men who are created in the image of God and
animated with an immortal soul destined to live
throughout the countless ages of eternity.—That
many of our great men, who are now occupying
distinguished positions in the world, are not
ashamed to acknowledge the spiritual benefit
they derived from such valuable Associations.
—That many young men take a great interest in
parading infidel sentiments. As a great writer
has said—"They question the truth of Christian-
ity because they hate the practice of it."—That
it is a pity that any one should become the

want of practical religion dwarfs the man and
hinders his spiritual development.—That no
young man can say he is ignorant who knows
His Bible true—
A truth the brilliant Frenchman never knew.

Poetry.

——:0:——

FIDDLER DOIG'S BACK AGAIN.

Air—"Highland Harry's back again."

Fiddler Doig's back again,
Fiddler Doig's back again;
There's no in Fife man, maid, or wife,
That hisna heard his cheery strain.

Wi' plaintive air he sings a sang,
That mak's the silent tear to fa';
An' though the drap whiles puts him wrang,
He's aye made welcome by us a'.

I've heard him sing a cheery sang
When winter's howling winds wud blaw;
Nae wonder though he takes a dram
To cheer his heart 'mang frost an' snaw.

Auld Doig has seen better days,
Afore the streets ere heard him sing:
Few laddies yet on Fife's green braes
Cud dance wi' him the Highland Fling.

Whin at the corner he begins
Tae screw his fiddle pins wi' glee,
The wee bit bairnies gather roon',
An' dance an' sing aboot his knee.

But though his een are dark an' dim,
A sprightly, social cock is he;
Though growin' auld, he's swank o' limb,
Like ony laud o' twenty-three.

There's no a toon in bonny Fife,
That's heard his elevating strain,
But to the auld blind fiddler gi'es
A cheery welcome back again.

S. P. T.

WHAT THE FOLKS ARE SAYING. — That the obscene and disgusting language employed by some of our young men in the streets of our burgh on a Saturday evening is a disgrace to our boasted civilisation.—That so many of them escape condign punishment is not the fault of our vigilant and energetic policeman.—That it would require an omnipresent eye and a watchful ear to secure the punishment of every filthy speaker.—That no young man with the least self-respect would be guilty of uttering language which might bring the blush of shame to the face of a pandemonium devil.—That modern swearing is not of that gentlemanly stamp which Milton characterises as one of Satan's most sublime inventions. — That delicate and pure-minded females are compelled to listen to tirades of disgusting language.—That one wonders where such *elegant* and refined young men have been educated. — That vicious companionship must lower the morals of young men.—That a pure morality makes its way directly to the understanding and feelings of every enlightened mind. —That our municipal authorities must do everything in their power to clear and purify our atmosphere from the seductive breath of impurity. — That the virtues of humanity and benevolence — the principles of morality and religion—exercise little influence upon a man who is steeped to the lips in the trough of filth and impurity.—That the loud laugh and boisterous expression bespeaks the empty skull and vacant mind.—That the pulpit and the press should speak out and cause their influence to be felt against a vice more deadly than the pestilence that walketh in darkness.—That the long summer nights are come again.—That our famed brass band is making our streets and squares to ring with the melody that gladdens the hearts of our labouring swains —That we have the musical material for the making of a splendid band.

—That they should devote their spare time to that practice which makes perfection.—That if they pay attention to their skilful and energetic teacher, Mr Carmichael, they would be second to no band in the kingdom of Fife.—That music is a universal language understood by all nations. —That its cultivation amongst the people of the burgh might prove instrumental in lessening the dirty language we so much deplore.—That strong drink gets the blame of creating much of this filthy talk.—That no publican in the burgh would tolerate in his house for a moment men capable of belching forth torrents of obscenity. —That the English language is sufficiently expressive for the most of men.—That when

Gleamin hour is calm and still,
And silence reigns o'er mead and hill,
'Tis very painful for the ear
Such vile and filthy words to hear.

PIC-NIC.—Last Friday an interesting group of young ladies and gentlemen assembled in a field belonging to the genial and kindly old farmer, Mr Anderson, Cartmore. Upwards of thirty young ladies displayed their inestimable charms before their youthful admirers. After partaking of the good things of this life—gingerbread, lemonade, sweeties, candy rock, and cocoa-nuts —they sported their little airy figures over the grassy sward to the delightful strains of a brass band, conducted by Mr Harry Baxter, Lochgelly. Very sweet and appropriate songs for the occasion of a May gathering were sung by Bella Baxter, Jeanie White, Dody Baxter, Andrew Baxter, and Willie Craigie. Their place of rendezvous was visited during the afternoon by many interested spectators. Much credit is due to Miss Agnes Baxter for making the meeting a success. After enjoying a most delightful day they returned to their homes about ten p.m., every one well pleased with the innocent pleasures of their rural pic-nic.

Poetry.

THE PAPER GIRL'S DREAM.

If you're waking, call me early,
  Call me early, mother dear ;
By eight o'clock to-morrow
  The *Advertiser's* here.
I intend to rell a thousand sheets
  Through our Lochgelly toon,
So don't forget, dear mother,
  To call me very soon.

There's mony lads in our braw toon,
  And smiling lassies, too,
Wha like to read the poetry
  O' S.P.T. and Hugh.
Although the *Advertiser's* young,
  The time will come, I ken,
When it's praises will be sung
  By a' our workin' men.

Good-night, mother dear ; call me up
  Before the day is born,
For I intend to be the first
  Upon the streets the morn ;
And I will sell a thousand off
  Before the sun gang's doon,
For, mother, I intend to beat
  Their Cowdenbeath lang toon.

I dreamed last night, dear mother,
  That I sel't six score and ten
O' papers to our lassies
  And thrifty working-men.
So, mother, call me early,
  When the cock begins to craw ;
I like the *Advertiser* weel—
  I'd sel'd through frost an' snaw.

Lochgelly.   THE SUNNY MUSE.

Poetry.

THE BARDS O' LOCHGELLY.

You brag o' your bards so learn:d an' braw,
   And pure in their diction an' grammar,
But nae bard ava' that ever I saw
   But whiles wad gie a bit stammer.
The au'dest you hae is no muckle worth—
   Indeed, you hae nae bard, that's true, man;
But I can write rhyme, grand, sweet, an' sublime,
   In spite o' S. P. T. or Hugh, man.

Your bards in the Moor write lines pretty pure,
   An' twa frae Rotten Raw street, man;
But though I'm a youth, I tell you the truth,
   Your scribblers a' I can beat, man.
I hae read Hogg, Byron, Shelley, an' Scott,
   Nae wonder I'm very sublime, man;
Although I don't drink, I'll lay you a pot
   You dinna get poems like mine, man.

To print their songs the way you have done
   Shows lit le discretion av.', man;
But ow you maun see a great bard in me,
   Able to outshine them a', man.
Y u hae found at last a real child o' song,
   Sweet, calm, delicious, and mellow;
One that can soar through the realms o' love,
   Aboon puny bards in Lochgelly.

Lochore, 9th June, 1891.

                          H. SHANKIE.

TO H. SHANKIE.

I laugh'd until my sides were sore
At the bouncing bard frae green Lochore
His diction pure, and language true,
Must shame our S.P.T. and Hugh.

There's mony bards like him, I ken,
Wha eats the grass upon the plain ;
He cocks his lugs, then gie's a roar--
This poet*ass* frae green Lochore.

The poets o' the Rotten Raw,
You'll never fill their shoon ava ;
As for the bards doon in the moor,
You're no like them, sublime and pure.

You are a vain conceited thing ;
How dare you try wi' bards to sing ?
Now cower your flight, and write no more
Impudent scribbler frae Lochore

You've eaten *Hogg*, I dinna doot,
And kissed our Burns on the snoot,
But your brains are rather shallow
To match the bards o' Lochgelly.

I'm neither S.P.T. nor Hugh,
Nor any o' the bardie crew ;
Now, Shankie, hide your head, an' never
Interfere wi' bards so clever.

WHAT THE FOLKS ARE SAYING. — That strangers paying a visit to our elegant and compact little burgh cannot fail to notice the great number of beautiful and interesting lasses which adorn every street and thoroughfare of our dignified and exalted city. — That these young ladies are looking forward to the happy auspicious day when they will have the privilege of entering the holy and sacred circle of matrimony.—That being deeply interested in the spiritual and moral welfare of our handsome lasses, we would advise them to pause, think, and reflect before embarking on a voyage of such momentous importance to all concerned.—That the young man who is inclined to exhibit a spirit of thoughtless living and folly is hardly the proper person to secure domestic happiness for a young woman voyaging down the stream of time. —That every young man should look with abhorrence upon everything vulgar and mean, and endeavour to attain to a dignified position of a pure morality.—That such a man ought to make a loving and a virtuous wife a happy companion.—That our young lasses should be able to exercise discretion and prudence in selecting a mate for a voyage which is a combination of hurricane, sunshine, and storm.—That we have every reason to believe that our bonny lasses will give ear to the beauty of wisdom, and despise not the precepts of truth.—That our fair young daughters should make the beauty of mind and soul synonymous with the sweet fascination and captivating charms of their soul-enrapturing forms.—That an old Chinese writer informs us of "young women walking in maiden sweetness, with innocence in their minds, and modesty on their cheeks; that they are clothed with neatness, and filled with the fruits of temperance; that humility and meekness are as crowns of glory encircling their heads; that on their tongues dwelleth music, harmony, and love; that submission and obedience are the

lessons of their lives."—That no young woman
would wish to link her fate with a man primed
with malice, hatred, anger, and with a whole
host of selfish affections.—That misery, disgrace,
poverty, and degradation must accompany every
woman who becomes the companion of the grace-
less, the profligate, and the abandoned.—That
the issues of marriage are unspeakably im-
portant.—That it is the bounden duty of every
young woman to repel the advances of any man
who takes up an attitude of hostility towards the
Christian religion, or shirks the obligations im-
posed upon us by the revealed will of God.—
That no man knows what a ministering angel a
woman is until he has gone hand and hand with
her down through the gloom and sunshine of an
earthly pilgrimage.—That many of our Scottish
poets were able to appreciate the virtuous beauty
and matronly kindness so characteristic of our
bonny Scotch lasses. Scott songs—

O woman, in our hours of ease,
Uncertain, coy, and hard to please:

When pain and anguish wring the brow,
A ministering angel thou.

That our national bard knew the sterling
qualities of a thrifty lass when he sung in the
following strain—

A bonny lass, I will confess,
Is pleasant to the e'e;
But without some better qualities,
She's no a lass for me.

That our own village bard has struck the true
key-note of poetical inspiration when he sings of
bonny lasses in such a beautiful strain of elegant
simplicity as the following sweet words can
testify—

O, lovely is the stream that flows
From Mary's breast to me,
And true is she that owns the name—
The treasure o' my e'e.

That the young and unfortunate Tannahill, whose short career in this world was unblest with the sunshine of matrimonial felicity, could sing of his Jessie in the following delightful measure—

How lost were my days till I met wi' my Jessie,
  The sports of the city seemed foolish and vain ;
I ne'er saw a nymph I cud ca' my dear lassie
  Till charmed wi young Jessie, the flower o' Dunblane.

That by the time the next census is taken we hope to see our present smiling girls the mothers of a healty, virtuous, and promising generation. —That we sincerely hope,

Ilka bonny smiling lass.
  That blooms in auld Lochrelly,
May to her gentle bosom strain
  Nae wild illiterate fellow.

THE WARNING VOICE.

Here I'm sitting sad and weary,
Pockets light and spirits dreary,
Sans a glass to make me cheery,
    Of the drink I no r deplore.
While I thus sat rapt in thinking
How to carry on my drinking,
    Down I fell upon the floor ;
And I heard a voice repeating,
Though the keyhole of my door—
    " Drink, oh brother—nevermore."

Forth I rushed into the street,
Nor shoes upon my tender feet,
Crying, " Stranger, come now tell me—
    Thy business I implore !"
But the voice kept on repeating,
While my heart was throbbing, beating—
    " What hath brought thee to my door ?'
Still the voice went on repeating,
Through the keyhole of my door —
    " Drink, oh brother—nevermore."

I rushed with fear back to my room,
Now shrouded close in midnight gloom,
And silent as the lonely tomb,
    Was all my cheerless floor.
Towards the keyhole I kept peeping,
For my eyes had gone from sleeping ;
Still I heard the strange voice keeping
    Up the words I heard before ;—
The mysterious words of warning
Through the keyhole of my door—
    " Drink, oh brother—nevermore."

Terrible infatuation,
Slave to drink's intoxication,
Misery and degradation

Fills my cup to running o'er.
Onward still I went careering,
Neither God nor demon fearing,
Virtuous actions ever jeering —
    Was the character I bore ;
Still the angel voice kept pleading,
Through the keyhole of my door—
    Drink, oh brother—nevermore."

Though the voice keeps on repeating,
Am I from the fiend retreating ?
Still it gets a welcome greeting
    From the s'ave-drink's mangled sore—
Drink can change me to a devil,
Make my life and actions evil,
Henceforth may my feet not travel,
    But shun the paths they trod before.
"Hurrah ! hurrah !" the voice repeated,
Through the keyho'e of the door—
    "My brother vows he'll drink no more."

Lochgelly.
                                            S. P. T.

WHAT THE FOLKS ARE SAYING. That our
burgh having the honour of giving birth to the
late Professor Page, the great exponent the
geological science, it is an incumbent duty
upon parents to watch and detect the spurious
and soul-killing literature dished up in our
weekly papers for the moral and mental improve-
ment of the youth of the present generation
—That penny horribles of every description
should be denounced in no measured language
by every one who wishes to see human nature
soaring towards an ethereal perfection.—That
one weekly paper read over the whole of Scot-
land furnishes its young readers with such soul
stirring stories as the following, viz.—" The
Body Snatcher ; a True Story of the Glasgow
Resurrectionists ;" " James Macpherson, the
Highland Robber," etc.—That we are thorough

convinced that such trashy, sparkling, and
deceptive litterature must have an injurious
effect upon the tender and susceptible nature of
our young men and women.—That our ministers
should try and do something to stem the
destructive tide of impure literature which is
snapping the very foundations of social morality.
—That George Gilfillan of Dundee was wont
to hurl forth from his pulpit terrible denuncia-
tions against a soul-killing literature.—That so
long as ecclesiastical divisions and jealousies
divide the churches in Scotland, our preachers
are powerless to present a combined front
against many forms of wickedness in the land.—
That we might well exclaim in the language of
the weeping poet, Jeremiah, " Oh, that my head
were waters, and mine eyes a fountain of tears,
that I might weep day and night for the slain of
the daughters of my people."—That we ought
to do everything we can to counteract the evil
tendency of much of the questionable fiction of
this great and wonderful age of scientific
thought and intellectual development.—That it
behoves us to keep up the credit of our brave

fatherland, which has long been distinguished for all the virtues which exalt and adorn human nature.—That at present we yield to no country for our patriotic devotion for the glorious land which has given birth to a Burns, a Chalmers, a Wallace, and a Bruce.—That every patriotic Scotchman must deplore the decay of family worship among our Presbyterian families, and the neglect of parental instruction.—That a parent who brings up a child without faith will soon learn that he has got a young devil on his hands.—That that was the opinion of Martin Luther.—That we must believe that our distin- guished countryman, Robert Burns, had he now been living, would have given a cold shoulder to the fashionable Agnosticism and Materialism of the present day.—That it is the duty of married men to commit to memory his "Cotter's Saturday Night."—That no insidious poison of modern scepticism lurks in the family worship in that pious Ayrshire home.

The cheerfu' supper done, wi' serious face,
They round the ingle form a circle wide ;
The sire turns o'er, with patriarchal grace,
The big ha' Bible, ance his father's pride.
His bonnet rev'rently is laid aside,
His lyart haffets wearing thin and bare :
Those strains that once did sweet in Sion glide,
He wails a portion with judicious care,
And, "Let us worship God," he says, with solemn air.

That it would be well for young Scotchmen who rejoice and glory in the name of our national bard, to study the religious side of his character. —That Burns never forgot, even in his moments of gaiety, that

An atheist laugh's a poor exchange
For Deity offended !

That many things in the world, both religious
and political, seem to indicate that we are still
far from the millennium era, **far from that**
Glorious period when man to man the world o'er
         Shall brithers be for a' that.
That the young men of Lochgelly will exercise
their minds with books calculated to enlighten,
instruct, and purify.—That though we condemn
the pernicious penny horrible, that we have no
objection to the pleasant, pure, and delightful
works of Scott, Galt, and Annie Swan.—That
great men have been amongst us,
hands   that penned, and tongues that uttered wisdom.